Rodger Beaubouman

LEADERSHIP
FOR
SAINTS

LEADERSHIP
FOR
SAINTS

RODGER DEAN DUNCAN
AND ED J. PINEGAR

Covenant Communications, Inc.

Covenant

Published by Covenant Communications, Inc.
American Fork, Utah

Printed in the United States of America
First Printing: August 2002

08 07 06 05 04 03 02   10 9 8 7 6 5 4 3 2 1

ISBN 1-59156-062-4

DEDICATION

We appreciate all the models of great leadership in our lives: apostles, prophets, bishops, teachers, coaches, parents, and others. Many men and women have deeply blessed our lives. And we dedicate this book to the two leaders who have had by far the greatest influence upon us: Rean Robbins-Duncan and Patricia Peterson Pinegar.

Though well educated, our dear wives have never had formal training in leadership. Most of their life's work has been invested in nurturing our families. That proves the point: great leadership is not about theory or title, and it's certainly not about "technique." Great leadership is about all the things that make Rean and Pat so magnificent: faith, vision, integrity, love unfeigned, charity, courage, gratitude, love unfeigned, patience, humility, optimism, love unfeigned, dedication, affirmation, caring, love unfeigned. And, oh yes, did we mention love unfeigned?

When people are around Rean and Pat, they simply want to be better and to do better. *That* kind of influence is what great leadership is about.

You can do it, too!

Rodger Dean Duncan
Ed J. Pinegar

ACCLAIM FOR
LEADERSHIP FOR SAINTS

"This is a book for our time. It has been said that, 'Membership in this Church is a call to leadership.' In our shared responsibility to become more effective leaders, I highly recommend this book for all members of the Church."

from the foreword by
Ardeth Greene Kapp

"As good people search for ways to add value, this book provides the basic currency. Filled with wise, reinforcing quotes, it's brilliantly insightful, illuminating, instructive and inspiring. It's profound, yet user-friendly. It's visionary, yet highly practical. It's seasoned with powerful stories and examples that bring the principles to life. It's full of hope and optimism. It's written with wonderful sensitivity, yet it minces no words in connecting the dots between good intentions and great performance. *Leadership for Saints* captures the essence of what we should be and do when we're called to serve—written by two very experienced, wise, orthodox, faithful leaders and great human beings."

Stephen R. Covey, Ph.D.
author of *Seven Habits of Highly Effective People*

"This is a multiple-vitamin book, enriched with calories that count, and no extra fat. A daily dosage will upgrade one's vital signs and skills in all the dimensions of leadership."

Truman G. Madsen, Ph.D.
Professor Emeritus of Philosophy, Brigham Young University

"The practice of righteous, effective leadership is a critical test of our Christianity. It requires a deliberate ascension from mediocrity. True leaders are principle-driven, selfless, incorruptible, and they get things done by bringing out the best in others. *Leadership for Saints* shows the way."

Hugh Nibley, Ph.D
Professor Emeritus of Religion, Brigham Young University

"Developing leadership skills rapidly is vital to moving the Lord's work forward. Some come into the Church with great abilities. But many need help in learning the important skills that will enable them to influence others to come unto Christ and to remain strong themselves when tested. As President Hinckley said: 'You can be a leader. You must be a leader.' Leadership for Saints will help in this worthy purpose. It will deepen the knowledge and bless the lives of members as well as investigators or new converts. I recommend this book to everyone—including those now serving in leadership positions."

Mary Ellen Smoot
former General President of the Relief Society

"This is a page-turner. It's easy reading for busy people, with depth and scope of content to satisfy the serious gospel student. Rodger Duncan and Ed Pinegar, outstanding teachers and leaders, apply contemporary methods to eternal principles that strengthen effectiveness. These *rules for Godliness* are valuable for sisters and brethren alike. Here you will find a fresh definition of what great leadership *is*, what great leaders *are*, what they *see* for those they are committed to help, and what they *do* about it. This book will be quoted and re-quoted all across the Church in every training situation, and it can work for you."

Elaine Cannon
former General President of the Young Women

"This is a book of vision and hope for any person seeking to become an effective leader. Written with that end in mind, its pages pulse with an assurance and practical knowledge that invigorates leadership. Every reader will discover insights and wisdom that are pure gold."

Michael W. Barker
former Stake President

"The first paragraph of *Leadership for Saints* got me hooked. The stories, quotes, and pearls kept me reading even when I thought I was too busy, too tired, and too discouraged to be taught anything. And as I read, I kept thinking, "I can do that!" And I will. If I were a bishop or stake president, I would give a copy of this book to every person I called to serve."

Glen C. Griffin, M.D.
author of *It Takes a Parent to Raise a Child*

"The insights of *Leadership for Saints* are a welcome resource for people who are as interested in their *being* as they are in their *doing*. This book can help you in your family, in your Church responsibility, community service, and leadership in the business world."

Brent Barlow, Ph.D.
Educator and Marriage Counselor

"Basically, the plan of salvation is a leadership training seminar. Being a covenant people is a pledge to be leaders. Instead of groping in the dark or using trial and error, read this book, which gives both the vision and the nitty-gritty skills, to fulfill this call to leadership."

Maurine Proctor
Editor-in-Chief, *Meridian Magazine*

"Those who want to improve their leadership skills should to do two things:
1 - Read *Leadership for Saints*
2 - "Do it"

Wesley M. Bitters
Director, Center for the Advancement of Leadership

"*Leadership for Saints* offers the means and motivation to all of us who would be better servants in the kingdom. Rodger Duncan and Ed Pinegar make complex issues of Church leadership understandable. Their book's unique design reinforces correct principles by placing quotes from great leaders alongside their text. This gives the reader the benefit of two books in one. Their work will be a valued addition to every member's home library."

Bruce L. Christensen
Senior Vice President of Bonneville International
and former President of the Public Broadcasting Service (PBS)

"*Leadership for Saints* will find its way to the briefcases, desks, nightstands, bookshelves and libraries of every Latter-day Saint who values leadership and recognizes the need for physical, mental, emotional and spiritual renewal. It should be read and pondered by everyone searching for effective answers in the quest to balance personal, family, Church, and professional commitments."

Steven Hall
Assistant Dean, Utah Valley State College

"*Leadership for Saints* is a great read as well as an incredible tool. I will use it extensively, and I'm immediately sending copies to my children and grandchildren. The entire membership of the Church will benefit from this book."

Beverly Campbell

"*Leadership for Saints* is a valuable tool; whether you're working to strengthen your marriage, raise your children, run a company, or magnify your Church calling, its insights will inspire and direct you. Its pages ring true."

Ahmed and Juliette Qureshi
Parents and Church Workers

"Principled leadership is one of the most significant needs in the world today. *Leadership for Saints,* with its delightful blend of principles, stories, examples, scriptures, humor, and inspiration will help decrease the leadership deficit. The authors, who live these principles themselves, deliver their message with great conviction, practicality and experience. Whether leading a family, a ward Relief Society, an elders quorum, a neighborhood committee, a stake, a company, or a first-grade class, this book gives sound guidance for improving your leadership capabilities."

Ned C. Hill, Ph.D.
Dean, Marriott School of Management
Brigham Young University

"This marvelous book has the power to turn leadership into love and service into sacred stewardship. It's packed with wisdom and insights that will lift Saints from ordinary to extraordinary performance. What a gift to all who lead at Church, in the community and at home."

Gary and Joy Lundberg
co-authors of *I Don't Have to Make Everything All Better*

"Two of this generation's great leaders have created a leadership tool of magnificent proportions. The abundant quotations from General Authorities and other prominent leaders make this book a marvelous resource for the seasoned leader. And the thoughtful, thorough presentation of leadership fundamentals will be of great value to the beginning leader. This is a balanced blend of original information drawn from the abundant experiences of the two authors, and carefully researched and documented material drawn from the leadership experts of the world. *Leadership for Saints* will quickly become one of the most valued books in every LDS home and office."

William R. Siddoway
former Dean of Continuing Education and Associate Dean of
the Marriott School of Management
at Brigham Young University; former Stake President, former
Mission President

"I served as bishop on three successive occasions. Other than raising a family, my leadership experience was limited. Even though I had good mentors and an array of handbooks, I needed help improving myself as a leader, as a teacher, and parent. *Leadership for Saints* would not only have assisted then, but can assist me now. Anyone who is called to serve in the Church, as well as those presiding over families, will find this book a source of inspiration."

a former bishop in Sydney, Australia

"How to shepherd? This is one of the most pressing concerns of a rapidly expanding international leadership. Rodger Dean Duncan and Ed J. Pinegar share with us practical and inspiring principles and methods to help us learn Christlike ways to lead and lift. From mutual teacher to stake president, from one giving a talk to one counseling, there is thoughtful advice for all. *Leadership for Saints* would have helped me in every calling I've ever held!"

Deirdre M. Paulsen

"This book reinforces time-honored principles in an enticing way. The examples included and the organization of the chapters lead readers to improve their personal leadership style, whether in a family, a Church calling, or in a business environment. *Leadership for Saints* is a valuable resource. It contains both valid doctrine and compelling spiritual insight. The concepts are timeless. I know they work!"

Elaine L. Jack
former General President of the Relief Society

THE CALL FOR LEADERSHIP

You can be a leader. You must be a leader, as a member of this Church, in those causes for which this Church stands. Do not let fear overcome your efforts. . . . Cast that fear aside and be valiant in the cause of truth and righteousness and faith. If you now decide that this will become the pattern of your life, you will not have to make that decision again. You will put on "the armour of God," and raise your voice in defense of truth, whatever the circumstances now and in all the years that lie ahead.[1]

—President Gordon B. Hinckley

The need for leadership through the wards and stakes of Zion (is increasing) dramatically. What is needed is not just young people of training and skill, but rather we will need a generation of great faith, those who have learned discipline and discipleship. What will be needed is a generation who understand not only how to organize a ward but also how to build faith, how to sustain the weak and faltering, and how to defend the truth.[2]

—President Howard W. Hunter

Yours is a great responsibility in this day when the need for courageous leadership is so urgent. *You* can become those leaders. . . . Our (people) need to develop qualities of leadership. They need to learn the value of staying power—stick-to-it-iveness. They need to learn devotion to duty—the devotion to duty that keeps a good doctor on the job right around the clock in an emergency; the devotion to duty that leads a scientist or a teacher to persevere in a low-paying position in public service because that is where his maximum contribution can be made.[3]

—President Ezra Taft Benson

Jesus was not afraid to make demands of those he led. His leadership was not condescending or soft. He had the courage to call Peter and others to leave their fishing nets and to follow Him, not after the fishing season or after the next catch, but now! Today! Jesus let the people know that he believed in them and in their possibilities, and thus he was free to help them stretch their souls in fresh achievement.[4] . . . if we desire to lengthen our stride in the management of the kingdom at all levels of its operation . . . we must be more willing to expend more of our time, talent, and means in providing leadership training.[4]

—President Spencer W. Kimball

There is an urgent need for leaders of the Church at all levels to spiritualize their leadership more so that our overarching purposes are not lost in the mechanics of meetings, organizations.[5]

—President Harold B. Lee

. . . the Church has no corps of professionals. It must depend upon leaders developed from within the membership as a whole . . . the Church's need is greater than ever now, both in terms of numbers and a requirement for greater devotion and skill . . . so must the need for more capable and responsible leadership multiply.[6]

—Elder Neal A. Maxwell

The first great need of any quorum is efficient leadership, a leadership that will say, "Come, let us go;" a leadership that will strive to emulate the Great Teacher who said: "I have given you an example, that ye should do as I have done."[7]

—Elder John A. Widtsoe

Leadership is what we need . . . Good leadership means effective work; poor leadership means poor work. That is a rule that will always be in force.[8]

—Elder Rudger Clawson

Looking forward to an enormous increase in membership and operating on a worldwide basis, we see great challenges, opportunities, and responsibilities. Our great need is leaders, and our greatest challenge is to develop them.[9]

—**Elder Franklin D. Richards**

Endnotes

1. "Stand Up for Truth," BYU Devotional Address, September 17, 1996. Also in Gordon B. Hinckley, *Teachings of Gordon B. Hinckley* (Salt Lake City: Deseret Book Co., 1997), 138.

2. Howard W. Hunter, *The Teachings of Howard W. Hunter,* edited by Clyde J. Williams (Salt Lake City: Bookcraft, 1997), 122.

3. Ezra Taft Benson, *God, Family, Country: Our Three Great Loyalties* (Salt Lake City: Deseret Book Co., 1974), 9.

4. Spencer W. Kimball, "Jesus, the Perfect Leader," *Ensign*, August 1979, 5.

5. Harold B. Lee, *The Teachings of Harold B. Lee,* ed. Clyde J. Williams (Salt Lake City: Bookcraft, 1996), 466.

6. Neal A. Maxwell, *A More Excellent Way: Essays on Leadership for Latter-day Saints,* (Salt Lake City: Deseret Book Co., 1967), Foreword *iii.*

7. John A. Widtsoe, *Priesthood and Church Government* (Salt Lake City: Deseret Book Co., 1939), 144.

8. Rudger Clawson, *Conference Report,* October 1941, Afternoon Meeting, 123.

9. Franklin D. Richards, *Conference Report,* October 1967, Afternoon Meeting, 147.

FOREWORD

This is our time. This is a book for our time. We live in a remarkable season with greater opportunities than ever for Latter-day Saints with leadership skills, attributes, and vision that can make a difference. In the home, in our Church callings, in the community and professionally, we have opportunities and responsibilities unique to this time and season.

It has been said that "Membership in this Church is a call to leadership." We must prepare to respond to the call. In the words of President Gordon B. Hinckley, "The purpose of all our work is to help the sons and daughters of God find their way along the road that leads to immortality and eternal life. When all is said and done our greatest responsibility as leaders in this Church is to increase the knowledge of our people concerning their place as sons and daughters of God, their divine inheritance and their divine eternal destiny" (*Teachings of Gordon B. Hinckley*, 111).

Leaders with this eternal perspective will be guided by principles that lift and build. The uniqueness of *Leadership for Saints* is that it is written by authors who have a deep appreciation of the resources available with every calling in the Church through "study and also by faith." For many years it has been my privilege to know and associate with Rodger Dean Duncan and Ed J. Pinegar. They write from decades of effective and successful leadership experience in the Church and otherwise. They are men of integrity, motivated by a sincere desire to build the Kingdom and help others do likewise.

This book teaches leadership principles and practices with practical application, examples, and self-help questions that motivate and provide vision. Specific guidelines are offered to help you evaluate progress, build confidence in your gifts and talents, and extend your natural ability.

Leadership for Saints is written for the seasoned leader, introducing principles that invite careful analyses as well as forward-looking concepts that expand vision and possibilities. It is also written for the novice in search of simple steps to measure effectiveness and plan for success. As a bonus, this book includes an impressive collection of relevant quotes on leadership by apostles and prophets, as well as other renowned leaders. These extensive quotes, placed as sidebar information, give focus and context to the principles and practices developed within each chapter. All the principles are reinforced with doctrinal support using scriptural references and personal testimonies.

Application of the principles presented here will prepare leaders to step up to a new level of performance and meet the challenge of President Hinckley: "We can do better!"

The message of *Leadership for Saints* is comprehensive, developmental, and easy to follow with one principle leading naturally to the next. It begins with the role of a leader and concludes with a very insightful and quick reference to the most commonly asked questions with thoughtful responses from these experienced leaders.

While this work is a valuable text for the serious student of leadership, it is also an inspiring book for the leader seeking inspiration and direction. It is a story book for the one who enjoys following the process that helps inexperienced leaders become more effective leaders and in turn help others to become leaders. This book is informational, inspirational, instructional, practical, and very stimulating as one chapter invites anticipation of the next.

Leadership for Saints is a declaration of purpose. In our shared responsibility to become more effective leaders, I highly recommend this book for all members of the Church.

Ardeth Greene Kapp
former General President of the Young Women
and author of *Lead, Guide, and Walk Beside*

PREFACE

Effective leadership has always been a vital part of the Lord's work. As the restored Church continues to expand at unprecedented rates around the globe, effective leadership is today more critical than ever.

In offering this book on leadership, we acknowledge that we are no different from you who are reading it. Like you, we are simply trying to do better and be better in our service to the Kingdom of God. In these pages, we share some of the teachings, nurturing moments, and training that people and the Spirit of the Lord have given us. We esteem ourselves no better than anyone else (see Alma 1:26). Yet with a desire to serve and bless, we offer this work with the hope that it will help all who seek to be better leaders.

Leadership is stewardship. Faithful stewards:
- seek the will of Heavenly Father and share that vision with the people they serve.
- live by every word that proceedeth from the mouth of God (D&C 84:43–46).
- draw strength from the grace of God and from the infinite and eternal Atonement of the Savior Jesus Christ.
- measure every thought and act against the principles of righteousness.
- embrace the counsel to "Trust in the Lord with all thine heart; and lean not unto thine own understanding" (Proverbs 3:5).
- as always, are Spirit-directed in all things.

These are not simply "nice" things to do when convenient. They are absolutely imperative. Effective leadership stewards work hard to perfect their own gifts and skills *and* they constantly acknowledge and seek inspiration from the *source* of their gifts and skills.

No matter how new or how seasoned you are, you can do better. You can learn more. You can become a better leader—even a great leader as you rely on the Lord and work with all your heart, might, mind, and strength.

In these pages you will find principles and doctrines taught in the scriptures, wisdom shared by our Church leaders, and pertinent ideas regarding human relationships. Our intent is for this volume to provide a vision of what you can do as well as what you can become.

This is a book of vision and hope. *You* can become a great leader.

Rodger Dean Duncan
Ed J. Pinegar

Contacting the Authors

This book represents an ongoing exploration into the role of leadership in Latter-day Saint life. We welcome feedback from our readers in the form of thoughts, stories, examples, reflections, and testimonies. Though we are not always able to respond to every e-mail, we enjoy hearing and learning from our readers.

To reach us via e-mail, go to www.covenant-lds.com and click on the "Authors" section. This will enable you to link to our e-mail addresses and contact us directly.

TABLE OF CONTENTS

SECTION 1

UNDERSTANDING
THE ROLE
OF LEADERSHIP

1

WHAT GREAT LEADERSHIP IS

Latter-day Saints who lead come in all sizes and shapes, with a wide range of experience, with many levels of confidence and competence, and with numerous titles. Some are called Mother or Father. Some are called Teacher or Coach. Some are called President or Bishop. Many are simply called Brother or Sister.

Virtually everything we do as covenant-keepers involves leadership. Great teaching requires leadership. Great missionary effort requires leadership. Great parenting requires leadership. The Lord's work moves forward as His servants exercise leadership by faith and obedience.

Leadership is much less a function of position than it is of influence. And while it is true that some "leadership traits" come as gifts or inherited attributes, it is also true that effective leadership can be learned.

In short, if you genuinely want to be a better leader than you believe you are now, you can improve if you (1) faithfully practice correct principles and (2) petition the Lord for the associated spiritual gifts. Just as our salvation is secured through the fine balance of grace and works, so great leadership is realized through our hard work and the Lord's merciful bestowal of gifts of the Spirit. In fact, if you

There is an urgent need for leaders of the Church at all levels to spiritualize their leadership more so that our overarching purposes are not lost in the mechanics of meetings, organizations.
—**Harold B. Lee**[1]

Yours is a great responsibility in this day when the need for courageous leadership is so urgent. *You* can become those leaders! This emphasizes the increasing need for leadership training and the wise delegation of responsibility.
—**Ezra Taft Benson**[2]

faithfully practice correct principles *and* make yourself eligible for spiritual gifts, you might even become a *great* leader. Great leaders are great leaders because they value the results of great leadership and because they are willing to pay the price of continuous improvement.

Leadership in The Church of Jesus Christ of Latter-day Saints is not just about conducting meetings or "sitting on the stand."

At every level, leadership in the Church is about learning how to become an instrument in the Lord's hands to minister to His children. In this way we can exercise a righteous influence.

Leadership in the Church is about vision and imagination and stretching for greater heights.

It's about affirmation and encouragement.

It's about teaching and correcting.

It's about good listening and good coaching.

It's about planning with a purpose and turning good plans into good results.

It's about changing lives for the better.

WE ARE HEIRS TO BLESSINGS

We love and serve the Lord best by loving and serving one another. This book is about service through effective leadership. Not the sheepherder kind of leadership. The *shepherd* kind. The scriptures are replete with direction, standards, and examples of excellent leadership. For instance, in D&C 38 we read:

> Verily I say unto you, teach one another according to the office wherewith I have appointed you;

I fear we have learned too much over the years about programs at the expense of insufficient understanding of principles. If we had learned more principles, priesthood leaders all over the world would be solving local problems with local resources without waiting for something to come from Church headquarters. Members would be helping each other without waiting for an assignment.
—**Glenn L. Pace**[3]

God will hold you responsible for those whom you might have saved had you done your duty.
—**John Taylor**[4]

And let every man esteem his brother as himself, and practice virtue and holiness before me.

And again I say unto you, let every man esteem his brother as himself.

For what man among you having twelve sons, and is no respecter of them, and they serve him obediently, and he saith unto the one: Be thou clothed in robes and sit thou here; and to the other: Be thou clothed in rags and sit thou there—and looketh upon his sons and saith I am just?

Behold, this I have given unto you as a parable, and it is even as I am. I say unto you, be one; and if ye are not one ye are not mine (D&C 38:23–27).

The theme of this revelation is *unity*—unity between us and the Savior, unity among those of us who have been called, and unity between us and those we've been called to serve.

Of course we all know that some people are simply not as easy to serve as others. Some are not as easily approachable or as easily loveable or as easily teachable. We can use these circumstances as marvelous reminders of our own human weaknesses and inabilities and nothingness without God. It is in these challenges that we draw closer to the Lord by begging to be filled with His love for the unlovable. These are the seasons of our greatest growth and humility. But they are still our Father's children. They are part of our family. (And we dare say that many of us

I know sanctification comes not with any particular calling, but with genuine acts of service, often for which there is no specific calling.
—**Glenn L. Pace**[5]

wouldn't be where we are today if someone at another place and time had not invested the time and trouble to approach us, to love us and to teach us.)

Now—just how do we go about serving those who are less eager to be served, as well as those who are eager and willing to accept our love and service? The answer is in D&C 50:14, a revelation in which the Lord tells us that we are called "to preach [His] gospel by the Spirit, even the Comforter which was sent forth to teach the truth." And then He adds:

> Verily I say unto you, he that is ordained of me and sent forth to preach the word of truth by the Comforter, in the Spirit of truth, doth he preach it by the Spirit of truth or some other way?
>
> And if it be by some other way it is not of God.
>
> And again, he that receiveth the word of truth, doth he receive it by the Spirit of truth or some other way?
>
> If it be some other way it is not of God.
>
> Therefore, why is it that ye cannot understand and know, that he that receiveth the word by the Spirit of truth receiveth it as it is preached by the Spirit of truth?
>
> Wherefore, he that preacheth and he that receiveth, understand one another and both are edified and rejoice together.

True shepherds nourish and care for each member of the flock and keep them in remembrance. They do not simply number them. Shepherds know and care for their flock. A shepherd cannot rest when even one of the flock is lost.
—**Robert D. Hales**[6]

Those who would lead in this Church must set the example of personal righteousness. They should seek for the constant guidance of the Holy Spirit. They should have their lives and homes in order. . . . They must be exemplary in all their conduct. They should be men of honor and integrity.
—**James E. Faust**[7]

And that which doth not edify is not of God, and is darkness (D&C 50:17–23).

As leaders we must make ourselves eligible for the influence of the Spirit so that He can inspire our prayers. He will tell us in our minds and hearts what gifts we need to better succor the challenging individuals we are called to serve. When the Spirit directs our asking, we can exercise confident and powerful faith that our pleadings will be realized and that both the servant and the served will be blessed. The greatest leaders recognize their dependence upon the Holy Spirit in every aspect of their stewardship.

BRINGING LIGHT TO OTHERS

Our challenge, then—as parents, as stake leaders, as bishoprics, as quorum presidencies, as Relief Society leaders, as missionaries, as nurturers of young men and young women, as single adult representatives, and as instructors in all of these areas—is to bring light into the lives of others. We can do that only when we have light in our *own* lives.

Therefore, hold up your light that it may shine unto the world.

Behold I am the light which ye shall hold up—that which ye have seen me do (3 Nephi 18:24).

His message is perfectly clear: *He* is the light which we must hold up. We are just the candles. He is the flame. We are the Lord's disciples, and with the calling and charge we

Consider now, even at this moment, the brother or sister next to you, or one nearby, through the hall, across the street, or down the road. Will you put yourself so in tune that you can try to see in that person what the Savior sees? Will you share with that brother or sister something that would ease their load or brighten their day, or expand their vision, or increase their hope, and try to do it the way you think the Savior might do it? Could you? Would you?
—**Ardeth Greene Kapp**[8]

have a responsibility as leaders to be willing and worthy to share His light unto the people—

> Ye are my disciples; and ye are a light unto this people, who are a remnant of the house of Joseph (3 Nephi 15:12).

> Verily, verily, I say unto you, I give unto you to be the light of this people. A city that is set on a hill cannot be hid.

> Behold, do men light a candle and put it under a bushel? Nay, but on a candlestick, and it giveth light to all that are in the house;

> Therefore let your light so shine before this people, that they may see your good works and glorify your Father who is in heaven (3 Nephi 12:14–16).

Our duty is clear. We are the light of the world, for we follow Christ, we preach of Christ, we bring the light of the gospel of Jesus Christ to all mankind. It is evident in the Doctrine and Covenants that we are commanded to be a light and a savior of mankind. If we do otherwise, the consequence of being "good for nothing" is our reward.

> For they were set to be a light unto the world, and to be the saviors of men;

> And inasmuch as they are not the saviors of men, they are as salt that has lost its savor, and is thenceforth good for nothing but to be cast out and trodden under foot of men" (D&C 103:9–10).

You cannot light a fire in another soul unless it is burning in your own soul. You teachers, the testimony that you bear, the spirit with which you teach and with which you lead, is one of the most important assets that you can have, as you help to strengthen those who need so much, wherein you have so much to give.
—**Harold B. Lee**[9]

Ammon was this kind of leader. He brought the light of the Savior to King Lamoni.

> Now, this was what Ammon desired, for he knew that king Lamoni was under the power of God; he knew that the dark veil of unbelief was being cast away from his mind, and the light which did light up his mind, which was the light of the glory of God, which was a marvelous light of his goodness—yea, this light had infused such joy into his soul, the cloud of darkness having been dispelled, and that the light of everlasting life was lit up in his soul, yea, he knew that this had overcome his natural frame, and he was carried away in God (Alma 19:6).

We can be this kind of servant, too. The light of God's love and truths comes only when we are worthy and receptive. Each one of us is entitled to discernment within the scope of his or her stewardship and calling. In addition, Elder Bruce R. McConkie taught us:

> There is no perfect operation of the power of discernment without revelation. Where the saints are concerned—since they have received the right to the constant companionship of the Holy Ghost—the Lord expects them to discern, not only between the righteous and the wicked, but between false and true philosophies, educational theories, sciences, political concepts and social schemes. Unfortunately, in many instances, even good (people) hearken to the

> You have not done enough, you've never done enough, so long as you have something more to contribute.
> —**Dag Hammerskjöld**[10]

"traditions of their fathers" and rely on the learning of the world rather than the revelations of the Lord, so that they do not enjoy the full play of the spirit of discernment.[1]

The most effective quorum leaders seem to be those who consistently pray for their brethren—by name—and then seek them out. They consistently and faithfully hold personal priesthood interviews with home teachers—as part of the Lord's system of accountability and as an important way to stay close to the families whom they are called to bless.

The most effective youth leaders seem to be those who specifically pray for—and receive—the spirit of discernment as they teach and guide and serve as examples for our precious young people.

They've come to understand that service in the kingdom is rarely convenient, and they are called by the Lord Himself to serve *all* of His children, including those who rarely attend meetings and who require second- and third-mile efforts on our part.

Quite simply, we must *know* our people.

We must operate with love unfeigned.

We must validate and affirm each individual as a special son or daughter of our Father.

We must be prepared to "teach the one."

We must invite the Spirit to teach *us*. And then we must carefully and prayerfully *listen*.

When we do these things as faithful instruments in the hands of the Lord, He can bring about miracles through us. Our ministry bears wonderful fruit. Precious souls are rescued. Hearts and lives turn to the Savior. And the heavens rejoice.

When it comes to the work of the Lord and the attainment of his purposes, it is not enough to obtain a good result—it must be done in the right way.

—**Dallin H. Oaks**[11]

Underlying the ultimate capacity of any leader to lead is, of course, his capacity to love. As Kahlil Gibran observed, work is love made visible, and the quality of our work and our service to other people is a direct indication of our capacity for love. No leader can be fully effective without love, and those who try to serve without it will not be properly motivated and may even feel resentment and a sense of slavery.

—**Neal A. Maxwell**[12]

As leaders in the Church, we have many responsibilities. But our primary obligation, our primary *covenant*, is to "invite all to come unto Christ." (See D&C 20:59.)

CATALYSTS FOR THE MIGHTY CHANGE

In our individual ministries, we can choose to be either primarily transactional leaders or transformational leaders.

A transactional leader focuses on routine and regimented activities. He invests most of his energy in making sure meetings run on time, that administrative details are properly handled and that completed tasks are noted on check lists.

A transformational leader focuses primarily on initiating and "managing" change in those he serves. He invests energy in efforts that influence people to improve, to stretch and to redefine what's possible.

While the Church needs both kinds of leaders, it is the *transformational* leader who is most influential in bringing about "the mighty change" in people.

A good bishop, for example, will certainly ensure (mostly by delegating to other capable people) that appropriate information is gathered and accurate reports are generated, that music is prepared for sacrament meeting and that the ward social is planned and organized. Those are transactional matters that must be done properly. The bishop's primary responsibility, however, is to be a transformational leader—to be an instrument in the hands of the Lord in bringing about positive change in the lives of his people. He does this by doing what every good leader does—by loving unconditionally, by teaching

We can improve, and when all is said and done that's what this is all about: improvement, changing our lives so that we can help people change their lives and be better. And let's build Zion in the earth. That's what it is all about.
—**Gordon B. Hinckley**[13]

You give little when you give of your possessions. It is when you give of yourself that you truly give.
—**Kahlil Gibran**[14]

correct principles and by giving encouragement. He does it in confidential interviews where he listens with empathy and teaches with tenderness. He does it with a reassuring handshake or a pat on the shoulder. He does it with a kind smile. He does it when he addresses the entire ward and when he talks one-on-one with a child. He does it by boldly bearing witness to the saving principles of the restored gospel.

The same applies to all of us wherever we serve. We must be sure that the appropriate transactional things are done properly. They are an important part of our ministry. But more importantly, we must tend to the transformational things, the things that change lives and save souls. Transactional things involve making sure the train runs on time. Transformational things involve making sure the train is on the right track, that it is headed in the right direction, and that everyone who wants to make the trip has a ticket.

> I fear that some of what we do is of little worth from an eternal perspective. . . . Some of our numbers have been known to be busily engaged in the 'the thick of thin things.'
> —**H. Burke Peterson**[15]

LEADERS, FOLLOWERS, AND MORE LEADERS

The Lord is most eager that we understand and labor together to accomplish the mission of the restored Church: to invite all to come unto Christ and be perfected in Him. There are three important ways to accomplish this mission: (1) to proclaim the gospel; (2) to perfect the Saints; and (3) to redeem the dead. Everything we do should be aimed at fulfilling one or more of those purposes.

It's often said that a critical part of effective leadership is the development of effective followers. That is no doubt true, especially when considering "Are the followers reaching their potential? Are they learning? Serving? Do they achieve the required results? Do they change with grace? (Do they) manage conflict?"[2]

We believe another characteristic of effective leaders is the development of other effective leaders. Especially in the Church, which as a fulfillment of prophecy is growing at unprecedented rates, the development of a wider and wider army of influential, spirit-driven leaders is critical to the vitality of the people and the success of the work.

Our challenge is focus. For a variety of reasons, many of us who hold leadership positions in the Church suffer occasional bouts of blurred vision. On the surface, we are good "institutional" Latter-day Saints. We accept callings. We go through the requisite administrative motions. But do we have the genuine, Christlike caring for one another that is embodied in the covenants we have made? Sometimes, we simply need more *focus*.

There's a marvelous little book, long out of print, called *Markings*. It's essentially the personal journal of Dag Hammarskjöld, a wonderful Swede, a truly Christian gentleman, who served as Secretary-General of the United Nations. (He was killed in a tragic airplane crash in Africa in 1961.) In Hammarskjöld's little book are many powerful statements that have profoundly affected millions of people. One of those universal truths is this: "It is more noble to give yourself completely to one individual than to labor diligently for the salvation of the masses."[3]

Think about that. Embodied in that statement is unfiltered truth, the pure love of Christ. As the Savior himself taught, the key to the ninety-nine is the one.

Love of God is something that requires action, for men cannot have faith in God, nor love him, unless they are acting in his cause, with their whole heart constantly thinking of him and giving of their physical strength in love.

—Joseph L. Wirthlin[16]

And it is only too true that many persons drift so carelessly and aimlessly through the world as to allow their surroundings to rule them, instead of impressing the character of a determined human will and noble purpose upon every thing that comes in their way.

—Brigham Young[17]

UNDERSTANDING LINKAGES

Everything you do as a leader should have a purpose or it is extraneous. Great leaders know that time and influence are the primary currencies by which they bring about good. Great leaders also know the importance of focus. Can you imagine the spiritual *leverage* we could exert throughout the Church if every Latter-day Saint would genuinely *focus* on just one other person?

A young father tells of a conversation he overheard between his 10-year-old son and 6-year-old daughter. The subject was colors. Sarah asked her big brother what you get when you mix blue with yellow.

Ten-year-old Matthew said: "With blue and yellow you get green."

Then he decided to test his little sister by asking, "What do you get when you mix red with orange?" Without missing a beat, little Sarah replied, "You get a sunset!"

That little girl is one of those blessed souls who understands linkages.

Do *you* understand linkages?

Do you understand the linkage between a strong and effective and involved Sunday School presidency—and bringing people to Christ?

Do you understand the linkage between well-prepared Sunday School and priesthood and Primary and Relief Society lessons—and bringing people to Christ?

Do you understand the linkage between home teaching and visiting teaching done the right way for the right reasons—and bringing people to Christ?

Do you understand the linkage between carefully planned and executed social and

> In serving others, we "find" ourselves in terms of acknowledging divine guidance in our lives. Furthermore, the more we serve our fellowmen in appropriate ways, the more substance there is to our souls. We become more significant individuals as we serve others. We become more substantive as we serve others. Indeed, it is easier to "find" ourselves because there is so much more of us to find!
>
> —Spencer W. Kimball[18]

cultural activities in our wards and branches—and bringing people to Christ?

Do you understand the linkage between attending the temple—and bringing people to Christ?

Do you understand the linkage between teaching simple gospel principles to Sunbeams and Valiants—and bringing people to Christ?

Do you understand the linkage between working with hard-to-handle teenagers—heirs to everything God has—and bringing people to Christ?

Do you understand the linkage between rendering compassionate service—and bringing people to Christ?

Do you understand the linkage between personal obedience—and bringing people to Christ?

Our labor as leaders in the Church is *the Lord's* work. In every facet of our assignments we have the opportunity to help bring others—and ourselves—closer to Him. As Elder Marvin J. Ashton said, "No one ever lifted someone else without stepping toward higher ground."[4]

Perhaps the best-known statement on effective leadership in the Church came from the Prophet Joseph himself: "I teach them correct principles and they govern themselves."

Contained here are at least three basic elements: (1) There *are* correct principles. (2) The leader is teacher and servant. (3) People are capable of self-government.

Faith in and love for the Lord Jesus Christ are the first and most important guiding principles. They are necessary ingredients in all practices and all programs

The principles of the gospel of Jesus Christ will never change, but environment, circumstances, institutions, and cultural patterns do. Our challenge is to move forward in our present realms with commitment and enthusiasm. We must do our part to progress and enjoy life while we are in the process of meeting our situations.
—**Marvin J. Ashton**[19]

Some members assume that one can be in full harmony with the spirit of the gospel, enjoy full fellowship in the Church, and at the same time be out of harmony with the leaders of the Church and the counsel and direction they give. Such a position is wholly inconsistent, because the guidance of this Church comes not alone from the written word but also from continuous revelation, and the Lord gives that revelation to the Church through his chosen prophet.
—**Marion G. Romney**[20]

pertaining to our stewardship. With faith and love come commitment. The Savior Himself is our model. Everything He has ever said and everything He has ever done modeled perfect leadership principles. His gospel is the foundation of every good thought we should have, every good motive we should act upon and every good deed we should offer in the service to others.

Essential to our success is that we operate under the direction of the living prophets with personal guidance from the Holy Ghost. Note this from D&C 12:5–9:

> Therefore, if you will ask of me you shall receive; if you will knock it shall be opened unto you.

Exaltation is achieved by keeping covenants, not by holding high position.
—**Boyd K. Packer**[21]

> Now, as you have asked, behold, I say unto you, keep my commandments, and seek to bring forth and establish the cause of Zion.

> Behold, I speak unto you, and also to all those who have desire to bring forth and establish this work.

> And no one can assist in this work except he shall be humble and full of love, having faith, hope, and charity, being temperate in all things, whatsoever shall be entrusted to his care.

> Behold, I am the light and the life of the world, that speak these words, therefore give heed with your might, and then you are called. Amen.

PRINCIPLES AND PRACTICES

To be trained in correct principles allows infinitely more freedom than to be taught only *practices*. For each true principle there are an infinite number of correct *practices*. As the Prophet Joseph observed, "A man is saved no faster than he gets knowledge, for if he does not get knowledge, he will be brought into captivity by some evil power in the other world, as evil spirits will have more knowledge, and consequently more power than many men who are on earth. Hence it needs revelation to assist us, and give us knowledge of the things of God."[5]

We must constantly bear in mind that the leader is teacher and servant. As always, the Savior is the perfect model:

Ye call me Master and Lord: and ye say well; for (so) I am.

> If I then, (your) Lord and Master, have washed your feet; ye also ought to wash one another's feet.
>
> For I have given you an example, that ye should do as I have done to you.
>
> Verily, verily, I say unto you, The servant is not greater than his lord; neither he that is sent greater than he that sent him.
>
> If ye know these things, happy are ye if ye do them (John 13:13–17).

Self-government is an ongoing process. The Lord is actively engaged in helping each person do his or her best. "For behold, this is my work

> We are individually responsible and will be held accountable for … the breaking of covenants by others for whom we are responsible insofar as such breaking is *the result of our failure to teach them*.
> —**Marion G. Romney**[22]

> In light of this doctrine developmental discipleship assumes genuine significance, inasmuch as our individual spiritual growth is so vital to our happiness and salvation. These words of King Benjamin take on added meaning: . . . "and becometh as a child, submissive, meek, humble, patient, full of love, willing to submit to all things which the Lord seeth fit to inflict upon him, even as a child doth submit to his father" (Mosiah 3:19; see Alma 13:28).
> —**Neal A. Maxwell**[23]

Attitude is an impor-
tant part of the foun-
dation upon which we
build a productive life.
In appraising our
present attitude, we
might ask: "Am I
working to become
my best self? Do I set
worthy and attainable
goals? Do I look
toward the positive in
life? Am I alert to ways
that I can render more
and better service? Am
I doing more than is
required of me?"
—**M. Russell Ballard**[24]

As the Church moves
into the challenges of
the last decades of this
century, the need for
leadership through the
wards and stakes of
Zion will increase
dramatically. What is
needed is not just
young people of
training and skill, but
rather we will need a
generation of great
faith, those who have
learned discipline and
discipleship. What will

and my glory—to bring to pass the immortality
and eternal life of man" (Moses 1:39).

Individual growth depends on the
demands the individual makes on himself,
from accepting responsibility (stewardship),
fulfilling that responsibility and being
accountable for his commitments.

As a leader in the Lord's Church, can you,
will you—

- See yourself as a teacher to your people?
- Change from seeing *your* people as *your*
  helpers in getting your assignment done,
  to seeing yourself as a servant to help *them*
  in *their* stewardships?
- Resist managing by fear and threats
  (implicit or explicit)?
- Give people a job, with a specific time to
  return and report, and then allow them
  the freedom to succeed?
- Wait for the Holy Ghost before reproving?
- Correct with clarity and charity, not anger?
- Love those you serve, especially after
  correcting?
- Include persuasion, long suffering, gentleness, meekness, and love unfeigned, kindness, and pure knowledge with your
  management skills?

All of this requires that leaders serve with
"the heart and a willing mind" (see D&C
64:34), and that we listen constantly for the
promptings of the Spirit.

But does that preclude an understanding
of and the ability to benefit from specific
leadership *skills*? Of course not. In fact, for
generations of Saints, the General Authorities
of the Church have emphasized the need for
more skilled leadership in the kingdom. It is

true that success in Church leadership is measured in terms of souls saved and strengthened, not in profit and loss. The Lord's work must be done by faith, by prayer, and by the Spirit. But just as the Savior reminded Oliver Cowdery (D&C 9:7–9), *we are expected to do our part, too.*

Our part is the focus of this book. It is designed to help Latter-day Saint leaders in stakes, wards, branches and families increase the effectiveness of their service. The authors do not profess to cover everything there is to know about effective service in the Church. But this book does attempt to view such leadership through a wide-angle lens. Treatment is given to the importance of personal worthiness and self-mastery. Being a model, not a critic. Relying on influence rather than on authority. Listening with empathy. Ministering versus administering. Becoming a partner with those you serve. Nurturing through focused teaching and interviewing. Managing meetings in ways that excite and motivate the participants. Delegating tasks—and accepting tasks—in ways that build people and inspire performance.

In short, bringing others, and ourselves, to Christ

In all these things, continuous improvement should be our goal. After all, does the Lord—the leader of us all—deserve any less? Does he *desire* any less for us?

be needed is a generation who understand not only how to organize a ward but also how to build faith, how to sustain the weak and faltering, and how to defend the truth. What is needed is a generation whose glory comes from their capacity to comprehend light and truth, who can with that light and truth then enlarge their capacity to love and to serve.

—**Howard W. Hunter**[25]

Cultivate an attitude of happiness. Cultivate a spirit of optimism. Walk with faith, rejoicing in the beauties of nature, in the goodness of those you love, in the testimony which you carry in your heart concerning things divine.

—**Gordon B. Hinckley**[26]

APPLYING THE PRINCIPLES

1. Make a list of about a half dozen of your roles in life. The list should include your obvious leadership roles like Church call-

ings as well as roles you may not always associate with leadership, such as parent, friend, neighbor, community volunteer.

2. Under each role, write the word "Linkage." Then jot down two or three things in that role that you do (or should do) to invite others to Christ. These may not be obvious and overt "missionary activities." For example, under the role of "Young Men counselor" you might write something like "Stay positive and upbeat in working with the Aaronic Priesthood." Under "community volunteer" you might write something like "Avoid criticizing; always look for the good and how to make it even better."

3. Make three specific commitments to yourself regarding your own leadership development. Take responsibility. Follow through.

YOU CAN DO IT!

You realize that everyone is a leader—at home, school, work and in the Church. You are a leader by example, within your role, or by an assignment or calling. Sometimes you can feel overwhelmed. There is no need to fear, for the Lord will not only provide a way but also give you the strength to do the work. You should be of good cheer. You are His child, doing His work. You are empowered by your God. He will bless you and you shall have glory and joy in the work. You are filled with the Spirit that will show you what to do and how to do it. Just do your best, and your best will constantly improve. Enjoy the journey. The role of a leader can be a blessing to you and those you serve.

You can do it!—in the strength of the Lord.

ENDNOTES FOR MAIN BODY TEXT

1. Bruce R. McConkie, *Mormon Doctrine* (Salt Lake City: Bookcraft, 1966), 197.

2. Max DePree, *Leadership Is An Art* (New York: Dell Publishing, 1989), 12.

3. Dag Hammarskjöld, *Markings* (New York: Alfred A. Knopf, 1964), 142.

4. Marvin J. Ashton, *Conference Report*, October 1973, 131.

5. Joseph Fielding Smith, compiler, *Teachings of the Prophet Joseph Smith* (Salt Lake City: Deseret Book, 1976), 217.

ENDNOTES FOR SIDEBARS

1. Harold B. Lee, *The Teachings of Harold B. Lee*, ed. Clyde J. Williams (Salt Lake City: Bookcraft, 1996), 466.

2. Ezra Taft Benson, *God, Family, Country: Our Three Great Loyalties* (Salt Lake City: Deseret Book Co., 1974), 9, 129.

3. Glenn L. Pace, "Principles and Programs," *Ensign*, May 1986, 23.

4. John Taylor, *Journal of Discourses*, 26 vols. (London: Latter-day Saints' Book Depot, 1854–1886), 20: 23–24.

5. Glenn L. Pace, "Confidence in the Lord," *Ensign*, May 1985, 78.

6. Robert D. Hales, "Some Have Compassion, Making a Difference," *Ensign*, May 1987, 35.

7. James E. Faust, "These I Will Make My Leaders," *Ensign*, November 1980, 34.

8. Ardeth Greene Kapp, *I Walk by Faith* (Salt Lake City: Deseret Book Co., 1987), 11.

9. Harold B. Lee, *Stand Ye in Holy Places* (Salt Lake City: Deseret Book Co., 1974), 187.

10. Dag Hammarskjöld, *Markings* (New York: Alfred A. Knopf, 1964), 158.

11. Dallin H. Oaks, *The Lord's Way* (Salt Lake City: Deseret Book Co., 1991), 9.

12. Neal A. Maxwell, *A More Excellent Way: Essays on Leadership for Latter-day Saints* (Salt Lake City: Deseret Book Co., 1967), 14.

13. Gordon B. Hinckley, *Teachings of Gordon B. Hinckley* (Salt Lake City: Deseret Book Co., 1997), 726.

14. Kahlil Gibran, *The Prophet* (New York: Alfred A. Knopf, Inc., 1994), 19.

15. H. Burke Peterson, "A Thought from the Scriptures," *Church News,* January 25, 1992.

16. Joseph L. Wirthlin, *Conference Report,* April 1948, Afternoon Meeting, 147.

17. Brigham Young, *Contributor,* vol. 10 (November 1888–October 1889), September 1889, 422–423.

18. Spencer W. Kimball, *President Kimball Speaks Out* (Salt Lake City: Deseret Book Co., 1981), 43–44.

19. Marvin J. Ashton, "Choose the Good Part," *Ensign,* May 1984, 9.

20. Marion G. Romney, "Unity," *Ensign,* May 1983, 17.

21. Boyd K. Packer, "Covenants," *Ensign*, May 1987, 24.

22. Marion G. Romney, *Ensign*, Nov. 1975, 73.

23. Neal A. Maxwell, *But for a Small Moment* (Salt Lake City: Bookcraft, 1986), 95.

24. M. Russell Ballard, "Providing for Our Needs," *Ensign*, May 1981, 86.

25. Howard W. Hunter, *The Teachings of Howard W. Hunter*, ed. Clyde J. Williams (Salt Lake City: Bookcraft, 1997), 122.

26. Gordon B. Hinckley, "If Thou Art Faithful," *Ensign*, November 1984, 92.

2

WHAT GREAT LEADERS ARE

Great leaders are people of great character. Great character enables vision and empathy. Great character makes possible personal revelation. Great character results in credibility and moral authority. Character affects everything a leader says and does. What a leader *is* radiates to others.

By every word and deed in your leadership role(s), you project an image. For you to be effective, your image must be worthy of the confidence of those you serve. As you become more Christlike, the light of the Lord emanates through you because of His goodness.

In your quest to become like Jesus and to lead like Jesus, you progress line upon line and precept upon precept. You develop a Christlike character. You will not be perfect in all things, but you *can* be perfect in your overall approach to leadership. You can be perfectly consistent in seeking correct principles. You can be perfectly consistent in trying to be fair. You can be perfectly consistent in wanting to do the right thing. After all, character is about seeking and trying and wanting.

As people around you sense your genuineness, their confidence in you will increase. They will "give you slack" when you make

We need strong leaders of good character in all places—leaders who are examples of integrity, dependability, and righteousness.
—N. Eldon Tanner[1]

[The Savior] has identified the cardinal virtues of His divine character in a revelation to all priesthood holders who serve in His ministry. In this revelation, which was given a year before the Church was organized, He said, "Remember faith, virtue, knowledge, temperance, patience, brotherly kindness, godliness, charity, humility, diligence." (D&C 4:6.) These are the virtues we are to emulate. This is the Christlike character.
—Ezra Taft Benson[2]

Those whose hearts are pure do the right things for the right reasons. Their motives are pure and unsullied by self-interest, ambition, pride, or malice.
—Alexander B. Morrison[3]

There was to be no deviation from the outlined plan for the redemption of mankind. It is definite and specific in all of its requirements. Obedience is the price of salvation.
—Alma Sonne[4]

First, the successful leader has faith. He recognizes that the greatest force in this world today is the power of God as it works through man.
—Thomas S. Monson[5]

mistakes because they know you are seeking, trying and wanting great results in their behalf. Character is not about perfect results every time. Character is about constantly trying to do the right things for the right reasons.

We love the motto used by the elders and sisters in the Japan Fukuoka Mission:

- OBEDIENCE is the price.
- FAITH is the power.
- LOVE is the motive.
- THE SPIRIT is the key.
- CHRIST is the reason.

Of course this applies not only to missionary endeavors, but to every other kind of leadership in the Church. Let's consider each part and see how it applies to your leadership.

OBEDIENCE is the price. To be a great leader, you must be a worthy vessel. Great leaders are clean and guileless.. They obey the commandments and keep themselves free from the burden of sin and guilt. They lead in righteousness. Great leaders also obey principles of healthy human relationships. Violating such principles jeopardizes effective leadership. Great leaders understand true principles of every kind, and they gladly pay the price of obedience because they have discovered the "linkage" between obedience (to promptings and commandments) and increased endowments of personal revelation.

FAITH is the power. To be a great leader, you must be a person with faith in the Lord Jesus Christ. You must have rock solid faith in God, our Eternal Father, and in His Son Jesus Christ. You must have faith in the promises of God. And you must have faith in yourself as a child of God. To be a great leader, you must have a believer's heart. Great leaders perform with the assurance expressed by Nephi, who noted that the Lord gives us no task without enabling us to accomplish it (see 1 Nephi 3:7 and 1 Nephi 17:3). Great leaders are powered by faith.

LOVE is the motive. To be a great leader, you must exude love. You must lead because you genuinely love the cause you champion and the people you serve. You must work hard to build strong loyalty—not loyalty to you, but loyalty to the Savior. After all, bringing people to Christ is your primary purpose. Everything else is subordinate. Nothing should be done for your ego or self-promotion. Everything should be done to glorify God and to bring the Gospel of Jesus Christ to the forefront in the lives of those you lead. Great leaders are motivated by love.

THE SPIRIT is the key. Great leaders are able and willing to be guided by the Spirit (see 1 Nephi 4:6). To provide the quality of leadership your people want and expect from you, you must have the Holy Ghost as your constant companion and guide. Although certain skills are very important, great leadership is not a matter of "technique" or "style." Great leadership is primarily a function of connection—our connection with the Lord first and foremost, connection with correct principles, connection with a vision for the future, (closing the gap between present performance and desired future performance), and connection with the people we serve. All of these require discernment, and discernment comes from the Spirit. Great leaders seek and listen to and heed the promptings from the Spirit.

Faith . . . worketh by love. Love is the motive power underlying all things. The atonement, righteous living, all good things grow out of love—the love of God for his children and the love of his children for each other and their Creator.
—**Bruce R. McConkie**[6]

Actuated by that spirit, leaders will think more of men than of the success of a system.
—**David O. McKay**[7]

Let us never forget that we are disciples of the Lord Jesus Christ. He is our Leader and Exemplar.

—Stephen L Richards[8]

. . . leadership success is an appropriate combination of knowledge, attitude, skills and habits made effective through the instrument of the personality of the leader.

—Sterling W. Sill[9]

CHRIST is the reason. Great leaders focus on the Savior. They not only believe *in* Jesus, they *believe* Jesus. He is the central purpose of everything they plan and everything they do. In comparison, nothing else matters. They understand this is *His* work, not theirs. They recognize that they are merely vessels for Him to accomplish His purposes and designs among His children. After all the programs, meetings and planning are finished, a great leader would determine his success by observing whether the people under his stewardship had drawn closer to the Lord. For great leaders, all roads must lead to Jesus the Christ, who then leads us to the Father.

To be a great leader, your integrity will be beyond reproach. Your word will be your bond. Complete honesty will be your only policy. Righteousness will be your native tongue. You will be true to yourself and true to your God. There will be no duplicity in your life.

The cornerstone character traits of great leaders are integrity and honesty. We define integrity as "the integration of behavior and professed values." People of integrity are clear about what they stand for and what they will not stand for. People of integrity say what they mean and mean what they say. People of integrity adhere steadfastly to high standards of morality and personal ethics. Honesty, a sibling of integrity, involves being genuine and truthful.

As your character is developed, it becomes the launch pad of your performance as a leader. You willingly sacrifice for the greater good. Your ability to teach and persuade increases. Your perception and power of discernment are enhanced. Your goals are clear. Your preparation and planning in the strength of the Lord are done with an eye single to His glory and for the blessing of those you lead and serve. You are not concerned with receiving credit or accolades. Your ego is never a factor in your leadership.

Your success will be measured not in programs, but in the lives of the people you serve. As you realize your place as an instrument in the hands of God, your enthusiasm will be unrelenting. Your heart will be full of desire to bless and serve. Your conscience will be free from sin and your example will be a standard for those who depend on you. As a leader, you will go forward with dedication and steadfastness in the pursuit of excellence in the things you do and the people you serve.

As you ponder, pray, and meditate on becoming a servant leader, always remember that your character should reflect the love and light of the Lord Jesus Christ and our Heavenly Father. Determine to be "even as He is" (see 3 Nephi 27:27).

Your character (what you truly are) is based on your capacity and diligence in becoming like our Savior Jesus Christ. When you take upon yourself His name, always remember Him and keep His commandments, you have the blessing of His Spirit. So you should be anxiously engaged in a good cause—the cause of becoming a man or woman of God with character attributes like our Savior's.

- You will repent and be free from guilt.
- You will live a righteous life.
- You will exercise faith, live with hope and show an abundance of Christlike charity.
- You will seek to build up the Kingdom of God.

. . . leaders are to understand the nature of their stewardships and seek to fulfill their responsibilities in meekness and humility. Good leaders understand their roles as servants to others (Matt. 20:27). Thus, doubly benefited, persons gain from leadership experiences through unselfishly serving in a Christlike way and, through such service, come to know the Lord (Mosiah 5:13).
—**Paul H. Thompson**[10]

- You will strive continually to live by the Spirit, worthy of personal revelation.
- You will have the faith and courage to act upon the promptings of the Spirit.

How does all this begin? It begins with humility.

All of us are weak and, as we acknowledge our weaknesses, we will be moved to humility. We confess our total dependence upon our Heavenly Father and our Savior. We understand the divine relationship that binds us together. In the state of humility, we can be made strong (see Ether 12:27; 2 Corinthians 12:10). The Lord will make us strong, and in His strength we can do all things (see Alma 26:11–12). It is in Him that we can be strong enough to do the Lord's will and to magnify our callings. We can do all things by faith (see Moroni 7:33). We really can! There is nothing too difficult for the Lord and His servants to accomplish.

President Thomas S. Monson said, "He who is on the Lord's errand is entitled to the Lord's help. Whom the Lord calls the Lord qualifies."[1] With this encouragement from a prophet of God, should we not set our goals high? Should we not have confidence? Is not this the time to be in the pursuit of leadership excellence? The answer is a resounding yes. So, let's move onward and upward.

In one of the core covenants of our faith we promise, "to stand as witnesses of God at all times and in all things, and in all places that (we) may be in" (see Mosiah 18:9). This cannot be an idle promise. Standing as a witness of God involves much more than merely acknowledging His existence. It also

The leader who has integrity, who leads by example, will never suffer the scorn of disappointed youth who declare, "People are always telling us what to do but aren't doing it themselves." The apostle Paul counseled us wisely, "Be thou an example of the believers, in word, in conversation, in charity, in spirit, in faith, in purity" (1 Timothy 4:12).

—Thomas S. Monson[11]

involves doing everything humanly and heavenly possible to *be* like Him. Honoring covenants is a matter of love and a matter of character.

When you're asked the question, "Are you honest in your dealings with your fellowman?" how do you—how *can* you—respond?

You'll notice that the question doesn't read, "Are you *sometimes* honest?" or "Are you *usually* honest?" or "Are you honest only when everyone's watching?"

In a priesthood interview for worthiness, the question couldn't be more plain: "Are you honest in your dealings with your fellowman?" Period. We can't assume that this question covers only the more obvious integrity issues like bank robbery and cattle rustling. It also covers all the more subtle shades of honesty so often ignored by the rest of the world.

The covenant-keeping Latter-day Saint does not tell black lies, gray lies or even the so-called white lies. He tells only the truth.

The covenant-keeping Latter-day Saint does not cheat on his tax return. If he dislikes the tax laws, he works to get them changed. But while they are in force, he obeys them.

The covenant-keeping Latter-day Saint doesn't need a radar detection device in his car because he doesn't plan to cheat others out of their right to safety on the highways. He obeys traffic laws.

The covenant-keeping Latter-day Saint keeps his promises. When he says he'll finish a job, he finishes it. When he incurs a debt, he pays it—on time. When he accepts a responsibility, he is reliable. He performs. He can be trusted.

. . . people who have entered into a covenant with God have been known as "Saints" from the days of ancient Israel to the present. Such a lofty title is not presumptive or something to boast about. It is a means of identifying those who are striving to become sanctified through covenant-making and covenant-keeping (see D&C 125:2).

—**Carlos E. Asay**[12]

... all who have held positions of leadership will be required to give an accounting for that which they did with the office or position that was theirs. Righteous government is essential to the preservation of society, and leadership is a sacred trust.

—Joseph Fielding McConkie and Robert L. Millet[13]

Here are five things to remember when trouble strikes. They are among the most fundamental truths of a gospel-centered life.
1. Pray earnestly and fast with purpose and devotion. . . .
2. Immerse yourself in the scriptures . . .
3. Serve others. . . .
4. Be patient. . . .
5. Have faith. . . .
—Jeffrey R. Holland[14]

Honesty and integrity are not "sometime" things. They must be "all the time" things. Either we behave with integrity or we do not. Either we are honest or we are not. A half truth is a lie. A broken promise is a blemish on our reputation and a stumbling block in our progression.

President David O. McKay taught that it's more important to be trusted than to be loved. The covenant-keeping Latter-day Saint can be trusted because he is totally honest with his fellowman. And what could be more loveable or more Christlike?

Improving our character and becoming Christlike takes a lifetime. It is a constant journey, not a one-time event. It is continuous change and improvement. It is part of the grand process that begins in repentance and in applying the Savior's infinite and eternal Atonement in our lives.

USER-FRIENDLY CHRISTIANS

In the world of technology, the term "user-friendly" is often intended to denote a computer system that is easy to use, one that doesn't demand a lot of indulgence and pampering. In our roles as leaders in the Church, the Lord wants each of us to be a "user-friendly" Christian—or, in other words, a Christ-centered Saint.

We can be good "institutional" Latter-day Saints. We can be proud of the Church, its heritage, its programs, its traditions, even its university's football team. We can embrace the Church's culture, its social morés, its members' work ethic. That's all well and good. Membership in the Lord's Church is indeed a wondrous experience. It's a way of living. It's a way of life. But it is *not* adequate to ensure our eternal life. The Church is merely the vehicle to bring us to the Author of our salvation, Jesus the Christ. Too often members allow the "programming" to get in the way of their relationship with the Lord. This happens when our security rests in the outward performances of the law and not in the hidden issues of the heart. If we are to call ourselves "Saints" in the intended sense of the word, we must be—first and foremost—followers of Christ. We must be Christlike. We must make ourselves able and keep ourselves willing to be instruments for righteousness in the Lord's hands. We must be the Lord's hands on earth to bless and minister to His people. Then we will be Christ-centered Saints, leaders of destiny.

In what ways can this be done? You could compile a good list of your own. Here are three worth considering.

1. ACKNOWLEDGE THE DIVINITY OF THE SAVIOR AND THE NECESSITY OF HIS MISSION.

The plan of salvation is specific. It includes guidelines for our behavior and spiritual maturation. The key figure in this plan is Jesus Christ—our Father's only begotten Son in the flesh. Our Savior. Our Redeemer. The Holy Messiah.

Jesus loved us enough to die for us so we could, first, live again, and second, become exalted—the first automatically, the good with the bad, through His grace; the second upon condition of personal obedience and worthiness through His grace. As true Saints, we should acknowledge and bear witness of these things to the world.

Our lives must become a symbol of meaningful expression, the symbol of our declaration of our testimony of the living Christ, the Eternal Son of the living God.
—**Gordon B. Hinckley**[15]

The gospel is a program, a way of life, the plan of personal salvation, and is based upon personal responsibility.

—Spencer W. Kimball[16]

2. UNDERSTAND AND ACCEPT OUR OWN ROLE AND PERSONAL RESPONSIBILITY IN THE PLAN OF SALVATION.

Our third article of faith declares: "We believe that through the Atonement of Christ, all mankind may be saved, by obedience to the laws and ordinances of the Gospel." *We* must take the initiative to acknowledge our sins and forsake them. *We* must take the initiative to understand our Father's will and obey it.

3. BE ANXIOUSLY ENGAGED IN DOING THE LORD'S WORK IN THE LORD'S WAY.

J. Golden Kimball reportedly said there are three kinds of members in the Church: the Saints, the ain'ts, and the complaints. Our challenge, our opportunity, our *covenant*, is to be Saints.

Service to God and, thereby, to one another, is a fundamental tenet of our religion. That cannot be changed by any number of excuses or any amount of rationalization.

In D&C 101, through the allegory of the servants who second-guessed their master, the Lord underscores the consequences of failing to follow instructions.

It is a great work that we are engaged in, and it is for us to prepare ourselves for the labor before us, and to acknowledge God, his authority, his law and his priesthood in all things.

—John Taylor[17]

> They were slow to hearken unto the voice of the Lord their God; therefore, the Lord their God is slow to hearken unto their prayers, to answer them in the day of their trouble.

> In the day of their peace they esteemed lightly my counsel; but, in the day of their trouble, of necessity they feel after me (D&C 101:7–8).

A key to our progression—and a constant test to our character—is doing the Lord's work in the Lord's way. This does not mean we are to become automatons, each a clone of the other. There is great room for individuality in blessing those whom we're called to bless. But the Lord does expect us to serve in righteousness. And with that service there often must come sacrifice and consecration.

Elder Bruce R. McConkie wrote the following while serving as a mission president in Australia:

MY MISSIONARY COMMISSION
I am called of God. My authority is above that of the kings of the earth. By revelation I have been selected as a personal representative of the Lord Jesus Christ. He is my Master and he has chosen me to represent him. To stand in his place, to say and do what he himself would say and do if he personally were ministering to the very people to whom he has sent me. My voice is his voice, and my acts are his acts; my words are his words and my doctrine is his doctrine. My commission is to do what he wants done. To say what he wants said. To be a living modern witness in word and deed of the divinity of his great and marvelous latter-day work.[2]

Of course, one doesn't need to wear a missionary nametag to enjoy the benefits of such a commission. It applies to all Saints who righteously serve the Lord.

Throughout the Church, we see faithful members give up hobbies, favorite television

President Spencer W. Kimball stated: "We must lay on the altar and sacrifice whatever is required by the Lord. We begin by offering a 'broken heart and a contrite spirit.' We follow this by giving our best effort in our assigned fields of labor and callings. Finally we consecrate our time, talents, and means as called upon by our file leaders and as prompted by the whisperings of the Spirit. . . . And as we give, we find that 'sacrifice brings forth the blessings of heaven!'" (Hymns, no. 147.)

And in the end, we learn it was no sacrifice at all.

—Carlos E. Asay[18]

programs, lots of recreational reading, Saturday afternoon athletic events, home improvement projects and many other activities because they put the Kingdom of God first. Giving a full measure involves consecrating our time, talents, and means to building the Church, the Kingdom of God, on earth.

We are *not* counseled to neglect our families. Quite the contrary. We must work to save our families. As leaders we must always remember that we will be released from our Church callings but we will never receive a release from our divine appointment of father and husband, mother and wife. Stakes may be organized and divided anytime in our Church buildings but the sacred institution of families may be organized only in the holy temple. David O. McKay made it clear that a priesthood holder's first stewardship accountability from the Lord will be for his wife and then his children. With that said, neither are we counseled to use our families as an excuse for not giving full service to our Church assignments. The issue isn't choosing between success with our families and success with our Church stewardships—and "success" is defined as doing the best we can. Rather, the issue is recognizing that failure in one area invariably leads to failure in both. We cannot have celestial families unless we are living the celestial law of consecration. The Holy Spirit will lead us to balance our time and effort between family and Church responsibilities.

What does all this have to do with character? Everything. True Christianity is not just a matter of organizational affiliation. True

> No other success can compensate for failure in the home.
> – **David O. McKay**[19]

> True Christianity is love in action. There is no better way to manifest love for God than to show an unselfish love for one's fellowmen.
> – **Thomas S. Monson**[20]

Christianity is a matter of integrity to our relationship with God. True Christianity is a matter of character.

In every sense, great leaders in the Church are Christ-centered Saints. While their personalities, styles and skills may vary widely, the common thread of their character is faithfulness, devotion, love unfeigned, sacrifice and consecration. They live as though their lives depend on their character because they do.

This great statement by George D. Boardman really puts into perspective the process of building character: "Sow a thought, and you reap an act; sow an act, and you reap a habit; sow a habit and you reap a character; sow a character, and you reap a destiny."[3] It is a process that takes time and effort. It takes a value system based on moral principles. It takes self-discipline.

The leader who aspires to be better works to know *himself* better. He makes an effort to explore his spiritual roots.

The scriptures tell us we are children of God. This knowledge gives us precious perspective about our own worth.

In the parables of the lost sheep, the lost coin, and the lost son (see Luke 15), the Savior taught how much our Father loves *each* of us. In each parable, Jesus compared that which was lost to the soul of man, and pointedly declared that there is rejoicing among the angels over one repentant sinner.

Lethargy and despondency have no place in us. Instead, knowing what we know about our spiritual genealogy, we should be motivated to *change*.

Men and women who turn their lives over to God will discover that He can make a lot more out of their lives than they can. He will deepen their joys, expand their vision, quicken their minds, strengthen their muscles, lift their spirits, multiply their blessings, increase their opportunities, comfort their souls, raise up friends, and pour out peace. Whoever will lose his life in the service of God will find eternal life (see Matthew 10:39).
—**Ezra Taft Benson**[21]

Consider this perspective from C. S. Lewis:

Imagine yourself as a living house. God comes in to rebuild that house. At first, perhaps, you can understand what He is doing. He is getting the drains right and stopping the leaks in the roof and so on. You knew that those jobs needed doing and so you are not surprised. But presently He starts knocking the house about in a way that hurts abominably and does not seem to make sense. What on earth is He up to? The explanation is that He is building quite a different house from the one you thought of—throwing out a new wing here or an extra floor there, running up towers, making courtyards. You thought you were going to be made into a decent little cottage, but He is building a palace.[4]

Our loving Father, who is the greatest Architect and the greatest Builder, has a plan for us that's bigger and bolder than anything we can imagine.

As part of our climb to be better and to do better as leaders, we can expect some adversity. When we choose to follow the Savior, we should expect some suffering, some loneliness and even some occasional injustice. But in such times, it's good to recall the words of Orson F. Whitney, an apostle in the early 1900s:

No pain that we suffer, no trial that we experience is wasted. It ministers to our education, to the development of such qualities as patience, faith, fortitude and humility. All that we suffer and all we endure, especially when we endure it patiently, purifies our hearts, expands our soul and makes us more tender and charitable, more worthy to be called the children of God. It is through (this) that we gain the education that we came here to acquire and which will make us more like our Father in heaven.[5]

We live in a time when the world has more distractions and temptations, more rapid change than ever before in the history of the human family. Sometimes fighting off worldly distractions feels a bit like trying to push water uphill with a rake. And yet we *can* make the journey safely. We *can* return home with our spirits intact. But the trip is fraught with many blind spots, and we must travel with great care. Part of that great care is being sure that our character is strong and constantly growing stronger.

One of the great blessings of leadership is that we often draw strength and insight from the very people we're trying to serve. We love the story told by our dear friend Ardeth Kapp, former general Young Women president in the Church. She received a letter from a participant of a Young Women's conference attended by several hundred mothers and daughters: "Dear Sister Kapp. I waited in line after the meeting and you gave me a hug and said some wonderful things to me. I was the girl in the green jumper on the second row. Could you please write and tell me what you said. I forgot and I want to write it in my journal so I can read it when I'm feeling down."[6]

> Every apostle, prophet, and legal administrator whom I have commissioned to offer the fruit of eternal life to men shall be cut off by my Father unless he carries forward my work; and every minister who is faithful in my service shall be pruned of dead foliage (divested of worldly distractions) and given power to bring forth more fruit.
>
> —Bruce R. McConkie[22]

Now that's the tenderness of youth because this young girl didn't fully understand what happened to her. What happened to her is she felt the Spirit distill upon the occasion and she wanted somehow to reach back to that spiritual moment. She wanted to recognize and enjoy—again and again—the tenderness of her brief time with a great leader.

Isn't that really what leadership is all about? Oh, they may say, "Do you remember me? I was the one in the green dress." But what they really mean is, "Help me feel again what I felt when we were together. Help me feel good about myself. Help me know that I matter. Help me know that Heavenly Father knows who I am and that He loves me."

When we allow ourselves to serve as instruments for righteousness in the Lord's hands, others among Father's children are comforted and strengthened. Their loyalties are not to us. Their loyalties are to the source that allows us to be part of the miracle. A great leader will always clarify that God is the true source of the love and light the people feel lest he (the leader) be guilty of holding himself up as the light.

We are part of God's miracle—as recipients and as conduits. We're also part of the wave talked about in the seventh chapter of Moses: "And righteousness will I send down out of heaven (the Lord says); and truth will I send forth out of the earth, to bear testimony of mine Only Begotten; his resurrection from the dead; yea, and also the resurrection of all men; and righteousness and truth will I cause to sweep the earth as with a flood, to gather out mine elect from the four quarters of the earth" (Moses 7:62).

Bless them with love. Let them know that you love them. It's so important. You are not generals running an army. You are servants of God, ministering to His people. Bless them with love.

—**Gordon B. Hinckley**[23]

It is *our* charge to be the beacons of righteousness spoken of in the Book of Mormon and echoed in the Doctrine and Covenants: "Hold up your light that it may shine unto the world" (see 3 Nephi 18:24). "Arise and shine forth, that thy light may be a standard for the nations" (see D&C 115:5).

As Christ-centered servants, we cannot walk or talk or do as people of the world. We have an *obligation* to bless and lift those without gospel truths unto fulfilling God's great purposes and destinies for them. Ours is a *covenant* requiring great character. Only then can we be great leaders.

QUESTIONS OF CONSCIENCE

- Am I willing to pay the price of obedience? Do I? In what areas do I resist?
- Do I exercise sufficient faith? Am I seeking to be endowed with greater faith through stricter obedience and increased sacrifice?
- Is love for God and for His Son *really* the motive for everything I do and say?
- Am I genuinely worthy of the promptings of the Spirit? Am I submissive to the Spirit?
- Do I not only believe *in* the Savior, but do I also *believe* the promises He has extended to me? Do I trust Him? Am I worthy of *His* trust?
- Is integrity one of my defining characteristics?
- Do I honestly strive to do my duty, even when it's difficult or inconvenient?
- Do I do the right thing, even when no one is watching?
- Am I teachable?

- As a leader, do I constantly remember that I am a servant?
- Am I seeking the specific guidance from the Spirit to divide my energies and time between family and Church responsibilities?

APPLYING THE PRINCIPLES

1. Reflect on your favorite stories from the scriptures that illustrate the leadership style of the Savior and other great leaders like Moses, Nephi, Alma, and King Benjamin. Jot down the key learning you get from each story. Consider specific ways you can apply the learnings in your own leadership service.

2. Note the motto of the Japan Fukuoka Mission regarding obedience, faith, love, the Spirit and Christ. How do these apply to you? How can diligent application of these principles help you be better and do better? Make commitments. Take responsibility. Follow through.

3. Consider the C. S. Lewis quote on page 36. What do you suppose Heavenly Father's plan is for *you*? What are you willing to do to help translate His plan into reality?

YOU CAN DO IT!

You were destined to become "even as He is" (3 Nephi 27:27). You are hopefully engaged in the process of taking upon you His divine nature (see 2 Peter 1:3–12) by becoming a man or woman of God, possessed with a Christlike character. It is exciting. It takes time. It can be exhausting. It is often frustrating—but it is worth it. It is fulfilling. Find joy in knowing that each day is a day to prepare to meet God. You are not just a human being having a spiritual experience. You are a spiritual being having a human experience.

You can do it!—in the strength of the Lord.

ENDNOTES FOR MAIN BODY TEXT

1. Thomas S. Monson, *Live the Good Life* (Salt Lake City: Deseret Book Co., 1988), 116, 121.

2. Bruce R. McConkie, "How Great Is My Calling . . ." From a talk given as President of the Australian Mission.

3. Quote by Samuel Smiles. Sean Covey, *The 7 Habits of Highly Effective Teens* (New York: Simon and Schuster, 1998), 8.

4. C. S. Lewis, *Mere Christianity* (San Francisco: Harper Collins, 2001), 204.

5. J. Vaughn Featherstone, *The Incomparable Christ* (Salt Lake City: Deseret Book Co.,1995), 92–93.

6. Ardeth Green Kapp, *My Neighbor, My Sister, My Friend* (Salt Lake City: Deseret Book Co., 1990), xi.

For additional insight into the linkage between character and great leadership, see Spencer W. Kimball, "Jesus: The Perfect Leader," *Ensign*, August 1979, 5–7.

ENDNOTES FOR SIDEBARS

1. N. Eldon Tanner, "Why Is My Boy Wandering Tonight?" *Ensign*, November 1974, 85.

2. Ezra Taft Benson, *Come unto Christ* (Salt Lake City: Deseret Book Co., 1983), 48.

3. Alexander B. Morrison, *Visions of Zion* (Salt Lake City: Deseret Book Co., 1993), 19- 20.

4. Alma Sonne, *Conference Report,* April 1968, Afternoon Meeting, 41.

5. Thomas S. Monson, *Be Your Best Self* (Salt Lake City: Deseret Book Co., 1979), 116.

6. Bruce R. McConkie, *Doctrinal New Testament Commentary*, 3 vols. (Salt Lake City: Bookcraft, 1965–1973), 2:481.

7. David O. McKay, *Conference Report,* October 1944, Afternoon Meeting, 81.

8. Stephen L Richards, *Conference Report*, April 1939, Afternoon Meeting, 41.

9. Elder Sterling W. Sill, October 3, 1960, *BYU Speeches of the Year,* 6.

10. *Encyclopedia of Mormonism,* 1–4 vols., edited by Daniel H. Ludlow (New York: Macmillan, 1992), 815.

11. Thomas S. Monson, *Be Your Best Self* (Salt Lake City: Deseret Book Co., 1979), 116–117.

12. Carlos E. Asay, *Family Pecan Trees: Planting a Legacy of Faith at Home* (Salt Lake City: Deseret Book Co., 1992), 213–214.

13. Joseph Fielding McConkie and Robert L. Millet, *Doctrinal Commentary on the Book of Mormon,* 4 vols. (Salt Lake City: Bookcraft, 1987–1992), 2: 201.

14. Jeffrey R. Holland, *However Long and Hard the Road* (Salt Lake City: Deseret Book Co., 1985), 9.

15. Gordon B. Hinckley, *Teachings of Gordon B. Hinckley* (Salt Lake City: Deseret Book Co., 1997), 184.

16. Spencer W. Kimball, *The Teachings of Spencer W. Kimball.*, ed. Edward L. Kimball (Salt Lake City: Bookcraft, 1982), 28.

17. John Taylor, *The Gospel Kingdom: Selections from the Writings and*

Discourses of John Taylor, selected, arranged, and edited, with an introduction by G. Homer Durham (Salt Lake City: Improvement Era, 1941), 166.

18. Carlos E. Asay, *The Seven M's of Missionary Service: Proclaiming the Gospel as a Member or Full-time Missionary* (Salt Lake City: Bookcraft, 1996), 129–30.

19. David O. McKay, *Steppingstones to an Abundant Life* (Salt Lake City: Deseret Book Co., 1971), 284.

20. Thomas S. Monson, comp., *Favorite Quotations from the Collection of Thomas S. Monson* (Salt Lake City: Deseret Book Co., 1985), 44.

21. Ezra Taft Benson, *The Teachings of Ezra Taft Benson* (Salt Lake City: Bookcraft, 1988), 361. ("Jesus Christ—Gifts and Expectations," Christmas Devotional, Salt Lake City, Utah, 7 December 1986.)

22. Bruce R. McConkie, *Doctrinal New Testament Commentary*, 3 vols. (Salt Lake City: Bookcraft, 1965–1973), 1:745.

23. Gordon B. Hinckley, *Teachings of Gordon B. Hinckley* (Salt Lake City: Deseret Book Co., 1997), 339. (Berlin Germany Regional Conference, priesthood leadership session, June 15, 1996.)

3

WHAT GREAT LEADERS SEE

Great leaders have vision. With clarity, they see who they are and understand how they "fit" in the larger scheme of things. They are both humble and confident—humble as they lead with influence rather than authority or position, and confident as they acknowledge they are on the Lord's mission being used to accomplish His purposes.

Great leaders see potential everywhere. They see the people they lead as individuals, not as a mass of humanity. They see the individual pieces of detail as well as the broad brush strokes of the big picture. They see the gap between where performance is now and where it should be in the future. They are clear about the cause they champion. They envision, often in very specific terms, what they want to help their people do and become. They constantly practice the art of the possible. Great leaders are people of vision.

There's really nothing mysterious or complicated about vision. When you were a child, did you dream about what you wanted to be when you grew up? When you were in school, did you ever dream about what you hoped to accomplish in a particular class? When you became engaged, did you imagine the life you hoped to build with your sweetheart?

While it is true that our earthly councils can be effectively used to actually formulate plans of action, it is also true that the leader must come to the council with, at the very least, a sense of vision.
—M. Russell Ballard[1]

When a leader in the Church inspires council members with vision, he helps them focus on their real mission so that they are ministering to people rather than merely administering programs.
—M. Russell Ballard[2]

A real leader ought to be able to foresee what his policies will do to the next generation. Vision must have hope and optimism in it. The past must push us—never pull us.
—Thomas S. Monson[3]

If you answered yes to any of those questions, you already have a pretty good idea what a "vision" is and have had some practical experience in forming one.

Great leaders—in the family, in the community, and in the Church at every level from nursery workers to Sunday School teachers to bishops to high councilors to stake presidents to General Authorities—understand the notion of "vision." And no matter where they serve, great leaders *use* vision in blessing the lives of others.

INSIDE-OUT PERSPECTIVE

Great leaders have an inside-out perspective. Because they care deeply about the people and causes they serve, they work hard to ensure that their own heads and hearts are "in the right place." They place more importance on accomplishing good than on who gets the credit. They invest energy in solving (or preventing) problems rather than in assigning blame. They constantly encourage and affirm those around them. They tend to be coachable, always in search of ideas to improve their own performance. (Perhaps that's why you are reading this book!) They appropriately honor the past, but they work passionately in the present because of their hopes and dreams for the future. This is vision.

A popular story-poem tells of a steep cliff, just off a winding mountain road, responsible for the death or maiming of many people. The village leaders meet to discuss the problem and decide that they can take either of two approaches: They can erect a strong fence at the edge of the cliff, or they can place an ambulance in the valley below. They choose the fence.

The Church of Jesus Christ operates on this same positive premise. To rescue the fallen is good, but it's better to prevent the fall.

We know that we are created in God's image, that our potential is unlimited, that our progress is eternal, and that we are blessed in proportion to our obedience to God's commandments. And to help ensure our continued growth, Latter-day Saints have developed many resources to meet their needs.

It's been said that merely sitting in church on Sunday no more makes you a Christian than sleeping in a garage makes you a car. We believe in that adage, and ours is a "total immersion" religion—not just because we baptize that way, but because our faith engenders a lifestyle of seven-day involvement.

In a typical Latter-day Saint congregation, as many as 200 people may hold positions. In addition to those specifically designated as "leaders," these include teachers, musicians, librarians, clerks, and assistants called by God to strengthen the spiritual and temporal lives of men, women, fathers, mothers, teenagers, and small children.

Our common mission—regardless of our current position or "title"—may be expressed in a single word: Service.

> Oh, that all council leaders could understand the value of service one to another as taught in this powerful example of the Savior.
> —M. Russell Ballard[4]

SERVICE IS OUR COVENANT

For the committed Latter-day Saint, service is his covenant. It is his responsibility as well as his joy. It is his reason for being.

We came to this earth to grow, to develop, to learn, to progress, to prove our obedience to God's will and become eligible to return to the presence of our Father in Heaven.

The heaven-ordained vehicle for this increase of worthiness is *service*. Love is the ultimate concern that brings about righteous service.

Service is not just a by-product of our main duty. Service is not an offshoot of something else deemed more urgent by our leaders.

The Lord simply commands us to "love one another." That love cannot be passive. It must be active. Service is the demonstration of our love.

Basic as it may seem, love is why tens of thousands of Latter-day Saint missionaries set aside their routine activities for eighteen to twenty-four months to go—at their own expense—to remote places on the globe to teach the gospel of Jesus Christ.

Love is why a busy Latter-day Saint mother (and we realize the phrase is redundant) makes room in her hectic schedule to teach others the fine points of money management . . . world cultures . . . social graces . . . or the practical, day-to-day applications of the New Testament.

Love is why a Latter-day Saint man— whose daily calendar is already filled with the responsibilities of marriage, fatherhood, and earning a living—gladly devotes another four to thirty hours a week to his Church calling.

Love is why Latter-day Saints of every age are willing to alter, postpone, or even set aside other pursuits so they can honor the covenant to bear one another's burdens, to comfort, to teach, and to lead.

Now, let's be frank. If our love-motivated service is so glorious, you may ask, why do many Church members privately feel guilty about their service? In this context, we don't use the term *guilt* in the sense of moral transgression. We use the term *guilt* to connote

Service is the virtue that has distinguished the great of all times and which they will be remembered by. It places a mark of nobility upon its disciples. It is the dividing line which separates the two great groups of the world—those who help and those who hinder, those who lift and those who lean, those who contribute and those who only consume. How much better it is to give than to receive. Service in any form is comely and beautiful. To give encouragement, to impart sympathy, to show interest, to banish fear, to build self-confidence and awaken hope in the hearts of others, in short to love them and to show it is to render the most precious service.

—Bryant S. Hinckley[5]

something innocent though painful—the sense of inadequacy, frustration and even helplessness experienced by many Church members who feel overwhelmed by all the tugs on their time and energy.

Even for a seasoned worker, receiving and accepting a call to serve in the Church can be an intimidating experience. Most of us have a wide range of priorities tugging at us—our families, our friends, our community obligations, our occupations, our need for physical exercise, our determination to keep up with our scripture study. We have only so many hours in a day, and a lack of balance in handling these priorities can launch us on a guilt trip and hamper our effectiveness.

Service, of course, is a covenant responsibility. As Latter-day Saints we talk of "renewing our covenants" through partaking of the sacrament. This is very important because worthy participation in the sacrament gives us the opportunity to focus on the Savior's atoning sacrifice for us, on His promises to us, and on our promises to Him. Through the sacrament, we may resolve to *do* better and to *be* better. More importantly, we may claim the promise of having the Holy Spirit attend us to guide the allocation of our energies.

It is through *service* that we are able to put that resolve into action. Our baptismal covenants include our promise "to mourn with those that mourn . . . comfort those that stand in need of comfort, and to stand as witnesses of God at all times and in all things, and in all places that (we) may be in" (Mosiah 18:9). These covenants encompass the entire range of service from home teaching and

Bishop Hunsaker also said to be effective in a calling, members need to make an effort to understand their callings. "Sometimes people accept callings and don't understand what is expected. This can make them frustrated once they start the calling."
—*Church News*[6]

Holders of the Melchizedek Priesthood receive it upon a covenant to use its powers in the service of others (see D&C 84:33-40). Indeed, service is a covenant obligation of all members of the Church of Jesus Christ.
—**Dallin H. Oaks**[7]

visiting teaching to every kind of adminis-tering and ministering needed in our Father's kingdom on earth.

Although most service does not directly involve a priesthood ordinance, righteous service is also a renewing of our covenants.

A question commonly asked by those called to serve is "How will I ever find the time?" It's usually not that the servant is reluc-tant. More commonly, the servant is simply lacking the vision of what is possible.

MIRED IN THE THICK OF THIN THINGS

The things which matter most must not be at the mercy of the things which matter least.
— Johann Wolfgang Goethe[8]

What does this mean? It means that many of us fall into the trap of placing a priority on so many items that most items do not get the attention they need. It means that many of us become disheartened by our apparent inability to excel to the extent we would like. It means that many of us become mired in the thick of thin things. We are subject to the frustration spawned by values and priorities that seem to be in conflict. Quite simply, we are out of balance.

You've likely heard the old saying that "if you fail to plan, you plan to fail." As with many clichés, this one is true. Yet effective planning is much more than juggling sched-ules. The best planners and the most effective servants are those who establish a clear mission for themselves and operate from that mission every hour of every day.

In this context, "mission" does not mean a specific assignment, like going to Brazil for 24 months to teach the gospel. Mission is used here to connote the sense of personal vision and the clarification of personal values that enable us to *perform* more comfortably and more effectively and with a greater sense of balance. Even our Father in Heaven has articulated His mission: "For behold, this is my work and my glory—to bring to pass the immortality and eternal life of man" (Moses 1:39).

Albert Einstein reportedly said that the significant problems we face cannot be solved with the same level of thinking we were at when we created them. Most of our problems with conflicting priorities are of our own making. With good intentions we innocently accept layer upon layer of responsibility, then wake up one morning befuddled and overwhelmed by it all.

The beginning of our relief comes when we *strategically* plan our lives. At first blush, this may sound too businesslike. Aren't strategic plans what business organizations use to guide their activities? Yes. And strategic plans are what effective people use to guide *their* activities, too.

There are likely countless ways that an individual can "build" a strategic plan for his life. But we're going to discuss only one way—not because it's necessarily the very best way, but because it's simple, it's values-based, it's easily adaptable to many situations, and it works.

DISCOVERING YOUR ROLES AND VALUES

A root cause of the frustration many people feel with their time management is a lack of clarity on who they are and what they value. Now, you might argue: "Oh, I know very well who I am. And I know what my values are." But do you *really*? When we pose this question to some people, they respond with something fairly generic like "I'm Mike

> To be sure your life will be full and abundant, you must plan your life.
> —Spencer W. Kimball[9]

> Without a goal there can be no real success. Indeed, a good definition of success is: 'The progressive realization of a worthy ideal.'
> —Thomas S. Monson[10]

Wilson and I stand for integrity" or "I'm Louise Gardner and I value fairness and reliability." It's hard to find fault with that, but such generalizations provide only limited assistance in reaching the hundreds, maybe even thousands, of decisions we're required to make.

Here's a simple process we've found to be helpful in clarifying your roles and values.

First, take a sheet of paper and begin to write down your roles. If you're an adult male, your list of roles might go something like this: Husband. Father. Son. Brother. Accountant. Neighbor. Young Men President. Home Teacher. With only a little bit of work, you can likely make a list of twenty or more roles.

Now, take any one of those roles and break it down into sub-roles. With more careful thought, for example, you'll realize that the role of Father has a number of sub-roles such as Coach, Teacher, Friend, Referee, Chauffeur, Banker, Nurturer, Cheerleader, and so on. As you list these roles and sub-roles, you'll notice that you're actually addressing the subject of values. For instance, if you were to list something like Nurturer as a sub-role under your role of Parent, that says something about the way you view—the way you *value*—the role of Parent. It also says something about the way you really desire to invest your time.

Keep at it. Write down as many roles as you can think of, then under each one list the sub-roles pertaining to that role. You'll find that many of these sub-roles tend to overlap. For example, the sub-role of Friend is appropriate for the roles of Parent, Neighbor, Teacher, etc.

The next step might be to take each sub-role and list the character traits that you feel appro-

> May we ponder carefully, deeply, and prayerfully our roles in life, where we can give the greatest service, to whom we can make the greatest contribution, what we should do with our lives and with our special skills and training. Our success will be measured by what we can give of our lives and our contribution to others rather than what we can get and receive from others.
>
> —Spencer W. Kimball[11]

priately support the sub-role. Under the sub-role of Friend, you might list such characteristics as loyalty, reliability, patience, and so forth.

CLARIFYING YOUR ROLES

Through all of this, you are clarifying your values. You are not *creating* your values, you are discovering and possibly rediscovering them.

Why is such a process important to us? Because truly effective people base their decisions and responses on their values. They are value-based and principle-centered. Clarifying the values and principles we embrace enables us to live our lives more effectively. Without this clarification we run the risk of making decisions and responding to situations and circumstances that are not consistent with our values and principles. We go through life in the reactive mode.

The process of brainstorming on your personal roles and sub-roles is a first step to writing your personal Mission Statement or Constitution. Again, you might say that you don't need a written document to guide you because you already know what you want to accomplish in life. But we have worked with hundreds of people who thought the same thing. Then, after patiently and diligently working through the process of clarifying their roles and values and writing a personal Mission Statement or Constitution, they discovered the wonderful comfort of bringing their lives into better focus and balance.

We recommend that upon beginning such an exercise you write two words at the top of the page: "First Draft." Drafting a personal Constitution is not a quick-fix kind of thing.

When we find our values in life, things that are most worthwhile, things of greatest worth to us, then we begin to feel our individuality, our creativity, our freedom, our strength. We begin to get possession of life when we concentrate not on the whole of reality in which we feel insignificant, but when we select certain things we are determined to live for; it seems to me that's when we get hold of life again.

—Lowell L. Bennion[12]

When we set (and write down!) specific goals based on clearly defined values, we have more control over our lives. We reward ourselves with a sense of direction and a feeling of accomplishment. We fill our lives with the power of purpose . . . When we set goals based upon a recognition of our eternal worth, our goals more fully reflect God's goals for us—or our unique potential. The mission statements we write will become personal manifestos, written from the perspective of children of God. Goal-oriented improvement programs will become most effective not just because we have guideposts of improvement but more importantly because those guideposts are in harmony with God's plan for our eternal progress.

—Lloyd D. Newell[13]

It requires careful and prayerful thought and consideration. It is a winnowing process. It involves a sifting of the various things that can consume—or bless—our lives. In fact, the sifting or screening metaphor is especially appropriate. Picture your life as an opportunity to respond to—by embracing or rejecting in various degrees—a wide range of activities or principles. In its finished form, your personal Constitution or Mission Statement serves as a screening device. By carefully setting up that screening device, you're better prepared to make the countless decisions we all make each day. Without such a screening device, we run the risk of deciding by default or deciding in a way that is in conflict with our mission and values.

It really doesn't matter whether you call this guiding document a Mission Statement, a Personal Constitution, a Declaration of Purpose, a Written Creed or anything else. The point is that you will benefit from drafting and referring to the document. The power of such a process and the resulting document is that it helps you *clarify* who you are and what is genuinely important to you. Then, when you get caught up in the routine of daily living and find yourself slipping away from the *balance* you desire, you can always refer to your document of guiding principles. You will become more a product of your deliberate values-based decisions than of external conditions. You will escape the danger of merely reacting to situations. You begin to manage your life instead of letting it manage you.

KEEP IT SIMPLE

Most good Mission Statements (we'll now use this phrase for simplicity and consistency) contain two basic elements: a declaration of what you want to *do* and a declaration of what you want to *be*.

The value of such a document is fourfold:

1. It forces you to think deeply and strategically about your life. The process expands your perspective and causes you to re-examine your deepest thoughts. It challenges you to resolve the inevitable conflicts between the "wants" and the "shoulds" in your life. And it enables you to identify and clarify the purpose of your life and what is most important to you.

2. The very act of writing it all down seems to be therapeutic and clarifying in and of itself. Undergoing the discipline of succinctly expressing such important thoughts can help us understand better than ever what we stand for and what we don't and won't stand for.

3. The act of writing the document seems to imprint our values and purposes more firmly in our minds. Then they become more cemented within our identity us instead of just something we pondered about in one instance and then set aside.

4. The document provides a tangible tool that keeps before us our hope and vision—and strategic plan—for our lives.

Although the notion of personal Mission Statement has received a lot of attention in the popular press in recent years, it is an ageless idea. Consider these:

Today, most active members would express the mission of the Church something like the following: "The threefold mission of The Church of Jesus Christ of Latter-day Saints is to [1] proclaim the gospel to all peoples, [2] perfect the Saints in Christ's church, and [3] perform vicarious ordinances for the eternal spirits of our deceased ancestors and others."

—**Victor L. Ludlow**[14]

CREED

A declaration of purpose, a personal mission statement, or an organizational theme focuses attention upon the central objectives of the person or group. Such objectives encompass many areas of influence and should contain long-range perspective. A mission statement declares both what we want *to do* and what we want *to become*, and it will also probably suggest *why* we want to do it. Such a creed states the principles or values that motivate and give purpose to our activities.

—**Victor Ludlow**[15]

I believe in God, the Almighty Ruler of nations, our great and good merciful Maker, our Father in heaven, who notes the fall of a sparrow and numbers the hairs on our heads. I recognize the sublime truth announced in the Holy Scriptures and proved by all history that those nations are blessed whose God is the Lord. I believe that the will of God prevails. Without him, all human reliance is vain. With that assistance I cannot fall. I have a solemn vow registered in heaven to finish the work I am in, in full view of my responsibility to God, with malice toward none; with charity for all; with firmness in the right, as God gives me to see the right.

—Abraham Lincoln

RESOLUTION

Let then our first act every morning be to make the following resolve for the day:

I shall not fear anyone on earth.

I shall fear only God.

I shall not bear ill toward anyone.
I shall not submit to injustice from anyone.

I shall conquer untruth by truth.

And in resisting untruth I shall put up with all suffering.

—Mahatma Gandhi

MY TASK

To be honest, to be kind;

To earn a little and to spend a little less;

To make upon the whole a family happier for his presence;

To renounce when that shall be necessary and not to be embittered;

To keep a few friends, but those without capitulation;

Above all, on the same grim conditions, to keep friends with himself—

Here is a task for all that man has of fortitude and delicacy.

—Robert Louis Stevenson

MY SYMPHONY

To live content with small means

To seek elegance rather than luxury, and refinement rather than fashion;

To be worthy, not respectable, and wealthy, not rich;

To study hard, think quietly, talk gently, act frankly;

To listen to stars and birds, to babes and sages; with an open heart;

> Strategic planning is essential to the success of any enterprise. A clear mission statement with goals and objectives are necessary ingredients for progress in any organization.
> —*Church News*[16]

To bear all cheerfully, do all bravely, await occasions, hurry never.

In a word, to let the spiritual, unbidden and unconscious, grow up through the common.

This is to be my symphony.
— William Ellery Channing

Others who choose to draft personal Mission Statements often include declarations such as these:

"I'll do everything I can to make our home a place of refuge, of joy, of peace, of comfort and harmony."
"I will be a concerned and informed citizen, appropriately involved in the political process to ensure that my voice is heard."
"My money will be my servant, not my master. I will regularly save or invest a portion of my income. I will keep myself free from consumer debt."

We've observed that many people turn to an especially simple format for their Mission Statements. After identifying their key roles, they simply state guiding principles under each role in the form of "bullet" points. For example, one man drafted his Mission Statement like this:

As a Disciple, *I will—*
* *honor my temple and priesthood covenants*
* *study and obey the commandments*
* *adopt and follow Christlike habits*
As a Patriarch, *I will—*

The guiding principles to the realization of the higher life are not many nor complex. Indeed, they are few and simple, and can be applied by everyone in any phase of life.
First, is a recognition of the reality of spiritual values . . .
The second condition I name is a sense of obligation to the social group . . .
Next to the obligation to society I name the power of self-denial and the resultant self-mastery . . .
A fourth contribution to spirituality I will name is a consciousness that the ultimate purpose of life is the perfecting of the individual. . . .
—**David O. McKay**[17]

- *honor, love and respect my companion*
- *teach correct principles by precept and by example*
- *maintain trusting relationships with my children*

  As a Family Member, *I will*—

- *honor my progenitors for what they did and who they are*
- *remember the reality of the eternal family*
- *nurture relationships with extended family*

This man, who has carefully distilled his persona to half a dozen key roles, uses his personal Mission Statement as a guide or road map in living his life. This is done not merely in the sense of regarding the document as a list of broad brush principles. The man uses the document to deliberately plan the way he spends that precious and finite resource called time.

TRANSLATING GOOD INTENTIONS INTO SPECIFIC ACTIONS

For instance, notice the goals expressed as "bullet" points under his roles. Each denotes *action*—containing verbs like "honor," "study," "obey," "adopt," "follow," "teach," "nurture." At the beginning of each week, the man translates these values and goals into specific plans for the next seven days. He schedules a temple trip with his wife or an evening of family history work. He makes a place on his calendar for daily scripture study. He plans phone calls or letters to family members who live in distant cities. In other words, he translates his good intentions into specific actions. He transforms his high-sounding values and goals into real-life action

In the process of exchanging themselves for higher spiritual values, they "become." Action is of value in becoming; thought alone is not enough.
—**Bertrand Logan Ball, Jr.**[18]

and performance. He avoids the guilt trips that come with failure to make our dreams come true. He understands the reality that if we chase too many rabbits we catch none of them. So he has decided which "rabbits" are worth chasing and invests his energy and time where it does the most good. His is a mission that motivates.

Investing in a personal mission statement—and we strongly recommend that you do—pays huge effectiveness dividends. And remember the law of the harvest. Take no shortcuts. Don't expect to draft a meaningful mission statement at a single sitting. It is a process, not an event. The best mission statements tend to evolve over time. But you must start somewhere. Start now.

What does this have to do with vision? Everything. Remember, great leaders have an inside-out perspective. In order to understand and guide others, they must first understand and guide themselves. This requires a form of *pathmapping*—envisioning a desirable end result and deliberately mapping a route to get there. The perfect model is, of course, the Savior and the Plan of Salvation.

In addition to having a vision—and a plan—for your own performance, you must have a vision and plan for the labor to which you have been called. In later chapters we will address related topics like Creating a Performance Atmosphere in Your Calling, Planning and Organizing, Developing the Capacity of Others, and Stewardship Delegation. For now, let's focus on the "what" and "how" of using vision to bless those you're called to serve.

We have been given our free agency to choose for ourselves, it is vitally important that we carefully evaluate all aspects of life before making our choices.

—Victor L. Brown[19]

One way to develop a vision for your calling is to consider specific questions related to your stewardship. For example, if you are called to serve as bishop of your ward, the early questions that can trigger some productive thought might include:

- What specific impressions have I received from the Spirit?
- What counsel did my stake president offer when he issued the call?
- What are the strengths of my counselors and how can I help them develop?
- Who are the young men of the Aaronic Priesthood in the ward? What are their needs? What, specifically, can I do that will bless them most?
- Who are the young women in the ward? What are their needs? What, specifically, can I do that will bless them most?
- Who are the young children in the ward? What are their needs? What, specifically, can I do that will bless them most?
- Who are the Melchizedek Priesthood brethren in the ward? What are their needs? What, specifically, can I do that will bless them most? How can I help them be better husbands and fathers? How can I help them enjoy the blessings of the temple? How can I help them serve faithfully in all they are asked to do?
- Who are the Relief Society sisters in the ward? What are their needs? What, specifically, can I do that will bless them most? How can I help them be better wives and mothers? How can I help them enjoy the blessings of the temple? How can I help them serve faithfully in all they are asked to do?

We can ask questions to assess the needs of children so we can understand how best to encourage and love them.
—Patricia P. Pinegar[20]

. . . there are revelations dealing with the problems of the day. . . . the Church, directed by mortal men, needs divine guidance in the solution of current questions. Many of the revelations received by the Prophet Joseph Smith were of this character. . . . The Prophet presented his problems to the Lord, and with the revealed answer was able to accomplish properly the work before him.
—John A. Widtsoe[21]

- Who are the widows and singles in the ward? What are their needs? What, specifically, can I do that will bless them most?
- Which ward members are either inactive or less involved? How can we reach out to them to offer unconditional love, encouragement and friendship?
- What is the overall "culture" or tone of the ward? Is it friendly and outreaching, or do visitors and new members have to wait to be approached? What can I do to create a ward environment that is loving, welcoming and inclusive, a haven from the world?
- What is the reputation of the Church in our community? What are the opportunities for our ward members to offer themselves in community service?
- What are the missionary opportunities in our ward? How can I lead and inspire our members in proclaiming the gospel?

STOP: Compare your own list of questions for your own stewardship. Meditate on the "big picture" of your calling. And remember: great leaders often do not have the "title" of leader. Great leadership is not at all a function of title. It is a function of character and vision and behavior.

You'll notice that most of these questions (and you can think of *many* others) relate to people, not programs. They relate to individual children of God, not some abstract notion of "being in charge." As you consider such questions, you will begin to see your calling with both a microscope for the details and a wide-angle lens for the big picture. The vision you'll need to lead your ward requires both perspectives. As we mentioned in Chapter 1, your primary role is that of *transformational* leader—influencing positive change in the hearts and souls of real people with real challenges. You're also called on to be a *transactional* leader—you need to ensure that organizational details are appropriately handled. In other words, *ministering* is your primary role, while *administering* is also important but can be delegated to a large extent. That dual stewardship must be accommodated in your vision. And it must be accommodated by your personal mission during the season of your service as bishop.

Start with your vision. After writing down a couple of dozen questions like those suggested above, look for patterns. Certainly blessing the lives of individual people is one of the patterns. Other patterns might include developing others so they can enjoy—and provide—the blessings of service. Condense your vision to a few brief sentences. After all, it's not something you'll post on the wall of your office. It's primarily for your use as a picture of how you envision your ward and its people some time in the foreseeable future. At an appropriate time, you may wish to share your hopes and dreams with others—members of the ward council, for example—who can work with you and the Lord in making it come true. This kind of cascading sponsorship is what is meant by "catching the vision."

Remember: In developing a vision for your service stewardship, your all-important ally is the Lord. Seek the guidance of the spirit. Pray earnestly and often. You will not be disappointed.

. . . the council should spend most of its time pursuing such agenda items as the integration of new members, activation of the less active, concerns of the youth, the economic plight of individual members, and the needs of single mothers and widows. When organizational reports are given, they ought to be measured in terms of meeting those kinds of people-related goals.

—M. Russell Ballard[22]

We know that unless we match our programs to our people and their spiritual needs, we run the risk of unintentionally doing what the Master meant concerning the Jewish Sabbath—that "ends had been subordinated to means" until it seemed to the Master that the Jews apparently thought man had been virtually made for the Sabbath, not the reverse

—**Harold B. Lee**[23]

We should humble ourselves before the Lord and be in a position to be filled with the spirit of our calling, with the Holy Ghost, and with the revelations of Jesus Christ, that we may know the mind and will of God concerning us, and be prepared to magnify our calling and bring to pass righteousness.

—**John Taylor**[24]

When you have begun to develop your vision for your calling, we strongly recommend that you make appropriate adjustments in your personal mission statement. For example, as a new bishop, you might decide to include "Interviewer" as one of your roles that requires special focus (see Chapter 8). Much of your work as bishop will involve eye-to-eye, knee-to-knee confidential conversations with your ward members. You, and they, will be blessed if you deliberately include as part of your personal mission the development and use of specific gifts and skills that contribute to effective interviewing. Empathic listening, for instance, would be one such gift and skill.

This same pattern will help you regardless of your calling. In developing his mission and vision for service, a quorum president will need to address many questions regarding the spiritual and temporal welfare of the brethren he is called to lead. A counselor in a Young Women or Primary presidency will benefit from considering the strengths and needs of her president, the specific needs of the youth in her organization, the circumstances of all the families involved, and a range of other issues related to her stewardship. A stake high councilor must consider not only his own assignment but the assignments and interrelationships of all the other brethren on the stake priesthood executive committee. If he's assigned to work with the priesthood quorums in a particular ward, he needs to know the people and understand specifically what the priesthood leaders are trying to accomplish so he can be a useful resource. This will influence his own sense of mission and vision.

The scriptures teach that "Where there is no vision, the people perish"(Proverbs 29:18). To be effective instruments in the hands of the Lord, we must obtain and follow the Lord's vision for His people. We must understand the vision provided in the teachings of the living prophets. And we must operate daily from our own spirit-filled vision for our calling.

Great leaders accomplish great things because they have vision. As Thomas S. Monson said, "Vision without work is dreaming. Work without vision is drudgery. Work coupled with vision is destiny."[1]

QUESTIONS OF CONSCIENCE

1. Am I genuinely trying to discover the "big picture" vision the Lord has for my calling?
2. Do I look for gaps between current performance and what could—and should—be accomplished in the future?
3. Do I envision, in specific terms, how I can help others?
4. Do I avoid dwelling on what can't be done and instead practice the art of the possible?
5. Do I place more emphasis on accomplishing good than on who gets the credit?
6. Do I place more emphasis on solving (and preventing) problems than on assigning blame?
7. Do I have a personal mission statement— and is it in writing?
8. Do I use the promptings of the Holy Ghost to determine how and where to use my time?

9. Do I ask the Lord for clarity of vision in all the things I'm asked to do?
10. As a leader, do I constantly remember that I am a servant?

APPLYING THE PRINCIPLES

1. Re-read Mosiah 18 and other scriptures related to baptismal covenants. Consider your present calling(s) and the opportunities you have to provide comfort, to stand as a witness and to reflect the light of the Savior.

2. Use the ideas in this chapter to draft a personal mission statement. Consider the format that includes your various roles in life. Faithfully use the mission statement for at least three months in setting priorities and planning your activities. Test it. Refine it. You'll discover that it's a big help in translating good intentions into real results.

YOU CAN DO IT!

You can gain the vision of the work, and especially your role in bringing it to pass. A correct understanding of the worth of souls and the plan of happiness is essential to your true vision of purpose as a child of God and as a leader in the Kingdom. The Lord will give to you this vision when you study the manuals (follow the Brethren), when you pray mightily (see James 1:5–6), when you study the scriptures (see 2 Nephi 32:3), when you worship in the temple (see D&C 97:13–14), and when you heed the counsel of the living prophets (see D&C 21:4–6). He promised to give you this vision as you act with all diligence, exercise faith, give heed to all His instruction, and then be patient as He extends His arm toward you (see D&C 123:17). Heavenly Father knows you. He knows your name. He knows every person under your stewardship whom He wants to bless through you. He will give you the vision and all the inspiration necessary to fulfill your callings.

You can do it!—in the strength of the Lord.

ENDNOTES FOR MAIN BODY TEXT

1. Ezra Taft Benson, *The Teachings of Ezra Taft Benson* (Salt Lake City: Bookcraft, 1988), 200-201.

ENDNOTES FOR SIDEBARS

1. M. Russell Ballard, *Counseling with Our Councils: Learning to Minister Together in the Church and in the Family* (Salt Lake City: Deseret Book Co., 1997), 23.

2. Ibid., 23–24.

3. Thomas S. Monson, comp., *Favorite Quotations from the Collection of Thomas S. Monson* (Salt Lake City: Deseret Book Co., 1985), 80.

4. M. Russell Ballard, *Counseling with Our Councils: Learning to Minister Together in the Church and in the Family* (Salt Lake City: Deseret Book Co., 1997), 34–35.

5. Bryant S. Hinckley, "The Love That Never Ceases to Be," *New Era,* June 1975, 14.

6. "Church Callings Bring Blessings, Bishops Say," *Church News*, February 17, 1996.

7. Dallin H. Oaks, *Pure in Heart* (Salt Lake City: Bookcraft, 1988), 37.

8. Johann Wolfgang Goethe, quoted in Stephen R. Covey, *The 7 Habits of Highly Effective People* (New York: Simon & Schuster, 1989), 146.

9. Spencer W. Kimball, *Conference Report*, April 1974, 125.

10. Thomas S. Monson, *Pathway to Perfection* (Salt Lake City: Deseret

Book Co., 1973), 112 (emphasis added).

11. Spencer W. Kimball, *President Kimball Speaks Out* (Salt Lake City: Deseret Book Co., 1981), 44.

12. Lowell L. Bennion, *The Best of Lowell L. Bennion: Selected Writings 1928–1988,* edited by Eugene England (Salt Lake City: Deseret Book Co., 1988), 30.

13. Lloyd D. Newell, *The Divine Connection: Understanding Your Inherent Worth* (Salt Lake City: Deseret Book Co., 1992), 114.

14. Victor L. Ludlow, *Principles and Practices of the Restored Gospel* (Salt Lake City: Deseret Book Co., 1992), 558.

15. Ibid., 331.

16. "Blueprint for Spiritual Glory," *Church News*, September 14, 1996.

17. David O. McKay, May 10, 1961, *BYU Speeches of the Year,* 1961, 5–6.

18 Bertrand Logan Ball, Jr., Saint-Exupery and 444. *BYU Studies*, vol. 8, no. 4, Summer 1968. Saint-Exupery and "le culte du passe" by Bertrand Logan Ball, Jr.

19. Victor L. Brown, *Conference Report*, October 1970, Third Day— Morning Meeting, 124.

20. Patricia P. Pinegar, "Children: Our Priceless Converts," *Ensign*, February 1999, 10.

21. John A. Widtsoe, *Evidences and Reconciliations* (Salt Lake City: Improvement Era), 100.

22. M. Russell Ballard, *Counseling with Our Councils: Learning to*

Minister Together in the Church and in the Family (Salt Lake City: Deseret Book Co., 1997), 109.

23. Harold B. Lee, *The Teachings of Harold B. Lee.,* ed. Clyde J. Williams (Salt Lake City: Bookcraft, 1996), 563.

24. John Taylor, James R. Clark, comp., *Messages of the First Presidency of The Church of Jesus Christ of Latter-day Saints,* 6 vols. (Salt Lake City: Bookcraft, 1965–75), 3: 96.

4

WHAT GREAT LEADERS DO

Some might imagine that "what great leaders do" would comprise a very long list of complicated and even mysterious activities. The reality is that great leadership is relatively simple. Note that we didn't say *easy*. We said *simple*.

The best leaders emulate the Savior himself. They constantly remember their role as *servant*. They shoulder responsibility for the vision and direction of the people they serve. They may have "official" authority, yet they lead by influence instead of by position.

This chapter is a brief overview of what a leader does. It is not intended to be all encompassing, but rather a simple summary. We want this summary to be inviting, not overwhelming. We want you to remember that leadership is a developmental process. It is the process of becoming. *You* can become a great leader.

Great leaders use their vision to maintain a wise perspective on life around them and ahead of them. Dag Hammarskjöld, who served as secretary-general of the United Nations, had something to say that bears directly on the subject of righteous leadership: "The road to holiness necessarily passes through the world of *action*."

Being in power is like being a lady. If you have to remind people that you are, you aren't.
—**Margaret Thatcher**[1]

... the Church has no corps of professionals; it must depend upon leaders developed from within the membership as a whole . . . the Church's need is greater than ever now, both in terms of numbers and a requirement for greater devotion and skill, . . . so must the need for more capable and responsible leadership multiply.

—**Neal A. Maxwell**[2]

... the successful leader has faith. He recognizes that the greatest force in this world today is the power of God as it works through man.

—**Thomas S. Monson**[3]

... a feeling of deep responsibility to act as the Lord's agent, is perhaps the highest attribute of leadership . . . They seek only to serve, with no desire for self-aggrandizement or acclaim. They see themselves as the

FEED YOUR FAITH, STARVE YOUR DOUBTS

As we have interviewed and counseled with and learned from thousands of Church members over the years, we have often begun with two simple questions:

- "What is the health of your testimony?" and
- "How do you make it grow?"

The answers we've received from these wonderful Saints provide a simple tutorial on the kind of perspective (vision) that best serves great leaders: they feed their faith and starve their doubts.

Like any self-respecting verb, a good Latter-day Saint is active, not passive. Active verbs have *power*. Look around you. The people in your branch or ward or stake who exude the greatest happiness and who enjoy the most robust spiritual health are those whose character and habits are fueled by *power* verbs.

These are people who *honor* their covenants.

They *hold* to the rod of the word of God.

They *obey* the commandments.

They *choose* the right.

They *serve* their neighbors.

They *love* their enemies.

They *forgive* their trespassers.

They *repent* of their wrongs.

They *lengthen* their strides.

They *preach* correct principles.

They *practice* what they preach.

They *control* their tempers.

They *share* their talents and gifts.

They *resist* temptation.

They *proclaim* the gospel.

They *defend* the faith.

They *testify* of the truth.

They *listen* with empathy.

They *teach* with conviction.

They *lead* with power and energy and charity and hope.

These are the Saints who are able to feed their faith and starve their doubts because their lives are characterized by power verbs such as *renew, resolve, sacrifice,* and *consecrate.*

To one degree or another, all of us have faith. And in one way or another, each of us has doubts. It may be self-doubt, but it is doubt nonetheless.

Great leaders feed their faith and starve their doubts. Their sense of vision constantly reminds them who they are, *whose* they are, and what they can become.

With proper application of the principles of salvation, all of us can feed *our* faith and starve *our* doubts. This is particularly important in our family roles.

GREAT LEADERS DEVELOP CHRISTLIKE CHARACTER.

Great leaders are examples of goodness. They walk their talk and are consistent and reliable. They follow their own leaders, because all leaders must first be good followers. Their strength is in their humility and servant-oriented style rather than the building up of their egos. They willingly sacrifice for the greater good. Enthusiasm for the work is evident in their work ethic as well as in their discipline. They seek to be worthy to receive the blessings of the Spirit. They teach by precept and example. They are bold and courageous but not overbearing. They love

Lord's servants, on His errand, acting as His agents . . .

—Alexander B. Morrison[4]

Those who take seriously the covenants they make, who aspire to be numbered among the covenant people of God, wish only to be humble disciples of Jesus. . . . They recognize their dependence on God and His goodness . . . They voluntarily accept covenants that require both sacrifice and consecration.

—Alexander B. Morrison[5]

And what is the crowning glory of man in this earth so far as his individual achievement is concerned? It is character . . . his aim, the highest in life, should be the development of a Christlike character.

—David O. McKay[6]

those they work with and serve, and help instill lasting values in others. They honor the principle of agency, and practice persuasion with kindness and long-suffering. Their character, their whole being, literally teaches the principles of the gospel. In all their teaching, what they *do* speaks louder than what they *say*.

GREAT LEADERS HAVE VISION.

They know their purpose and their cause. They share their vision and invite their people to invest their hearts in the future. They identify what matters most. They know that the main thing is to keep the main thing the main thing. For leaders in the family and in Church, of course, "the main thing" is always the same: inviting people to come unto Christ.

> . . . a leader with no vision will dramatically limit his effectiveness.
> —Vaughn J. Featherstone[7]

GREAT LEADERS GET RESULTS.

The results we speak of are measured by the lives that are blessed, not by the extolling of numbers or percentages. Great leaders inspire allegiance and devotion to the cause. They unify people. They work to build a sense of order. Leadership can be lonely and it can be difficult. Great leaders are willing to exert "tough love" for the sake of the individual and for the sake of the cause. Popularity, though alluring, cannot be the ultimate goal. The ultimate goal must be the blessing of souls. Great leaders ask for and obtain commitment. They follow up for an accounting of performance. Great leaders get results.

> Remember that success results when preparation meets opportunity in our lives.
> —Joseph B. Wirthlin[8]

GREAT LEADERS PLAN AND ORGANIZE.

They are committed to excellence. They are careful not to waste time, energy or other

> When you learn to plan well, many other leadership skills will simply fall into place.
> —Shane R. Barker[9]

resources. They frequently ask questions like "What do we want to make happen?" "Are the vision and priorities understood?" "How will we measure success?" "What is our plan to strengthen their faith?" "What will we continually emphasize?" "What preparation is required?"

GREAT LEADERS MOTIVATE OTHERS.

They help others choose to do and give their best. They teach correct doctrine. They remind people that they are children of God and have infinite capacity to do good. They affirm and encourage.

GREAT LEADERS BUILD GREAT TEAMS.

Great leaders in the Church understand and use the "council form" of leadership. They build teams that build up the Kingdom of God. They know that unity of effort is always more powerful than division of labor.

GREAT LEADERS USE DISCERNMENT.

Some people pray for guidance, then they grab the steering wheel. Great leaders are different. They qualify themselves for the promptings of the Spirit, then they follow the promptings. Great leaders work as though everything depends on them, and they pray—and listen—as though everything depends on the Lord.

GREAT LEADERS TEACH AND NURTURE.

They are inspirational teachers. They teach true doctrine at every opportunity. They feed the lambs and sheep because they love and are unconditionally devoted to Heavenly Father and our Savior. Remember, the Spirit shows us all

> . . . the genesis of self- or inner motivation is faith-faith in one's own self, faith in one's God, faith in one's cause, and faith in one's leaders.
> —**Carlos E. Asay**[10]

> Real teamwork is created when leaders value the differences, encourage cooperation and involvement, and recognize that, like them, the people they lead are changing, growing individuals.
> —**Lloyd D. Newell**[11]

things to do as well as giving us the words to say at the moment we need them (2 Nephi 32:3, 5). As we teach and nurture those we serve, we must always root them to our Savior Jesus Christ. This is true teaching and ministering.

GREAT LEADERS COMMUNICATE AND COACH.

Prayerful leaders have discernment; they will know . . .
—Boyd K. Packer[12]

Communication—creating a "common-ness" with others—is a critical part of leadership. It is difficult to serve people unless and until you understand their needs and concerns. Great leaders listen with genuine empathy. They are open, patient, tender, understanding. They seek to be a light rather than always a judge. They communicate with kindness, with a soft voice, and with love unfeigned.

GREAT LEADERS DELEGATE.

. . . the leader who fails to teach and admonish must bear the burden of sins himself.
—Dallin H. Oaks[13]

They understand the principles of stewardship—having a responsibility with a trust. They know that holding people lovingly accountable for effective performance is one of the best ways to develop other leaders.

GREAT LEADERS MANAGE MEETINGS.

They know that every gathering of their people should have a specific purpose that is closely linked to mission and vision. Latter-day Saints gather often to be taught the word of God, to be edified, to make commitments, to renew their covenants, to organize and plan, to be trained. Meetings with a purpose are meetings that are effective and successful.

There is another reason to delegate, and that is to empower and prepare leaders for future service.
—M. Russell Ballard[14]

GREAT LEADERS MAINTAIN BALANCE.

They take time to smell the flowers. They make time to recharge their batteries, to renew themselves spiritually, mentally, physically and emotionally. Great leaders do not operate at a pace that will end in "burnout."

Great leaders orchestrate the simple—and important—things into a magnificent concert.

You can be a great leader!

QUESTIONS OF CONSCIENCE

1. Am I really willing to pay the price for being a great leader?
2. For me, is "leadership" about position or about influence?
3. Am I utilizing every opportunity to instruct and teach those around me?
4. Is helping people come unto Christ my first priority?
5. Do I lead to impress or to bless?
6. Am I improving at recognizing the promptings of the Spirit and following that inspiration?
7. Am I working hard to get the right results?
8. Am I aware of what the Lord is teaching me in my stewardship?
9. If I needed truly reliable help with something, would I ask someone like me?
10. Am I better than I was last year? Am I working to be even better next year?
11. Do I feel the Lord loving and blessing others through me?
12. Do I carefully observe and learn from other great leaders?
13. As a leader, do I constantly remember that I am a servant?

Keep balance in your lives. Beware of obsession. Beware of narrowness.
—**Gordon B. Hinckley**[15]

Every leader must keep current. He must read. He must study. In the Church he must know the scriptures and the handbook. He must read the bulletins. He must keep his eye fixed on new developments. If he does not he will soon find himself lagging behind and the work will suffer.

—Gordon B. Hinckley[16]

APPLYING THE PRINCIPLES

1. On page 72–73, note the list of habits that are fueled by *power* verbs. Consider how these can help you in your own leadership responsibilities. Develop a list of specific things *you* can do to improve your own spiritual health and character. Make commitments. Take responsibility. Follow through.

2. This chapter discusses a number of things that great leaders do. Reflect on some of the great leaders who have played a role in your life. Then consider how those great leaders applied some of these principles. Were they perfect? Of course not. But they tried. They used the gifts they had and they let the Lord make up the difference. So can you!

YOU CAN DO IT!

You can do every needful thing that is expected of a leader. Leaders are often required to be jugglers. They do many things at once. Remember that you can do several things in sequence as well as delegate many others. Be patient with yourself and with others. Recognize that all growth requires faith, diligence and a great amount of patience. Patience is your ally, with yourself as well as with others. Don't run faster than you have strength or time. One step at a time—one project organized with target dates, etc.—then another and another with adequate follow-through can bring success. Remember that people are always more important than programs. People are the *reason* for the programs. Our success with programs happens only when the people we serve are blessed and enriched. A day, a week, a month—one step at a time and you can become a great leader. Time and your desire are on your side.

You can do it!—in the strength of the Lord.

ENDNOTES FOR SIDEBARS

1. Quoted in James C. Hunter, *The Servant: A Simple Story About the True Essence of Leadership* (Rocklin, California: Prima Publishing, 1998), 15.

2. Neal A. Maxwell, *A More Excellent Way* (Salt Lake City: Deseret Book Co., 1967), iii.

3. Thomas S. Monson, *Be Your Best Self* (Salt Lake City: Deseret Book Co., 1979), 116.

4. Alexander B. Morrison, *Feed My Sheep: Leadership Ideas for Latter-day Shepherds* (Salt Lake City: Deseret Book Co., 1992), 21.

5. Alexander B. Morrison, *Visions of Zion* (Salt Lake City: Deseret Book Co., 1993), 122.

6. David O. McKay, *Man May Know for Himself: Teachings of President David O. McKay,* compiled by Clare Middlemiss (Salt Lake City: Deseret Book Co., 1967), 29.

7. Vaughn J. Featherstone, *The Incomparable Christ: Our Master and Model* (Salt Lake City: Deseret Book Co., 1995), 113.

8. Joseph B. Wirthlin, *Finding Peace in Our Lives* (Salt Lake City: Deseret Book Co., 1995), 150.

9. Shane R. Barker, *Youth Leading Youth* (Salt Lake City: Deseret Book Co., 1987), 31.

10. Carlos E. Asay, *The Seven M's of Missionary Service: Proclaiming the Gospel as a Member or Full-time Missionary* (Salt Lake City: Bookcraft, 1996), 109.

11. Lloyd D. Newell, *May Peace Be with You* (Salt Lake City: Deseret Book Co., 1994), 146.

12. Boyd K. Packer, *Things of the Soul* (Salt Lake City: Bookcraft, 1996), 135.

13. Dallin H. Oaks, *The Lord's Way* (Salt Lake City: Deseret Book Co., 1991), 228.

14. M. Russell Ballard, *Counseling with Our Councils: Learning to Minister Together in the Church and in the Family* (Salt Lake City: Deseret Book Co., 1997), 30.

15. Gordon B. Hinckley, *Teachings of Gordon B. Hinckley* (Salt Lake City: Deseret Book Co., 1997), 32–33.

16. Ibid., 309.

SECTION 2

GETTING THE
RESULTS YOU AND
THE LORD WANT

5

PLANNING THE WORK, WORKING THE PLAN

Great leaders have a clear vision of what they want to accomplish. And because they know it's often easier to conceive than to deliver, they invest plenty of energy in organizing and planning and executing. They tend to be very deliberate in their use of the finite resource called time.

You've probably noticed that "time poverty" is a challenge faced by every servant who cares. But you don't need to fall into what one Church worker described as "a chronic state of overwhelm." A more strategic use of your time enables you to serve with more passion and less panic. Making time decisions on the basis of mission and values boosts effectiveness and reduces guilt. Service then feels like the blessing it is instead of the burden it was.

It was the Spanish novelist Cervantes who reminded us that "by the street of By-and-By, one reaches the House of Never." The street of By-and-By, like another metaphorical thoroughfare, is paved with good intentions. Our progress and performance are frequently hindered by procrastination or frustration. Opportunity is lost. But a carefully crafted mission statement as we described in Chapter 3—a living document that can grow right

> The secret of success is constancy to purpose.
> —**Benjamin Disraeli**[1]

> The wise use of time helps to fit us for eternity.
> —**Neal A. Maxwell**[2]

> The soul that has no established aim loses itself.
> —**Montaigne**[3]

along with you—can help you reach "the House of Now." Good planning can also play a vital role in the quality of your marriage and family life. Even for a seasoned worker, receiving and accepting a call to serve in the Church can be an intimidating experience. Most of us have a wide range of priorities tugging at us—our families, our friends, our community obligations, our occupations, our need for physical exercise, our determination to keep up with our scripture study. We have only so many hours in a day, and a lack of balance in handling these priorities can launch us on a guilt trip and hamper our effectiveness. This is why we so strongly recommend crafting a personal mission statement—a mission that motivates.

We are not endeavoring to get ahead of others but only to surpass ourselves.
—Hugh B. Brown[4]

TIME MANAGEMENT MATRIX 1

In conjunction with your personal mission statement, a process that can help you bring better focus and balance into your life is to examine—precisely—how your time is used. Many time management specialists refer to the Time Management Matrix.[1] This is a simple box divided into four equal portions or quadrants. Notice that each quadrant is numbered and labeled.

Something that falls into Quadrant 1 is both Urgent and

1 Urgent Important	**2** Not Urgent Important
• Crises • Pressing problems • Deadline-driven projects • Some meetings • Some reports	• Planning & organizing • Preparation • Prevention • Relationship building • Steward development • True re-creation
3 Urgent Not Important	**4** Not Urgent Not Important
• Interruptions • Some meetings • Some phone calls • Some reports • Many popular activities	• Trivia & busy work • Irrelevant mail • Some phone calls • Time wasters • "Escape" activities • Excessive television

Important. It demands immediate attention. If you're a Sunday School president and a teacher fails to show up on Sunday, you are faced with an urgent and important matter. If you're a bishop and a married couple in the ward suddenly notifies you they are getting a divorce, you have a Quadrant 1 issue on your hands. If you're a parent and your teenager announces she's running away from home, you know full well what "urgent" and "important" feel like when they happen at once.

Quadrant 3 consists of those time-consuming activities that are Urgent but Not Important. This would include interruptions such as a ringing doorbell and even some meetings that are regularly on your schedule but have begun to lose their value.

Quadrant 4 includes those activities that are Not Urgent and Not Important. Much of what falls in this quadrant shouldn't even be done at all.

Quadrant 2 could be called the "power" quadrant. This is where the most productive activities occur. Quadrant 2 activities are Not Urgent, but they are Important. They include such things as planning, prevention, bridge painting (strengthening relationships), steward development and pursuing opportunities.

In this context, "Urgent" signifies something that appears to require immediate attention. "Important" signifies an activity that contributes to your mission and your significant goals.

Some people find themselves forced to expend an inordinate amount of their time on Quadrant 1 activities—crises and pressing problems. They are firefighters, constantly

> Life gives to all the choice. You can satisfy yourself with mediocrity if you wish. You can be common, ordinary, dull, colorless; or you can channel your life so that it will be clean, vibrant, progressive, useful, colorful, rich.
>
> —Spencer W. Kimball[5]

> Choices are the hinges of destiny.
>
> —Edwin Markham[6]

Time management is really self-management and discipline in how we manage ourselves in the time allotted. It involves making choices, and choosing how to use that time is sometimes difficult.

—Joseph B. Wirthlin[7]

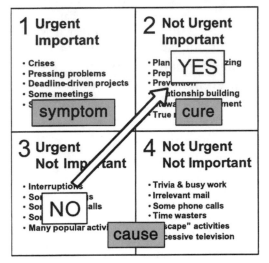

dousing the flames of problems that are mostly preventable. Investing more in Quadrant 2 activities—planning, prevention, steward development, etc.—tends to shrink Quadrant 1, preventing the fires of crisis.

In fact, we might look at the Time Management Matrix in this way. Quadrant 1 is the "symptom" quadrant. It is here that we see the symptoms of our poor time management. Symptoms include missed deadlines, poor meetings, low motivation, weak performance. Quadrants 3 and 4 are the "cause" quadrants. Time spent in Quadrants 3 or 4 inevitably results in less-than-desirable performance. Remember, regardless of your education, experience, age or any other factor, you still have only twenty-four hours a day. Every minute invested in Quadrant 3 or Quadrant 4 is a minute that's no longer available for investing in Quadrant 2.

When we neglect Quadrant 2, Quadrant 1 grows. It's that simple. When we neglect the activities represented in Quadrant 2, we seem to face more crises, more problems, more "fires" that must be extinguished. The key to effective management of our time, then, is to say "no" to Quadrant 3 activities and to say "Yes" to Quadrant 2 activities. We solve our time management problems by giving priority to Quadrant 2 activities—those that may not be Urgent but which are clearly Important.

Quadrant 2 activities take a variety of forms. The most important, of course, includes any and all activities that strengthen our relationship with the Lord. For the active Church worker, they also may include planning a Relief Society Enrichment meeting or a bishopric meeting or a Sunday School in-service lesson. They might include conducting a careful stewardship interview with a newly called servant, giving the worker a detailed understanding of the responsibilities and expectations associated with the assignment (see more on this in Chapter 9, Stewardship Delegation). They might include a carefully planned regimen of physical fitness to increase energy and vitality and to reduce stress. They can include pleasure reading or concert-going or any other worthy pursuit that brings needed balance to our lives.

Success requires a lot of careful planning and you are here to form these plans and make decisions to carry you forward in life.

—Howard W. Hunter[8]

IT'S A MATTER OF LEVERAGE

Don't expect Quadrant 2 ever to eliminate the other three quadrants completely. That's simply not reality. But with a careful and persistent application of your Mission Statement and with a more deliberate strategy in your planning, you'll discover that you're getting much more leverage from your time.

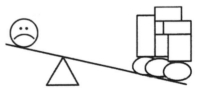

You've used leverage before. Remember playing on the teeter-totter in school? If the child on the other end was heavier than you, you simply moved the fulcrum (the center point carrying the entire load) closer to the heavier weight. That slight move affected the physics of the situation.

You can use the same principle in managing your time and responsibilities. As your load changes (your responsibilities increase), you face the frustration of being unable to lift the load.

Focusing on Quadrant 2 activities is the same as moving the fulcrum. Quadrant 2 activities provide the leverage with which you can lift your load. Remember, part of that leverage is saying "no" to Quadrant 3 activities—those that seem urgent but that in fact are not very important. Your personal mission statement will help you decide.

IT'S AN EVOLVING PROCESS

As your sense of vision evolves, undergirded by a well-developed personal mission statement (see Chapter 3), you're better able to make the myriad of daily choices regarding your time and other resources. This is an evolving process, not a flash point event. And one thing is certain: As you honor the law of the harvest, you will enjoy the fruits of continuous improvement. When you genuinely do your best, your "best" gets better and better.

Values clarification, visioning and time management are critical elements of your leadership. Effective organizing and planning cannot happen unless and until you are very clear about what you stand for (and what you will not stand for), what you hope and what you dream.

Make no mistake, big hopes and big dreams are not just the province of prophets, presidents, kings and others whose leadership is global in nature. Big hopes and big dreams

The daily choices we make are the foundation stones of our mansions of exaltation, or the perilous sands of calamitous failure.

—**Archibald F. Bennett**[9]

Are you farsighted? . . . This means "insight." . . . the ability to sense the long range values—to plan for them and to sacrifice the immediate pleasures for faraway rewards.

—**Mary Brentnall**[10]

can bring power and energy to any of Heavenly Father's children. Including you. Take your cue from one of our favorite bumper stickers: "Think globally, act locally."

The purpose of organizing and planning is to help us reach goals. Goals. Now there's a word that puts some people to sleep. Goal-setting can sound pretty boring, especially if your experience with it has been less than successful. How many times have you seen goals announced with great fanfare in a meeting, only to disappear and never be mentioned again? How many times have you heard someone announce a goal that was so unrealistic that everybody knew from day one that it could never be accomplished? How many times have you seen a goal that was so vague and nebulous that it would be impossible to know if you ever reached it?

> . . . most people do far too little goal setting, including the reflecting that precedes the setting of such goals.
> —**Neal A. Maxwell**[11]

GOALS THAT GET YOU SOMEWHERE MEANINGFUL

When it's done right, goal-setting provides direction and purpose. Goals help you see where you're going and how you can get there. After all, if you don't know where you're going, how will you know when you get there?

Lewis Carroll's wonderful book *Alice in Wonderland* offers some pertinent lessons. You may recall the exchange between Alice and the Cheshire Cat about the importance of setting goals. Consider this passage in which Alice asks the Cheshire Cat for advice on which direction to go.

"Would you tell me please, which way I ought to go from here?"

> . . . goals give purpose and direction to life.
> —**Carlos E. Asay**[12]

A prerequisite for "doing" is goal setting. Actions are preceded by thoughts and planning.
—Marvin J. Ashton[13]

"That depends a good deal on where you want to go," said the Cat.

"I don't much care where—" said Alice.

"Then it doesn't matter which way you go," said the Cat.

"—so long as I get *somewhere*," Alice added as an explanation.

"Oh, you're sure to do that," said the Cat, "if you only walk long enough."

It really takes no effort to get *somewhere*. Just do nothing and you're there. If you want to get somewhere *meaningful*, however, you must know where you want to go. Then you need to make plans on *how* to get there.

Suppose, for example, that you're in a Relief Society presidency and you have a vision of consistently providing high quality visiting teaching. How would you go about achieving that vision? You can hope and pray and show up on time for meetings, and some good will be accomplished. But if you hope and pray and show up on time for meetings *and* use a planned, goal-focused approach, your chances of real success are greatly enhanced.

Here are some reasons to establish goals whenever you want to accomplish something significant in your marriage, family community, business, and Church calling:

One ship drives east and another drives west with the selfsame winds that blow. 'Tis the set of the sails and not the gales which tells us the way to go.
—Ella Wheeler Wilcox[14]

• **Goals provide direction and traction.** For the example just used (consistently providing high quality visiting teaching), you can think of dozens of ways to improve visiting teaching. To get something meaningful done, though, you must have a definite road map—a target to aim for and to guide the efforts of you and the other sisters. Then you can translate that vision into goals that take you where you want to go. *Without* goals you are sure to spin your wheels going nowhere. *With* goals you can focus energy and effort on the activities that provide the best traction.

- **Goals help make your overall vision attainable.** Most visions cannot be reached in one giant leap. You need many smaller steps to get there. If a bishop's vision is for every endowed member of the ward to hold a current temple recommend, he probably can't expect to proclaim his vision on January 1 and then see every adult member on the ward temple trip in February. Many intermediate goals must be accomplished—from reactivation to building faith to strengthening marriages to re-teaching the law of tithing to scheduling interviews and counseling—before the overall vision can be attained. Goals enable you to achieve your overall vision. How? You divide your efforts into smaller pieces that, when accomplished one by one, add up to big results.

- **Goals provide measures for success.** Goals provide milestones along the road to accomplishing your vision. If you decide "consistently providing high quality visiting teaching" requires five intermediate goals to reach your destination and you complete four of them, you know you have one intermediate goal remaining.

- **Goals clarify everyone's role.** Effective goal-setting helps people avoid duplication of effort. Effective goals help you integrate and coordinate the use of your people

Recognition of intermediate goals reinforces our resolve to complete our annual goals.
—**Victor L. Ludlow**[15]

It concerns us to know the purposes we seek in life, for then, like archers aiming at a definite mark, we shall be more likely to attain what we want.
—**Aristotle**[16]

This empowerment process requires . . . modeling Christlike behavior; building caring, trusting relationships; setting up clear role and goal expectations; identifying sources of help; and requiring accountability.
—**M. Russell Ballard**[17]

resources, your time resources, and your budget resources. Effective goals include a designation of who does what. They bring clarity to mutual expectations. That way, each person understands his accountability and what others are depending on him to provide.

- **Goals give people something to stretch for.** When people are properly led and motivated, goals give them a sense of direction and purpose. And goals that require people to stretch—remember President Kimball's call to "lengthen your stride"?—tend to bring out the best performance.

How do you know what kind of goals to set? The whole point of setting goals, of course, is to *achieve* them. The best goals are *smart* goals. Actually, SMART goals is more like it. SMART stands for the five characteristics of well-designed goals.

Specific: Goals must be clear and unambiguous. Vague ambitions and platitudes have no place in goal setting. When goals are specific, they tell people precisely what is expected, when, and how much. Only with specific goals are you able to measure progress.

Measurable: What good is a goal if you can't measure progress? When goals are not measurable, you never know if or when or even how you're making progress toward their completion. Not only that, but it's very difficult for your people to stay motivated to complete the goals in the absence of milestones to indicate progress.

Attainable: Goals must be realistic and attainable. As we indicated earlier, goals

> Our goals should stretch us bit by bit.
> —Neal A. Maxwell[18]

> Only specific goals are useful.
> —Vaughn J. Featherstone[19]

> When performance is measured, performance improves. When performance is measured and reported back, the rate of improvement accelerates.
> —Thomas S. Monson[20]

should give people something to stretch for, but they should not be out of reach. Neither, of course, should goals be too easy. Goals that are set too high or too low become meaningless, and people tend to ignore them.

Relevant: Goals must be an important element in the overall plan of achieving your mission and reaching your vision. It's estimated that 80 percent of people's productivity often comes from 20 percent of their activities. You can guess where the remaining 80 percent of effort ends up. Relevant goals address the 20 percent of the effort that has the greatest impact on performance.

Time-bound: Effective goals have starting points, ending points, and fixed durations. People are better able to focus their efforts on goal attainment when they are committed to deadlines. Goals without schedules or deadlines tend to get lost in the rush of day-to-day life.

To illustrate how this approach adds value and power to goal-setting, let's compare a SMART goal with a not-so-smart goal. (This is vital in all councils, especially family councils.)

Let's say a ward council is discussing the Young Men and Young Women programs and the bishopric asks the YM and YW leaders to suggest a goal for the coming year. A not-so-smart goal might be something like "Get the youth more involved in activities." On the surface, this certainly seems like a worthy aspiration. But what does it really mean? Does "more involved" mean greater attendance? Does it mean having more fun? Does it mean cheering louder at basketball games? And what "activities" are included in this goal? You'll notice that this not-so-smart goal is not specific. It is not

Honesty with oneself and setting of desirable but attainable goals day by day can determine the paths we follow.
—**Marvin J. Ashton**[21]

We use so much of our time in rushing around, not thinking always what we ought to be, nor what it is that matters most. Sometimes we set our hearts on things we feel we have to have, and when we get them find they don't mean as much as once we thought they would.
—**Richard L. Evans**[22]

measurable because we don't know specifically what to measure. It is really not attainable because, lacking specificity and measurability, there's no way to know if and when the goal is reached. The goal is only marginally relevant because, although it alludes to involving the youth in activities, the lack of specifics dilutes it to "platitude" status. And the goal is not time-bound because it has no starting point, no ending point and no fixed duration.

> . . . set specific goals for what we would have to do in our lives . . . and then of course to reach our goals by the designated time.
> —Jay A. Parry[23]

For the sake of illustration, let's say that what the ward council members really *mean* is:

- We want our young men and young women to love the Lord, obey the commandments, build strong testimonies and have an unstoppable desire to serve missions, be married in the temple and raise righteous, eternal families.
- We want to do everything possible to fortify our youth against the evils of the world and help them live in the world without embracing the dangerous standards *of* the world.

> From these deep-seated beliefs, we develop specific goals and establish the standards for evaluating their accomplishment. We then proceed to *act, interact,* and *react* according to our determination of what is right and appropriate.
> —Kay P. Edwards[24]

While these are wonderful aspirations, they are not at all implied in the goal "Get the youth more involved in activities."

GETTING STARTED

If this goal is the starting point of discussion, good questions to ask would include:

"Exactly which 'youth' are we talking about?"

"Do we mean just the young men and young women who would be regarded as 'active,' or do we also mean those teenagers who are on the rolls but who rarely or never attend Church?"

"At what point do our less-active youth

seem to be slipping away? Is it right after the transition from Primary? What seem to be some of the root causes of inactivity?"

"Exactly which 'activities' are we talking about? Sunday YM and YW meeting? Midweek sporting events? Trips to the temple to do baptisms?"

"Exactly what would 'more involved' look like? Does this mean the deacons will participate in congregational hymn-singing during sacrament meeting? Does this mean that every priest will be an Eagle Scout? Does this mean all the Laurels will play a part in next summer's road show?"

"When will all this happen? Are we talking about accomplishing this 'goal' by Christmas, or by when today's youngest deacon has his missionary farewell seven years from now?"

Do you get the message? SMART goals— Specific, Measurable, Attainable, Relevant and Time-bound—have punch and power. A broad brush not-so-smart goal like "Get the youth more involved in activities" can be transformed into a series of SMART goals that actually contribute to the saving of souls.

STEPS ALONG THE WAY

For example: "Our goal is that every member of the Aaronic Priesthood will participate in the November 14 temple trip." Notice that this goal is Specific, Measurable, Attainable, Relevant and Time-bound. It also implies a number of intermediate goals. For instance, a complete list of all the Aaronic Priesthood boys must be compiled and clarified. Individual circumstances must be consid-

May we launch straightway toward setting goals that are gospel oriented, knowing that if we use the talents that are ours—that if we help others, strive for peace, avoid being overly sensitive or overly critical—strength upon strength will be added to our own abilities and we will move straightway toward greater growth, happiness, and eternal joys.
—**Marvin J. Ashton**[25]

ered. Adult chaperones must be invited. Schedules must be cleared and coordinated. Bishop's interviews must be scheduled. Transportation must be arranged. Every intermediate goal must be a SMART goal so it won't float out into never-never land. Getting all the young men to participate in the next temple excursion is not the absolute end of developing youth. But it is one of many steps to providing experiences that built faith, personal testimonies and a desire to honor covenants. The landscape of great leadership consists of countless smaller pieces that add up to a large mosaic. It is focusing on the smaller pieces—while keeping an eye on the larger vision—that enables ordinary people to accomplish extraordinary things.

Great leaders use SMART goals because they leave nothing to chance. They want their people to invest their energy and ingenuity in goals that are Specific, goals that are Measurable, goals that are Attainable, goals that are Relevant, goals that are Time-bound.

LESS CAN BE MORE

Every leadership meeting in the Church is attended by well-meaning people. In their desire to do good work, well-meaning people sometimes try to resolve *every* issue and fix *every* problem as quickly as possible. This usually results in the creation of too many goals. As a wise old hunter said, if you chase too many rabbits you'll catch none of them. No matter how great a leader you are, you simply cannot focus on everything at once. Delegation can help by off-loading some of your tasks, but that isn't the all-inclusive

Setting goals is an essential step toward change. . . . These include setting goals that are specific, focusing on positive behaviors, and describing goals in behavioral or action terms.

—Gary Steggell[26]

We don't need a quick fix. . . . Steady, sustained efforts will bring great results.

—James E. Faust[27]

answer either. Too many goals will eventually cause your people to be overwhelmed, frustrated, and ineffective.

When it comes to goal setting, less really is more. Here are some guidelines that will help you select the right goals—and the right number of goals—for your leadership role.

- **Select two or three goals to focus on.** Remember that you can't do everything at once, and you can't expect others to either. A handful of goals is the most you should attempt to address at any one time. Each major goal can (and should) of course have a number of intermediate or sub-goals, but your number of major goals should be limited.

- **Select goals with the greatest relevance.** Just as there is an aristocracy among true principles, there is an aristocracy among goals. Some goals are simply more relevant than others. Some goals are more critical in taking you further down the road to attaining your vision. Because your time and other resources are limited, it makes sense to concentrate your efforts on those few goals that have the greatest payoff.

- **Focus on goals with the closest linkage to your mission and vision.** It's tempting to tackle goals that are challenging and interesting but that are not directly related to your leadership calling. You, personally, can do very little to solve the problems of world hunger. But of course you can address such a huge issue if you break it down into smaller pieces. You could lead some young people or Relief Society sisters or a priesthood quorum in planting and tending a

. . . occasionally review the goals and objectives of your organization with your officers and teachers.

—Thomas S. Monson[28]

vegetable garden for that widow down the street. Think globally, then act locally.

- **Periodically revisit your goals and update as necessary.** Leadership is anything but static. Situations change. Resources change. Needs change. People change. As you work and serve, you gain fresh information and new insights. Periodically assess your goals to ensure that they are still relevant to the vision you're aiming at in your marriage, family and all other roles. When necessary, revise the goals and the schedules for attaining them. If you're the leader "in charge," be sure to involve your counselors and others when formulating plans and goals. When others have genuine opportunity to provide input, they gain ownership of the plan and enthusiasm for the result. Consider the following:

At the Church Regional Meetings held in the summer of 1978, the following instructions on goals were presented:

1. Goals should be prayerfully set with guidance from the Spirit.
2. Goals should be specific rather than general.
3. Goals should be written down.
4. Goals should be stated in terms of a specific time period.
5. Goals should be set by those responsible for their attainment.
6. Goals should be realistic and attainable but should also challenge us to lengthen our stride.
7. Goals should be reviewed frequently, and the results reported periodically.

8. Goals should be directed toward helping and serving other people as well as toward self-improvement.

—Marvin K. Gardner[2]

A story related by Elder Dallin H. Oaks illustrates the importance of careful organizing and planning:

> Two men formed a partnership. They built a small shed beside a busy road. They obtained a truck and drove it to a farmer's field, where they purchased a truckload of melons for a dollar a melon. They drove the loaded truck to their shed by the road, where they sold their melons for a dollar a melon. They drove back to the farmer's field and bought another truckload of melons for a dollar a melon. Transporting them to the roadside, they again sold them for a dollar a melon. As they drove back toward the farmer's field to get another load, one partner said to the other, "We're not making much money on this business, are we?" "No, we're not," his partner replied. "Do you think we need a bigger truck?"[3]

Most of us don't need more things to do. Like the two partners in Elder Oaks' story, our biggest need is a clearer focus on the challenges at hand and how we should value and use the resources we have.

In your zeal to accomplish as much as possible, avoid tackling too many goals. Too many goals can overwhelm you. Being over-

> Righteousness grows like a crop. . . . the sowing of the seed, of careful planning, of wise organizing; for, as you sow, so shall you also reap.
> —Spencer W. Kimball[29]

whelmed is not the model you want to give the people who depend on you for leadership. You, and they, are far better off setting a few significant goals and then concentrating on reaching them.

Remember that great leadership is not always a matter of huge success after huge success. Great leadership is a daily meeting of challenges and opportunities. Great leadership is about gradually but inevitably improving on the status quo. Great leadership is about seeing the big picture, yes. It is also about tending to all the pieces that make up the whole. *That* requires smart organizing and planning.

Wise individuals understand and seek change slowly and carefully. They set realistic goals, achievable goals. They also work on self-improvement each day.
—J. Spencer Kinard[30]

QUESTIONS OF CONSCIENCE

1. Do I value my time as the precious commodity it is?
2. Do I make careful, prayerful and discriminating decisions regarding the use of my time?
3. Do I really understand the leverage of investing in Quadrant 2 (Important, but Not Urgent)?
4. Do I carefully address the root causes of my time management challenges rather than treating just the superficial symptoms?
5. Do I use a personal mission statement to help me make wise choices about my resources?
6. Do I establish goals that really help me advance the work I've been called to do?
7. Are my goals SMART—Specific, Measurable, Attainable, Relevant and Time- bound?
8. Do I ensure that my goals are both ambitious and manageable?

9. Do I constantly consult with the Lord as I organize and plan my work?
10. As a leader, do I constantly remember that I am a servant?

APPLYING THE PRINCIPLES

1. Using the Time Management Matrix as a guide, honestly evaluate where you are currently investing your time. Make a list of specific Quadrant 2 activities that will contribute in a positive way to your leadership efforts. Make these a priority. Schedule them. Do them.
2. Honestly evaluate the goals you typically establish. Are they SMART goals? If not, apply the principles and practices discussed in this chapter. You will see a marvelous difference.

YOU CAN DO IT!

Effective organizing and planning are primary on the list of things great leaders do. You cannot afford not to plan. You cannot afford to be a "brush fire" leader, hopping from one crisis to another. You will burn out. You will never be focused. Your team will not function at its best because you failed to pay the price to plan. In any project or program, planning translates the vision into action. In every role you have—whether it's in the family, at work, at school or in the Church—planning is the beginning of all your success. The scriptures bear this out from the councils in Heaven, which by no accident includes the *plan of happiness*. The time you spend in planning will make you efficient and, most importantly, effective. Why? Because you will then be in a better condition to hear the quiet whisperings of the Spirit. We are unable to hear those divine directions when we are frantically putting out brush fires. Make the time to plan. You can do it!—in the strength of the Lord.

ENDNOTES FOR MAIN BODY TEXT

1. A number of excellent works use variations of the Time Management Matrix. We recommend *Connections: Quadrant II Time Management,* by Roger Merrill (Publishers Press: Salt Lake City, 1987). Two other good sources are *First Things First,* by Stephen R. Covey, A. Roger Merrell, and Rebecca R. Merrill (New York: Simon & Schuster, 1994); and *The 7 Habits of Highly Effective People,* by Stephen R. Covey (New York: Simon & Schuster, 1989).

2. Marvin K. Gardner, *Ensign,* July 1978, 72.

3. Dallin H. Oaks, "Focus and Priorities," *Ensign,* May 2001, 82.

ENDNOTES FOR SIDEBARS

1. John Bartlett, comp., as quoted by Benjamin Disraeli, in *Famous Quotations* (Boston), 10th ed.

2. Neal A. Maxwell, *Even As I Am* (Salt Lake City: Deseret Book Co., 1982), 56.

3. John Bartlett, comp., as quoted by Montaigne, in *Famous Quotations* (Boston), 10th ed.

4. Lloyd D. Newell, as quoted by Hugh B. Brown in *The Divine Connection: Understanding Your Inherent Worth* (Salt Lake City: Deseret Book Co., 1992), 111.

5. Spencer W. Kimball, *The Miracle of Forgiveness* (Salt Lake City: Bookcraft, 1969), 233.

6. Edward Markham, http://popup.matchmaker.com/titan1/lycos-now.html.

7. Joseph B. Wirthlin, *Finding Peace in Our Lives* (Salt Lake City: Deseret Book Co., 1995), 224.

8. Howard W. Hunter, April 26, 1961, *BYU Speeches of the Year,* 1961, 2.

9. Archibald F. Bennett, *Saviors on Mount Zion* (Salt Lake City: The Church of Jesus Christ of Latter-day Saints, 1950), 17.

10. Mary Brentnall, "The Right Age to Marry," *Improvement Era,* 1949, vol. LII. June, 1949, no. 6: 369, 400.

11. Neal A. Maxwell, *That My Family Should Partake* (Salt Lake City: Deseret Book Co., 1974), 73.

12. Carlos E. Asay, *In the Lord's Service: A Guide to Spiritual Development* (Salt Lake City: Deseret Book Co., 1990), 106.

13. Marvin J. Ashton, *Be of Good Cheer* (Salt Lake City: Deseret Book Co., 1987), 56–57.

14. Ella Mae Wilcox, http://www.cp-tel.net/miller/BillLee/quotes/Aristotle.html.

15. Victor L. Ludlow, *Principles and Practices of the Restored Gospel* (Salt Lake City: Deseret Book Co., 1992), 320.

16. Aristotle (384–322 BC), http://www.cp-tel.net/miller/BilLee/quotes/Aristotle.html.

17. M. Russell Ballard, *Counseling with Our Councils: Learning to Minister Together in the Church and in the Family* (Salt Lake City: Deseret Book Co., 1997), 59.

18. Neal A. Maxwell, *Deposition of a Disciple* (Salt Lake City: Deseret Book Co., 1976), 33.

19. Vaughn J. Featherstone, *Commitment* (Salt Lake City: Bookcraft, 1982), 31.

20. Thomas S. Monson, comp., *Favorite Quotations from the Collection of Thomas S. Monson* (Salt Lake City: Deseret Book Co., 1985), 61.

21. Marvin J. Ashton, *Ye Are My Friends* (Salt Lake City: Deseret Book Co., 1972), 91.

22. Richard L. Evans, "Where Are You Really Going?" *Conference Report*, June 1971, 73.

23. Jay A. Parry, "The Best Day of Their Lives," *Ensign*, January 1977, 63.

24. *As Women of Faith: Talks Selected from the BYU Women's Conferences* (Salt Lake City: Deseret Book Co., 1989), 242.

25. Marvin J. Ashton, *Be of Good Cheer* (Salt Lake City: Deseret Book Co., 1987), 62.

26. Gary Steggell, "Changing Me, Changing My Marriage," *Ensign*, January 1997.

27. James E. Faust and James P. Bell, *In the Strength of the Lord: The Life and Teachings of James E. Faust* (Salt Lake City: Deseret Book Co., 1999), 373.

28. Thomas S. Monson, comp., *Favorite Quotations from the Collection of Thomas S. Monson* (Salt Lake City: Deseret Book Co., 1985), 58.

29. Spencer W. Kimball, *The Teachings of Spencer W. Kimball,* edited by Edward L. Kimball (Salt Lake City: Bookcraft, 1982), 162.

30. J. Spencer Kinard, *A Moment's Pause* (Salt Lake City: Deseret Book Co., 1989), 99.

6

COUNCILS:
STRENGTH IN UNITY

The suspension bridge is one of the most impressive accomplishments of modern engineering. It begins as individual wires not much stronger than the ones you'd use to hang pictures on your living room wall. Spun together, these individual wires become strands. Then several of the larger strands are combined into a giant wire rope or cable that can bear thousands of tons of weight and safely cross enormous obstacles like canyons and rivers.

This same principle is part of the miracle of Christian service in the Lord's Church. In wards and branches and families around the globe, ordinary people achieve extraordinary things because they have discovered strength in unity.

The principle of strength in unity is especially evident in the council form of leadership. Councils involve an assembly of people who sit in consultation with one another. This does not preclude a leader of the council nor the leader's authority to direct all things. Rather, a council is a setting where important matters are addressed and counsel is sought and received.

We are encouraged today, both in our families and in our Church callings, to sit in council. Elder M. Russell Ballard clarified this when he wrote:

> Zion was not redeemed earlier in this dispensation because the Saints were not united, nor can it be until we practice the strength found in unity.
> —**Alexander B. Morrison**[1]

The genius of our Church government is government through *councils* . . . I have had enough experience to know the value of councils. Hardly a day passes but that I see the wisdom, God's wisdom, in creating councils . . . to govern his Kingdom.

—**Stephen L. Richards**[2]

The Lord has given us the broad organization outline, the purposes, and the objectives. But he leaves to us much of the working out of the methods. And this is where correlation and leadership training come in . . .

—**Ezra Taft Benson**[3]

Church and family councils are one of the best resources available to us in winning the battle for the souls of our Father's children. I feel strongly that the best way to help lift the burden of leadership—both in the Church and in the family—is to invite council members to assist in finding the answers and implementing the solutions that the gospel of Jesus Christ provides.[1]

This statement underscores the vision we need concerning councils. We must understand that priesthood councils, ward councils, presidencies in council and family councils are *the* method by which we share the burden of leadership. The council form of governance is simply the best way to use teamwork in our service to the Lord.

It's also important to remember that while counseling through councils is critical to the success of Church government, this is government different from what we hear about on the evening news. In Church government there is no "majority rule." There are no veto overrides. The council form of leadership and government invites input and discussion from all the council members. Then, through direction from the Holy Spirit, those who hold priesthood keys make decisions. In the Lord's Church, even the most "learned" dialogue never supercedes revelation.

THE POWER OF ALIGNMENT

Coordination is a constant challenge for most leaders. In the Church we call it "correlation." Correlation involves careful communication and collaboration among the organizations and their parts. It's much more than just scheduling the cultural hall or getting a ward social on the calendar. These are of course administrative details that need attention. But true correlation is about all the parts of the organization operating in complete harmony, each drawing strength from the others, all contributing to the effectiveness of the whole. The opposite of correlation is fragmentation. This is when the various parts of the organization "do their own thing" with little regard to their effect on the whole. Fragmentation always results in wasted effort and missed opportunity, and frequently leads to frustration and even discouragement. Unfortunately, there's a temptation to apply a temporary bandage rather than identify and address root causes. This kind of "tampering" often produces a cure that can be as frustrating as the original ailment.

Example: If you walked into an overheated control room of a nuclear power plant and began adjusting dozens of instruments randomly, the results could be catastrophic. So it is with organizations.

It's been said that *every organization is perfectly aligned to get the results it's getting.* A sobering thought. And doesn't it apply to your quorum, your council, your presidency, your bishopric, your family?

If your organization is perfectly aligned to get the results it's getting, and if you're not satisfied with those results, alignment—or correlation—is not a luxury. It is an imperative.

Think of your organization not as a machine to be "fixed," but as a living organism with many interrelated elements. Now think of yourself—the leader—not as a

Shepherds should use self-imposed discretionary time for important things: to plan and meditate, to think about what really must be done if they are to be successful, to make certain their priorities are in full alignment with the mission of the Church.
—**Alexander B. Morrison**[4]

If the Grand Council provides us with an excellent illustration of gospel governance through large councils (such as ward councils and stake high councils), another premortal council teaches important lessons about working with smaller, more intimate groups (such as presidencies and bishoprics).
—**M. Russell Ballard**[5]

mechanic but as a gardener. Successful leaders invest energy in "growing" rather than in "fixing." Successful leaders are gardeners. They don't rely on position or authority. They create a nurturing environment where people can learn correct principles, perform great work, and love each other in doing it. The council provides an ideal gardening place. The council is where we are most able to view the big picture of our organization as well as the individual needs of the people we serve. The council is where good ideas are cross-pollinated and allowed to germinate. The council is where plans are formed and assignments are given and accepted. The council is where we cultivate relationships of trust and cooperation that flow like refreshing water to the rest of the organization.

In our Church and family work, strong correlation—all the parts working in harmony—is clearly a critical key to effectiveness.

For the sake of illustration, let's consider a typical Latter-day Saint ward. The ward council consists of the bishopric, the priesthood quorum leaders, the ward mission leader, the ward activities chairman, and the presidents of the Relief Society, Young Men, Young Women, and Primary. The council meets regularly to *correlate* the programs and activities in the ward and to *align* their efforts with sound principles and policies. The graphics that follow show what weak and strong correlation look like.

VISION

Weak	Correlation		Strong
"Where there is no vision, the people perish" (Proverbs 29:18) There is some talk of vision, but it is not done in the context of any integrated effort to develop and implement plans that "make it happen."	The leaders have worked on vision, but there is negligible involvement and/or "ownership" by the rank and file followers. Effort is made to develop plans and activities in consideration of "the whole," but they are fragmented and lack a unifying purpose.	The vision is generally accepted by members of the council who use it as a guide in developing specific action plans. Good collaboration is evident among council members, but the work is still not integrated to the extent that fosters peak performance and effectiveness.	A clear vision provides purpose and direction that are understood, accepted and used by all members of the council. All ward leaders are very effective at translating "vision" into plans and activities that genuinely promote the work of bringing souls to Christ. Council members identify and deal quickly with problems and effectively remove barriers.

PURPOSE AND DIRECTION

Weak	Correlation		Strong

Although council members are committed to the Lord, there is some confusion about their purpose as a group. There's disagreement about what should have priority, where the greatest needs or opportunities are found.

Day-to-day activity is only loosely tied to goals and objectives.

There is some general agreement on purpose and direction. Plans, programs, and activities are beginning to be developed, but they are still fragemented.

The bishopric has sketched out some general goals and objectives, but they are not widely known.

A written plan is developed by the council, undergirded by a universally accepted vision for what the ward members need most. There is general integration of plans, programs, and activities.

A number of vision-based goals and objectives have been articulated and agreed upon. Some are measurable.

There is widespread agreement among council members on the most important issues and improvement needed in the ward. The norm is to seek continuous correlation and alignment by surfacing differences for resolution. Clear direction is provided by the bishopric.

Goals and objectives are specific, clear, and understandable. Results are measured at every level. All efforts are carefully integrated and clearly linked to vision.

COMMUNICATION

Weak	Correlation		Strong

Council members do not feel free to say what they think, especially in the presence of the bishopric. A hyperactive rumor mill exists, with council members constantly trying to find out through the "grapevine" what is in store for them and for the ward. A genuine spirit of "we're all in this together" seems to be missing.

Open communication is evident only in "pockets." Council members carefully pick and choose "safe" opportunities to express their opinions. Turf protection, or guarding the interests of one's individual stewardship, is a key criterion of what is said and shared. There is some headway in breaking down these barriers.

Communication is open between and among the council members, although communication is still somewhat constrained between and among the quorums and auxiliaries.

Open, authentic communication is evident between and among all council members, as well as between and among the counselors to quorum leaders and auxiliary presidents outside the council meetings. Relationships are characterized by active listening and encouragement of input. Council members know that effective communication is a key part of their stewardships; and they behave accordingly. Quality of communication is emphasized over quantity, although quantity is also abundant.

PLANNING INVOLVEMENT

Weak	Correlation		Strong

Planning communication is restricted by a semi-permeable membrane. Ideas flow downward only. Only a few council members participate in the establishment of plans and programs for the ward. New policies and procedures are "announced from the mountain top."	The bishopric consults with some members of the council, but there's still evidence of a one-size-fits-all communication mentality.	Most planning involves input from every member of the ward council.	All planning accommodates a bottom-up as well as a top-down flow of ideas. Information is appropriately available to all members of the council, tailored to the special needs and stewardships of the recipients.

COUNCILS WORK BEST WHEN

- They allow for discussion and a free exchange of ideas.
- Each council member is an integral part of the whole, with opportunity to participate and contribute.
- They address the real problems and challenges of people and carry out specific plans to bless lives.
- They provide a regular time and place to deal with issues that need focus.
- They ensure that calendared items are carefully targeted to strengthen families and those with special needs. All good planning begins with a purpose.
- They create synergy and enthusiasm for the work of the Lord.
- They fulfill the teachings of Paul regarding everyone's being a part of the body and the need for every part to work in concert with the others (see 1 Cor. 12:14, 18, 20–21, 26).
- They increase commitment, with individual council members—as well as the whole—"owning" the council's goals and decisions.
- They constantly reinforce the spirit of unity through respectful exchanges and Christlike behavior.

Councils are truly the Lord's way for us to be "undershepherds." For a council to be effective, each member of the council must feel personally responsible for the success of the group. Never doubt the value of your own input. Never fail to invite others to participate. You may initiate a discussion above and beyond the scope of your comment that will result in breakthrough thinking.

It seems that there are three keys to making stake councils work in the way they were designed and intended to work. First, beginning with the stake presidency, stake leadership must be committed to the council concept and to doing everything in their power to see that the councils are formed and operating as they should. Second, they must empower their councils; that is, give council members meaningful work to do. And finally, they have to get out of the way and allow the stake council to function.

—M. Russell Ballard[6]

That Jesus is committed to the council concept cannot be questioned. Twice in ancient times He personally organized His Church on the earth, and both times He established it with governing councils. In both the Holy Land of the New Testament and the promised land of the Book of Mormon, He spent considerable time teaching and instructing and training His councils and council leaders, and then He sent them forth to share what they had learned with others. Although the circumstances surrounding the two experiences were different, they both share at least two key similarities that illustrate the Savior's exemplary administration of councils. First, He taught His ancient councils carefully—by precept and by example. . . . Second, He loved those with whom He served in council. "As the Father hath loved me, so have I loved you," (John 15:9) . . .

—M. Russell Ballard[7]

TRAINING YOUR COUNCIL, COUNSELORS, OR TEAM

For your council to be effective, each person should receive instruction and training. Some of this is done during the call to service interview (see Chapter 8, "Communication: Building Bridges to Their Hearts"). Much of the instruction and training are part of the on-going process of service.

The purpose of training is to enhance people's ability and to boost their performance related to their callings or tasks. This improves both efficiency (doing things right) and effectiveness (doing the right things). Training can be of a general nature or it can be specific, depending on the needs and concerns of your people. As they review reports and observe performance, leaders can discern things that need attention. Then they can tailor the training to address issues with the biggest payoff.

Training sessions are ideal setting for boosting people's spirits. Make sure all your training has a firm footing in sound doctrine. Bear personal testimony of the relevance of the task at hand and the linkage between individual effort and forwarding the Lord's work. Express sincere love for your fellow workers. Offer frequent gratitude and affirmation for their contributions and commitment. Teach by the spirit so your people will draw closer to the Savior.

Training should be informational as well as inspirational. Abstract ideas with no specific "things to do" are usually ineffective. Statements like "Let's all do better," "We know we can improve," or "Let's gird up our loins" are pulpit pleas that seldom result in meaningful change. Effective training is a process that takes time and effort on the part of everyone involved. (See Chapter 5, "Planning the Work, Working the Plan" for ideas on developing and accomplishing goals. Then see Chapter 7, "Creating a Climate of Hope and Energy" for ideas on building an atmosphere that invites high performance.) In a word, good training requires *focus*.

EFFECTIVE TRAINING OCCURS WHEN:
- The Spirit is present and people feel the unconditional love of their leader.
- Appropriate feedback has helped determine where the "trainees" need assistance.
- The current situation and/or the performance of the group are thoroughly and candidly discussed.
- Ideas, strategies, and goals have been discussed with the individuals or group to pinpoint needs.
- The training format provides time for questions and discussion of the topics—and, when appropriate, practice of what is taught.
- It's done under the direction of the Spirit.
- The trainer provides good information *and* genuine enthusiasm for the importance and value of the training.
- There is time for introspection so people can make personal commitments to do better.
- Accountability is emphasized and follow-up training is carried out to emphasize the "return and report" nature of stewardship.

Successful training creates a feeling of self-worth and increases self-confidence. An increase in competence then tends to follow. First and foremost, training should strengthen testimonies.

> When we are without the proper training and discipline, our minds themselves may become addled, mixed up, and confused.
> —Sterling W. Sill[8]

[In training session role playing] without exception, the "bishop" would take charge of the situation and say, "Here's the problem, and here's what I think we should do to solve it." Then he would make assignments to the respective ward council members. This was a good exercise in delegation, I suppose, but it didn't even begin to utilize the experience and wisdom of council members in addressing the problem. Eventually I would suggest to the bishop that he try again, only this time asking for some ideas and recommendations from the members of the his council before making any decisions. I especially encouraged him to ask the sisters for their ideas. I tried to teach the concept that although men and women shoulder different responsibilities, they bring to their Church service varying background, talents, experiences, and points of view. . . .
—**M. Russell Ballard**[9]

DECISION MAKING

One of the most important responsibilities of your council or group is decision making. Decision making is even more critical than problem solving because, by definition, problem solving requires good decisions. The council is an ideal setting for good decision making. In reality, however, many councils seem to avoid their decision-making role by (a) deciding by default, i.e., waiting until their options are limited by time or other factors, (b) dealing with only the most perfunctory issues and side-stepping the more challenging matters, or (c) deferring all decisions to the leader. When we fail to reach our goals, the root cause frequently involves a failure to make smart, clear and timely decisions.

Like most every other element of leadership, decision making can benefit from a series of introspective questions. Here are some we suggest.

CLARIFYING THE ISSUE

- In specific terms, what is the problem or issue we need to address?
- What are the implications or effects of the problem or issue?
- Is this problem or issue really the most critical, or does another deserve our attention first?
- Are we focusing on the root causes or just the symptoms? How can we be sure?
- Is our information accurate, relevant and complete? How can we be sure?
- Are we resisting the temptation to jump to conclusions?

- How does this problem or issue link with the other matters on our agenda?

FINDING SOLUTIONS
- Are we appropriately involving people who will be affected by our decision?
- Is our solution or decision supported by everyone on the council?
- Do we have a SMART goal (see Chapter 5 for details)?
- Have we carefully considered budget, time, equipment, transportation and all other relevant issues?
- Does our plan include encouragement and positive reinforcement for the people we serve?
- Are we allowing for feedback and redirection so we can adapt to dynamic change?
- Are we confident our solution or decision is compatible with related matters such as calendared events, Church policies and solid principles?
- Have we asked enough open-ended or "what if" questions to ensure that we've considered all contingencies?
- Do we understand and accept both the short- and long-term implications of our solution or decision?
- Have we prayed in faith and unity to receive a witness of the Spirit that this solution or decision is acceptable to the Lord?

MIND MAPPING

As we've pointed out, one of the great advantages of the council form of leadership is that it combines the best thinking of a number of people. (It's especially true in fami-

Regardless of the size or makeup of the family council, the things that really matter are loving motivations, an atmosphere that encourages free and open discussion, and a willingness to listen to the honest input of all council members—as well as to the whisperings of the Holy Spirit as it comes to confirm truth and direction.
—**M. Russell Ballard**[10]

But let us not underestimate the worth of input from council members in the deliberation process. This is part of the miracle of Church councils . . . the best leaders are not those who work themselves to death trying to do everything single-handedly; the best leaders are those who follow God's plan and counsel with their councils.
—**M. Russell Ballard**[11]

lies.) This does not occur just by gathering people in a room. It requires skillful leadership and a lot of open communication.

One method found useful by many councils or groups is called "mind mapping." It's a simple and effective form of brainstorming that's especially practical in a group setting. When facilitated correctly, mind mapping is informal and non-threatening. Furthermore, it tends to energize the group and helps them explore a wide range of options. An added advantage of mind mapping is that it is a visual approach, and many people think more creatively with visual aids.

The only "equipment" needed for mind mapping is a chalkboard, white board, flip chart of some other writing surface. First, the group selects a "scribe," who places the issue in the middle of the writing surface. Then the discussion facilitator engages the group in dialogue about the issue. This should be a rather free-form discussion, with an agreement that no idea is a bad idea and that every idea has the potential to trigger an even better one. You'll be pleased by how enjoyable and productive this approach can be.

For the sake of illustration, here's a graphic showing how one council used mind mapping to address the issue of retention of a family of new converts to the Church.

Notice the simplicity of this approach. The primary issue (strengthening the Wilson family) is represented in the center. The available resources are represented on one "arm" that extends from the center. These may seem self evident, but it's always a good idea to be specific. Other areas on the mind map signal specific

When they make wise use of committees and councils, lives are blessed. This is particularly true on the ward or branch level, where leaders are in a position to have daily hands-on influence on the eternal well-being of families and individuals.
—M. Russell Ballard[12]

actions to be taken regarding friendship, stewardship and nurturing. These cover the recurring themes of President Gordon B. Hinckley in his teachings about strengthening people who have accepted the gospel message: Each new convert needs a friend, a responsibility, and to be nurtured by the Good Word of the Lord.

In addition to its utility in energizing and involving a group in problem solving and decision making, the value of mind mapping is that it enables the group to *visualize* the available resources, options and specific actions. The visual representation helps with integration and correlation. This often suggests ways to collaborate, avoid duplication of effort, and ensure that the issue at hand is considered holistically.

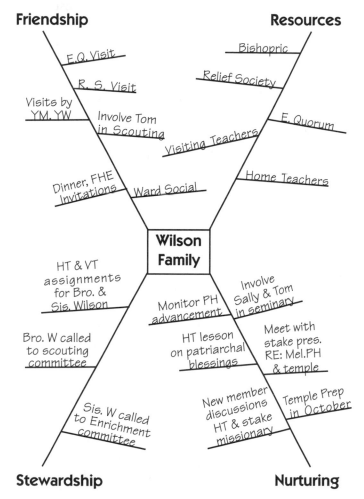

Friendship

E.Q. Visit

R. S. Visit

Visits by YM, YW

Involve Tom in Scouting

Dinner, FHE Invitations

Ward Social

Resources

Bishopric

Relief Society

E. Quorum

Visiting Teachers

Home Teachers

Wilson Family

HT & VT assignments for Bro. & Sis. Wilson

Bro. W called to scouting committee

Sis. W called to Enrichment committee

Stewardship

Monitor PH advancement

HT lesson on patriarchal blessings

Involve Sally & Tom in seminary

Meet with stake pres. RE: Mel.PH & temple

New member discussions HT & stake missionary

Temple Prep in October

Nurturing

THINGS TO REMEMBER IN
STRENGTHENING YOUR COUNCIL

- **Always work for unity.** "Divide and conquer" is one of Satan's favorite strategies. Constantly focus on your common goal of bringing your people closer to Christ. Emphasize the positive. Backbiting, complaining, faultfinding and contention have absolutely no place in your council. If there's a concern, always address it with positive solutions. Loving and kind communication goes a long way in teaching love and kindness. If contention or any other brand of negativity enters a council meeting, the leader should quickly step in and redirect the conversation in a more positive and productive vein. In one ward council meeting, a participant differed with the rest of the group and announced that he was "playing the devil's advocate." Before the conversation strayed further, the bishop said, with a friendly twinkle in his eye, "Bob, I think the devil already has too many advocates in this world. As a member of the Lord's team, what ideas do you have for making this plan work?"

- **Tend to the individual.** It's vital that you, the leader, understand and appreciate each individual's concerns, needs, anxieties, personal challenges, stress-producing factors, frustration, hopes and dreams. It's also helpful to understand each individual's self-worth and self-confidence issues. This knowledge—which comes from careful observation, sensitive interviews and promptings from the Spirit—

At periodic council meetings both individual and organizational needs are considered. Recognizing the unique circumstances surrounding a particular unit, geographical area, or set of individuals, the council identifies the programs and activities that need to be planned and correlated.
—**M. Russell Ballard**[13]

enables you to provide better guidance to your team. (See the ideas on situational leadership in Chapter 9, "Stewardship Delegation: The Great Multiplier.")

- **Tend to the whole.** Every group has a "chemistry." It's the way people relate to each other, the tone of their interaction, the spirit that's in the room when they meet. It's your responsibility as leader to ensure that the chemistry is positive and affirming. This is not to suggest that everything is syrupy sweet. It means that your council will be most effective when its individual members genuinely love and respect each other. You can and should be the model of behaviors that contribute to the feeling of oneness. Embrace the counsel of Paul: "Now I beseech you, brethren, by the name of our Lord Jesus Christ, that ye all speak the same thing, and that there be no divisions among you; but that ye be perfectly joined together in the same mind and in the same judgment" (1 Cor. 1:10).

- **Be a ready listener.** Solicit and respect each individual's input. Be especially attentive to people who tend to stay silent. They may have some especially valuable ideas or insights. Sometimes the more vocal council members inadvertently monopolize the discussion. It's up to you to manage the interaction so the whole benefits from each of the parts. You may need to establish a policy that "everyone is heard" so the quiet members expect to be asked for input and so the vocal members will be less prone to monopolize.

The ideal model is straightforward and simple: call good people to serve with you, listen carefully to their counsel and consider their input, and then listen to the whisperings of the Holy Spirit as it leads you to make good decisions.
—**M. Russell Ballard**[14]

- **Be patient.** Patience is a virtue that every leader must practice with the council. Peace and love cannot prevail in an atmosphere of impatience. Your primary concern must always be for the growth of your people, not just "let's get the performance up." Good performance is a natural by-product of effective councils. (For further ideas on effective councils, see Chapter 11, "Gatherings of Saints: Think *Purpose,* Not Meeting.")

> . . . we enjoy life when we have the ability to praise others for their good works.
> —**Howard W. Hunter**[15]

- **Affirm. Affirm. Affirm.** Always look to inspire, show gratitude and genuinely praise your people individually as well as collectively. Positive reinforcement pays amazing dividends. This must be done in purity and sincerity, not with manipulation.

- **Provide plenty of context.** Remember our discussion about "linkages" in Chapter 1? Ensure that your people understand the "why" of their stewardships as well as the "what." Help them grasp the linkages between their efforts and the efforts of their fellow workers. Make sure they have clear answers to questions like "What is my purpose?" "What should be my goals?" "What am I specifically responsible for?" "When are my reports due?" "What—and who—are my resources?" A good sense of context helps your team members understand their interconnecting roles and stewardships.

- **Maintain good humor.** Great leaders know how to laugh, especially at themselves. They tend to be firm with principle and flexible with people.

- **Calibrate for result.** As we discuss in Chapter 7, it's a good idea to make frequent checks or course corrections to ensure that you and your team are accomplishing the things you set out to do. It's easy to get caught in the hustle and bustle of holding meetings and lose sight of the *specific* blessings we're trying to bring to the lives of people.

FINAL THOUGHTS ON EFFECTIVE CHURCH COMMITTEES AND COUNCILS

The following principles have general application not only to all committee and council meetings held in the Church, but to any council meeting in any Latter-day Saint family.

- Council meetings should focus on accomplishing the mission of the Church and helping members live the gospel and come unto Christ.
- Council meetings should ensure that no parent or Church member is left to perform his or her labors without help from others.
- Presiding leaders should plan and make adequate time available for effective council meetings.
- Time spent in council meetings on calendaring and programs should be minimal. The major emphasis should be on assisting the Lord in His work and in meeting the needs of the individual people.
- While respecting confidentiality, presiding officers should encourage free and open discussion.
- *All* council members should be made to feel their input is valued and that they are

. . . our council meetings are about duties and responsibilities, not turf. They provide an opportunity for the priesthood quorums and auxiliary organizations of the Church to come together in a spirit of loving cooperation to assist Heavenly Father in accomplishing His very work and glory: "to bring to pass the immortality and eternal life of man" (Moses 1:39). The same is true of our family councils, only there it is a matter of parents and children joining forces in an energetic and dynamic way to ensure that there are no empty places at our eternal family tables.

—**M. Russell Ballard**[16]

The presidents and bishops who utilize Church councils most effectively are those who do a lot of listening in council meetings. . . . Furthermore, each council member has a responsibility to be spiritually in tune when taking part in council meetings so that he or she can make a positive contribution to the issues being discussed.
—M. Russell Ballard[17]

One bishop learned firsthand how destructive it can be when council members are not careful to safeguard the things that are discussed in meetings. A council member inadvertently left a copy of the council agenda on a church bench. On the agenda were penciled notes about a family who had been targeted for the special attention of the council. It was found there by a teenage member of the family. Imagine the effect such a careless thing had on the family members.
—M. Russell Ballard[18]

full partners in the council and full participants in discussions and decisions.

- Participation in councils is both a privilege and a responsibility. Each council member should feel personal accountability to prepare for and participate in council meetings. By doing so, council members help lift the load from the shoulders of the bishop and other presiding officers.
- Each council member should prayerfully seek solutions to all problems and matters brought before the council, and come to the meeting prepared with ideas.
- Council members should support one another, respect the role of the presiding officer, and be unified in decisions reached.
- Councils should be conducted in the spirit of love and follow the example of the Lord who "counseleth in wisdom, and in justice, and in great mercy" (Jacob 4:10).
- Councils can consider matters beyond their specific unit, such as community matters and general Christian service.
- All Church councils should assist and strengthen the family.

Nothing about effective work in councils is particularly complicated. It's all based on the timeless principles of faith, hope, charity, patience, brotherly kindness, humility and diligence. Mix those principles with some good organizing and planning, and you and your team can accomplish most anything you can imagine.

There really is strength in unity.

QUESTIONS OF CONSCIENCE

1. Do I really understand the principle of

strength in unity, and do I constantly work to help my people enjoy the blessings that flow from the principle?

2. Do I stay alert for signs of fragmentation, and do I work to enhance genuine correlation, coordination, and cooperation among my team members?

3. Am I primarily a "gardener" in my leadership role, or do I frequently behave as a "mechanic?"

4. Do I rely mostly on my position and authority in leading, or do I appropriately involve others in decisions and plans?

5. Does my leadership style accommodate a bottom-up flow of ideas as well as a top-down flow of ideas?

6. Do the members of my council or group enjoy real enthusiasm in working together? Are they committed? Are they effective? Are they growing?

7. Do I really understand the training and coaching needs of the members of my council or group? Do I see that they receive what they need?

8. Do the members of my council or group feel plenty of affirmation and appreciation?

9. Do the members of my council or group clearly understand the linkages between their individual stewardships and the work of the whole? Do they clearly understand the linkage between their efforts and bringing people to Christ?

10. As a leader, do I constantly remember that I am a servant and that others are depending on me?

Applying the Principles

1. Note the statement that "every organization is perfectly aligned to get the results it's getting." Apply that principle to *your* organization—your family, your quorum, your community group, etc. If your organization needs improvement (and whose does not?) prayerfully consider where and how there may be misalignment between professed values and actual practices. Look especially for ways that you can make positive changes in *your* behaviors.

2. Consider this chapter's material on making decisions, clarifying issues and finding solutions. Do your councils focus on these? How can you improve?

3. Note the example of mind mapping on page 123. Use this approach in brainstorming with other council members.

You Can Do It!

Great leaders create great teams. Being on a team is one of the most enjoyable and rewarding experiences one can have. The camaraderie and friendship last forever. Working together in a common cause brings a sense of belonging, and achieving your goals gives one the fulfillment and joy of being a Kingdom builder. As a leader you can inspire and motivate your people to do the work of the Lord. Members of your group, council, presidency, or committee will learn to care for each other and share the load. They will cheer for and support each other in their individual tasks. Your common goals and purpose will help you develop a sense of "family." You will be unified. With time and effort and with a good dose of patience, you can create a wonderful team.

Remember, you can do it!—in the strength of the Lord.

ENDNOTES FOR MAIN BODY TEXT

1. M. Russell Ballard, *Counseling with Our Councils: Learning to Minister Together in the Church and in the Family* (Salt Lake City: Deseret Book Co., 1997), flyleaf.

ENDNOTES FOR SIDEBARS

1. Alexander B. Morrison, *Visions of Zion* (Salt Lake City: Deseret Book Co., 1993), 13.

2. Stephen L. Richards, *Conference Report*, Oct. 1953, 86 (emphasis in original).

3. Ezra Taft Benson, *God, Family, Country: Our Three Great Loyalties* (Salt Lake City: Deseret Book Co., 1974), 129–130.

4. Alexander B. Morrison, *Feed My Sheep: Leadership Ideas for Latter-day Shepherds* (Salt Lake City: Deseret Book Co., 1992), 155.

5. M. Russell Ballard, *Counseling with Our Councils: Learning to Minister Together in the Church and in the Family* (Salt Lake City: Deseret Book Co., 1997), 25–26.

6. Ibid., 85.

7. Ibid., 33–35.

8. Sterling W. Sill, *Principles, Promises, and Powers* (Salt Lake City: Deseret Book Co., 1973), 248.

9. M. Russell Ballard, *Counseling with Our Councils: Learning to Minister Together in the Church and in the Family* (Salt Lake City: Deseret Book Co., 1997), 157.

10. Ibid., 19–20.

11. Ibid., 99.

12. Ibid., flyleaf.

13. Ibid., 5.

14. Ibid., 68.

15. Howard W. Hunter, *The Teachings of Howard W. Hunter.,* ed. Clyde J. Williams (Salt Lake City: Bookcraft, 1997), 68.

16. M. Russell Ballard, *Counseling with Our Councils: Learning to Minister Together in the Church and in the Family* (Salt Lake City: Deseret Book Co., 1997), 10.

17. Ibid., 65–66.

18. Ibid., 64.

NOTE: As you can tell by the number of sidebar quotes from Elder Ballard's fine book, *Counseling with Our Councils*, we regard that work as an important resource for the subject of this chapter. We highly recommend it.

7

CREATING A CLIMATE
OF HOPE AND ENERGY

Great leaders know that people thrive best
in a climate of hope and energy. Like Nephi of
old, they know that with every commandment
the Lord prepares a way to accomplish the
work at hand. To help in that divine process,
great leaders work hard to create a "We Can
Do It!" atmosphere for the people they serve.

Make no mistake, this is not about platitudes and cheerleading. It is much deeper and
more strategic than that. It is about carefully
managing the *climate* at work in your leadership
setting. To translate good ideas and good intentions into break-through performance, you
must engage your people in ways that spark
their imagination. You must build their confidence. You must tap their energy and enthusiasm. And you must hold yourself—and
them—to a standard worthy of the Lord's work.

WHAT'S THIS ABOUT *CLIMATE*?

Let's take a quick look at what is involved
in the *climate* of your leadership setting.

Climate includes traditions and rituals of
the organization. In the Church, this includes
calling each other "brother" or "sister,"
sustaining new workers by common consent,
releasing workers with a public vote of thanks,
and many other practices that seem such a

natural part of being a Latter-day Saint. Climate includes our habitual ways of behaving. In some wards, for example, promptness is clearly not a priority and people are habitually late for meetings. In other wards, members habitually come to meetings on time or even a bit early. New members tend to adopt the behaviors they see modeled.

Climate includes group and individual norms. In some Church settings, members tend to bring their scriptures and lesson manuals to class. In others, members seem to rely solely on the instructor for all materials and preparation. In some priesthood quorums, home teaching seems to be a constant struggle and performance is always spotty. In other quorums, the brethren have the vision of home teaching and obviously regard their assignments as a blessing rather than as a burden. Group and individual norms make all the difference.

Climate includes reinforcement systems. One quorum president helps his brethren catch the vision of priesthood service, then commends them for stalwart performance. Another quorum leader chides his brethren for not getting their work done, then he and his counselors do the work for them. Here we see two different reinforcement systems and two very different results.

BEHAVIORS, VALUES, "UNWRITTEN RULES"

Climate, in short, is the "frame of reference" of your organization (your family, your quorum, your Relief Society, your Primary, your activities committee, your Sunday School, your ward, your stake, etc.).

For all of us, to "hold on" includes, therefore, holding on not only to our beliefs but also to our proven and tested patterns of behavior and Christian virtues under cultivation, and seeking to deepen even further their development.
—Neal A. Maxwell[1]

Climate is the collective patterns of behaviors, values and "unwritten rules."

Behaviors are specific actions—what you and your people *do*.

Values are the guidelines for the decisions you and your people make. Every behavior is preceded by a (sometimes unconscious) decision. *"Unwritten rules"* are the way things *really* work in your organization.

Behaviors are easily observable, so they don't need a lot of elaboration here. Values and unwritten rules, on the other hand, can benefit from some explanation. So let's turn our attention to them.

In a wide range of settings—in Church meetings, in the news media, in political campaigns, in our families—people talk a lot about values. As mentioned earlier, in this particular context we define "values" as "guidelines." Values direct our thoughts and actions as individuals, and as a family, quorum, or ward. The way we act on our values defines our individual and collective character. Our values help describe and define what we stand for. Our values suggest the behaviors that are critical for our success.

In terms of actual behavior, unwritten rules are closer to the reality. For example, a stated value might be something like "we love and respect the Savior," while the unwritten rule (the reality of what we *do*) might be behaviorally expressed as "it's okay to walk noisily into the chapel during the administration of the sacrament"—something that implies less than respect and reverence for the Savior.

What We Profess, What We Practice

In developing his vision for the spiritual growth of his ward members, a new bishop prayerfully considered the *climate* needed for great performance. He met with his ward council. He lovingly engaged his fellow leaders in a nonthreatening and candid discussion about where performance was and where it needed to be. They discussed what they valued, and they discussed what they observed as the ward's current unwritten rules. Here are some of the unwritten rules they were able to identify:

> People may talk and never teach, unless they practice what they preach.
> —Thomas S. Monson[2]

- "It's okay to call a meeting without an agenda and without a list of desired outcomes."
- "Many of our meetings lack real direction or leadership. They are merely opinion forums that fail to result in solid decisions or action plans."
- "We invite people to meetings because we want them to feel included and because their attendance is specified in the handbook. But then we fail to involve them or hold them accountable for results."
- "You're expected to attend meetings, but it's okay to come unprepared."
- "We are friends. It's not 'nice' to hold your friends accountable."
- "People who don't perform are allowed to slide, or they're simply released with a vote of thanks."
- "It's okay to emphasize 'process' (going through the motions) to the detriment of getting real results."
- "Coordination takes time, so we often just 'fly solo.'" (This is a variation of "It's easier to get forgiveness than to get permission.")

The bishop counseled with his ward council. He explained how *climate* affects everything we do in an organization. He taught them the importance of modeling and reinforcing behaviors that get positive results. To clarify, he used the "CPR" model. In most environments, CPR stands for Cardio-Pulmonary Resuscitation, a method for "breathing life" into a person who has stopped breathing. In this instance, CPR stands for *Converse, Practice,* and *Reinforce*—a method for breathing life and vitality into an organization. In the typical Church climate, we are very good at the *Converse* part. We do a good job of talking about principles and values. Most of us can competently teach a lesson on any of the values we profess to embrace.

Converse   **Practice**

Values

Reinforce

The *Practice* part is a bit more challenging. This involves actually doing what we say we value. A critical element of the integrity of our Christianity is the degree to which what we profess and what we practice are in precise alignment.

The *Reinforce* part requires even more effort. Reinforcement is a critical element of our leadership ministry. This involves specific and deliberate application of affirmation, encouragement and "rewards" for positive behaviors. It also involves specific, deliberate and *loving* correction of negative behaviors. It's this latter point that many leaders in the Church find especially difficult. In their understandable eagerness to be kind, they mistakenly equate correction with unkindness. In reality, failing to correct poor performance is itself unkind. Note the example of the Savior. He taught eternal principles without a hint of apology, and He never missed an opportunity to provide loving correction. In the context of all the wonderful encouragement He offered for positive behavior, His correction of negative behavior never seemed harsh. That is the very model we should follow.

PUTTING CPR TO WORK

No matter what words they may use to describe this process, great leaders deliberately and consistently engage in CPR.

One quorum presidency used CPR to improve the quality of home teaching. First, they taught their brethren the core doctrines related to watching over the Church. They engaged their brethren in discussions about the oath and covenant of the priesthood. They invited a couple of highly successful home teachers to bear testimony regarding the blessings of service and the assistance they had been privileged to render in their callings. They invited a single mother to share with the quorum how her home teachers had helped her dyslexic son with his reading program. This *Converse* part of their leadership was not a one-time event. It was an ongoing process. At every opportunity, this quorum presidency taught and re-taught the value of giving and receiving excellent home teaching service.

Second, the quorum presidency was deliberate in their *Practice* related to excellent home teaching. In every possible way, they modeled excellence. They did not "strut their stuff" or brag about their own performance, they simply carried out their duty quietly and faithfully. This faithful practice of excellence applied to everything they did. Their example set the standard for the rest of the quorum.

Third, the quorum presidency was careful to *Reinforce* excellent behavior when they observed it in others. They took nobody for granted, and they freely and genuinely commended brethren who visited their assigned families, who delivered spiritual messages to their families, and who rendered other service. Their praise was not of the generic variety. It was situational and specific, such as "Brother Willis, that home teaching lesson you gave to the Palmer family was right on target. Brother Palmer said it really helped his children understand the law of the fast." Reinforcement for positive behavior is generally easy to accomplish. Even reinforcement for seemingly minor things has an effect, such as "It's great to see you at priesthood today, Tom. And thanks for bringing your lesson manual. It really helps with our discussions." A good leader constantly makes reinforcement a deliberate and natural part of his own leadership behavior.

So what about reinforcement of *negative* behavior? Actually, some leaders inadvertently reinforce the negative. This is what happens when a quorum presidency gets frustrated with poor home teaching and goes out to perform someone else's duty for them. Such filling in may be all right in an emergency, but as a general practice it is guaranteed to reinforce poor home teaching performance. A better investment of energy is to consistently

> . . . we enjoy life when we have the ability to praise others for their good works. George Matthew Adams said: "He who praises another, enriches himself more than he does the one praised. To praise is an investment in happiness. The poorest human being has something to give that the richest cannot buy."
>
> **—Howard W. Hunter**[3]

teach correct principles (*Converse*), model correct behaviors (*Practice*) and affirm excellent performance (*Reinforce*). CPR really can breathe life and vitality into your organization. It will help you create an atmosphere of hope and encouragement with your people.

Reliance on the Spirit is critical to our success as leaders. The challenge is that many "leaders" in the Church seem to expect the Spirit to do it all. This book contains frequent references to the need for spirituality—it provides ideas on what the leader himself can and should do. Skill is also critical. President Spencer W. Kimball himself counseled us to be more "professional" in our leadership service.

REINFORCEMENT IS THE KEY

A good portion of a leader's effectiveness comes from the *Converse* part of CPR—what the leader says and teaches. Even more of a leader's effectiveness comes from the *Practice* part–the actual behaviors that the leader personally models. And perhaps the most critical portion of a leader's effectiveness comes from the *Reinforce* part—how the leader encourages positive performance and corrects negative performance.

Reinforcement is really not complicated.

You might ask, "Should I reinforce my people for their little day-to-day successes, or should I save up my reinforcement for when they accomplish something really major?"

The answer to that question lies in the way most Church volunteers (remember, we're *all* volunteers!) get their work done. The simple fact is that, for most of your people, work is not a string of dazzling successes that they

How often do you and I also give what the scriptures call the "garment of praise" (Isa. 61:3)? The "garment of praise" is often more desperately needed than the physical cloak. In any case, as we all know, these needs are all around us, every day. There are so many ways we can "lift up the hands which hang down, and strengthen the feeble knees" (D&C 81:5).

—**Neal A. Maxwell**[4]

produce one right after the other. Instead, the majority of their work consists of somewhat routine activities. They perform most of these quietly and without fanfare.

For example, in a given week a good Primary teacher will read two or three lessons in advance (to get a sense of context for the current lesson). She will visit the meeting-house library to retrieve visual aids for next week's class. She will prepare other materials and activities to enhance the lesson. She will read and study all the pertinent scriptures. She will pray for her children, by name, asking the Lord to touch their young hearts with the truthfulness of what she will teach. And then on Sunday she will actually devote precious time in face-to-face contact with the priceless children entrusted to her. While this face-to-face contact has the greatest impact, it is only part of the Primary teacher's work. Her leaders must remain constantly aware of the teacher's "behind the scenes" effort.

Then they'll be in a position to follow the first rule of positive reinforcement: "Make a big deal about little things." In fact, giving frequent, specific and genuine reinforcement on positive behaviors tends to crowd out negative behaviors.

Earlier, we said that the perfor-mance climate you establish—consists of the collective patterns of behaviors, values, and "unwritten rules" at work in your organization. Note in the graphic here how CPR—*Converse, Practice,* and *Reinforce*—fits into the whole. The

. . . In short, each of us has to purge from his life those values, traditions, customs, and attitudes that do not conform to the principles of the celestial kingdom.
—*Ensign* **Editorial**[5]

I believe with all my heart that if we can abound in the virtues of effective leadership exemplified by the Savior, he will make us equal to the challenge.
—**Joseph B. Wirthlin**[6]

way you as a leader articulate, practice and reinforce values has a powerful effect on the behaviors of the people you lead. At the same time, to get the positive performance you want, the "unwritten rules" at play must be consistent with the professed values. In other words, your own CPR efforts impact the way values are perceived and acted on. The "acted on" part is the behavior of the people you lead. Simultaneously, their behavior is impacted by the "unwritten rules" that they observe. The behavior also *becomes* the "unwritten rules"—or "the way things really work around here." You can now see that it's critical for these three elements—Values, Behavior, and "Unwritten Rules"—to be carefully managed. Let's return to the bishop we told you about earlier. He and his ward council members identified some of the "unwritten rules" at work in their ward. One of them was *"Coordination takes time, so we often just 'fly solo.'"* The ward council agreed that this "rule"—this *practice*—was diluting the effectiveness of their collective leadership. In trying to serve a family in need, for example, it often appeared that the left hand didn't know what the right hand was doing. This resulted in duplication of effort, or no effort at all. When the activities committee planned a ward event without appropriately informing and involving the priesthood quorums, the Relief Society and the youth leaders, great opportunities for service and inclusion were often missed.

So a new "unwritten rule" was agreed upon:

> *"We carefully use the council system of the Church to bless the lives of our people. We keep each other informed and appropriately involved. We correlate all activities. We*

*always consider the big picture. Our success
is a result of unity of effort, not division
of labor."*

Then this group of faithful leaders worked
hard to keep their behavior in alignment with
the new "unwritten rule." They quickly
discovered the blessing of counseling in their
council. And with this new clarity, they found
it easier to work together for the benefit of
those they were called to serve.

This Values, Behavior, and "Unwritten
Rules" model can be very helpful in
reminding us of the alignment required for
good leadership. It should not be applied in
an academic, pedantic way. It works best when
used as a general roadmap. A good priesthood
quorum leader probably won't leave for a
meeting by saying, "Honey, I'll be back later. I
need to go do some CPR with the brethren."
Regardless of the language patterns he uses, he
will simply understand that effective leadership consists of persistently teaching correct
principles, modeling positive behaviors, reinforcing good performance and occasionally
correcting poor performance. He may never
even use the term "unwritten rules," but he'll
be alert to the assumptions his people have
about performance, and he'll work to adjust
those assumptions in the direction of great
performance. Great leadership is no accident.
It's the result of very deliberate effort and
acknowledgement of our dependence upon
the Lord's graces.

Clearly, creating a positive "We Can Do
It!" climate is not a one-time event. It is a
constant process. And in addition to having
the right "climate" in which to perform their

service, your people need to have confidence in their collective implementation. As someone said, "Planning is everything. Execution is everything else."

SIX STEPS THAT HELP

Do you remember the SMART goals we discussed in Chapter 5? Your leadership goals must be *specific, measurable, attainable, relevant* and *time-bound.* And to make the journey from good idea to great performance, your people expect to have a reliable "travel guide."

As you lead your people down the road of Christian service, here are six things you can do to help them march with confidence.

1. Validate the Journey. Even though Latter-day Saints are very faithful in taking instruction from their leaders, they always appreciate having information and "context" on what they're asked to do. When President Gordon B. Hinckley announced the establishment of the Perpetual Education Fund, he didn't just rely on his position and title to persuade the people to participate. To provide context, he carefully related the marvelous ripple effect of the historic Perpetual Emigration Fund. He gave an overview of the needs of Church members in parts of the world today where education and training resources are scarce. He shared a vision for helping members with limited opportunity escape the cycle of poverty. He spoke of faith and devotion. He taught pertinent doctrine. He explained that the new Perpetual Education Fund required no new organization and would be administered by volunteers.

The Elders everywhere will instruct the brethren both in public and in private, in the principles and doctrines . . . so that every individual in the Church may have a perfect understanding of his duty and privileges.

—Joseph Smith Jr.[7]

In other words, President Hinckley was careful to validate the journey.

We should do no less in exercising our own leadership. When we ask people to make a change or transition, when we ask them to do something different, when we ask them to accept a new challenge, when we ask them to do better, we should always build a solid case for action. Make the journey meaningful and relevant to them. Give them context. Give them encouragement. Give them hope. Give them vision.

2. Scan for Speed Bumps. What happens if you're racing down the street and suddenly hit a speed bump that you didn't know existed? You're surprised, your teeth are rattled, and you might even lose control of your car. At the very least, your ride is disrupted. The same thing happens when you are unaware of speed bumps in the path of your leadership journey.

Scan for speed bumps. Carefully assess the climate. Analyze the history of implementation in your organization. Let's say you're a new Relief Society president. You are eager to have successful Home, Family, and Personal Enrichment meetings. In the past, these meetings have been only sparsely attended, and many of the sisters have never come at all. Do you simply rush headlong into the situation, hoping your own enthusiasm will save the day? No. History does tend to repeat itself, and unless you adjust the method of implementation you're likely to get the same result as in the past. So you scan for speed bumps. You gather information. You identify the points of resistance. You listen. You assess the

> . . . the vision was granted to him by the Lord for a wise and merciful purpose— that he might, through a better understanding of his duty, be able to remain steadfast thereto.
>
> —**George Q. Cannon**[8]

> . . . may I suggest that you *evaluate carefully*. Before you speak, consider what you have heard. Consider the course you are going to recommend . . .
>
> —**Thomas S Monson**[9]

impact of competing events and circumstances. You pray. You listen some more. *Now* you're better able to make the adjustments that will lead to success.

Incidentally, in one ward with low attendance at Enrichment meeting, the solution was relatively simple. The Relief Society president brought the situation before the ward council. She learned that a key to the issue was support by husbands and fathers. A special lesson on the Relief Society Enrichment program was prepared and presented to the brethren during priesthood meeting. When the husbands and fathers caught the vision, their level of cooperation (availability for baby-sitting, etc.) increased dramatically. A "speed bump" was avoided and implementation ran smoothly.

An early assessment of the environment is a smart investment of your time. Your implementation strategies will greatly benefit from your heightened awareness of possible obstacles.

3. Chart the Course. A big part of leadership is managing change and transition. *Change* is situational: the new class curriculum, the new calling, the new team roles. *Transition* is the psychological process people undergo in coming to terms with the new situation. Change is external. Transition is internal. Unless *transition* occurs, *change* will not work. Even positive change can produce stress (just ask anyone who's planned a wedding). Very few things undermine leadership effectiveness as much as the failure to think through who will need to let go of what when change occurs. Transition starts with an ending. A person is asked to let go of his previous calling or way of doing something. Even if he didn't particularly

What we need, as we journey along through this period known as mortality, is a compass to chart our course, a map to guide our footsteps, and a pattern whereby we might mold and shape our very lives.

—Thomas S. Monson[10]

enjoy or wasn't particularly successful with his previous way of performing, he may experience some anxiety with the letting go.

The next step in transition can be called the *neutral zone*. This is kind of a no-man's land between the old reality and the new. It's the limbo between the old sense of identity (the previous calling or performance standard) and the new. It's when the old is gone and the new doesn't feel quite comfortable yet.

It's during this neutral zone time that your people are "getting ready to get ready." Uncomfortable though it may be, the neutral zone is often the individual's best chance for creativity, renewal and development. This is an especially critical time for attentive listening, leadership, training, and coaching.

The final step in transition is the new beginning. This is when a person has successfully let go of the old and has come to terms with the new. So you have Ending—Neutral Zone—New Beginning.

In charting the course for the people you lead, two main approaches to transition are available to you: *compliance* and *commitment*. Compliance is when you simply instruct someone to do something and expect them to obey. Commitment is when you lead a person to "catch the vision" of a particular course of action. Good leaders carefully match the approach to the type of change they're trying to create. If the building catches on fire and you want people to exit immediately, you won't engage them with exploratory questions like "Do you have any particular opinions about smoke inhalation?" You will alert them to the fire and lead them to the quickest and safest escape route.

While the principles of the gospel are divine and do not change, the methods in dealing with the problems change to meet the circumstances, and so our methods have had to be flexible.
—Harold B. Lee[11]

Consider this experience by one of the authors:

Years ago our family was on a vacation in the Rocky Mountains. I was having difficulty with allergies, so I drove down the road to a small grocery store to buy some over-the-counter medicine. I found what I wanted and headed toward to checkout stand. In front of me was a little lady, probably about 80 years old, examining a display of eyeglasses. These were not sunglasses; they had clear lenses like you would use to read small print or do needlework. This lady tried on two or three pairs of glasses, each time carefully checking the focus by looking at a card on the display that had different sizes of print. Obviously she was very eager to select the perfect pair. Finally, with a very self-satisfied expression on her sweet face, she found a pair of glasses that seemed to work. "These will do," she said, and headed toward the cash register. I said to her: "Ma'am, I've never seen anyone buy a pair of eyeglasses in a grocery store. I suppose it's really hard to find a pair that's just right." And she answered: "Yep, it sure is, mister. Especially since I'm buyin' 'em for my neighbor!" I was delighted by this lady's attentiveness to her neighbor's view of the world. Although I can't recommend her method of optometry, I applaud her care and concern for others. We can learn a lot from that. As leaders, our constant challenge is to see the world through the lenses of the people we serve.

—Rodger Dean Duncan

Although the commitment approach—helping people "catch the vision"—is certainly the most advisable in most of our leadership situations, a compliance component is frequently part of the mix. For example, when a new teaching curriculum is developed and announced by Church headquarters, it's not the local leaders' prerogative to use it or toss it. Their responsibility is to ensure that the new curriculum is appropriately introduced and that transitions to its use are smooth and timely.

One of the truly marvelous things about service in The Church of Jesus Christ of Latter-day Saints is that *commitment* is an overwhelmingly large part of our performance climate. Yes, our people do *comply* with policies and handbooks and a wide range of operational instructions. And they comply because of their high levels of commitment. Again, leadership is about managing change and transition. People make new beginnings only if they first make an ending, then spend sufficient time in the neutral zone. Yet many would-be leaders try to start with the new beginning rather than first having an ending. They pay little or no attention to endings. They ignore the existence of the neutral zone. Then they wonder why people find change so difficult.

President Gordon B. Hinckley clearly understood *transition* when he outlined the three primary needs of a new convert: to have a friend, to be given an opportunity to serve, and to be nurtured by the Good Word of God. That is precisely what's needed by every person we lead through an ending, through the neutral zone, and to a new beginning.

> . . . wise shepherds understand that even in situations where perception does not agree with the facts, it is perception, and not reality, that determines behavior.
>
> **—Alexander B. Morrison**[12]

Frame of reference is so critical here. Frame of reference comes from past experience, from various social "filters," and from the way "facts" are perceived and sorted. To lead effectively, we must understand the frames of reference of our people. We must understand how they see the world and how their current experiences feel to them. Only then can we chart the course. (For related issues, see Chapter 9, "Communication: Building Bridges to Their Hearts," and the ideas on situational leadership in Chapter 10: Stewardship Delegation: The Great Multiplier.")

4. Build a Coalition. At General Conference and in other public settings, the president of the Church speaks with great power and clarity and influence. Faithful Latter-day Saints around the globe listen carefully to his message. And yet the prophet does not rely on "leadership by announcement." To ensure continuity and commitment regarding policies and programs, he wisely uses the organizational infrastructure at his disposal. He enlists the reinforcing sponsorship of the Quorum of the Twelve, the Seventy, the general auxiliary presidencies and their boards, area authorities, mission presidents, stake presidents and on down the line through bishops and branch presidents, home and visiting teachers, and right into the family. In irrigation terms, he makes sure the water gets to the end of the row.

This is the very model that should be followed in Church leadership at the "local" level.

One stake president was concerned by the dwindling number of young men in his stake who were making themselves eligible for full-

So we are one, my beloved brothers and sisters, united in this cause and in the glory of Him who has sent us forth on His errand.
—**Russell M. Nelson**[13]

time missionary service. In the past, as many as 50 missionaries from the stake were in the mission field at any given time. Recently, that number had shrunk to only about a dozen. The pool of Aaronic priesthood boys was still the same, so the issue was one of commitment, not demographics.

The stake president discussed the matter with his counselors. They concluded that a root cause of the situation was a drifting away from the core doctrines of sacrifice and consecration. But how do you make such lofty ideas appealing to teenaged boys who are distracted by sports, popular music, and other worldly things?

You do it with lots of love, lots of concentrated teaching, lots of focus, and something called cascading sponsorship.

The stake presidency first engaged the stake council. The group immediately caught the spirit of the matter, and their discussions were animated and enthusiastic. The primary symptom was clear: fewer and fewer young men were choosing to serve missions. At age twelve, most of them were excited and teachable deacons, eager to serve the Lord. Seven years later, many of them seemed to regard priesthood service as "a drag" and were more interested in less eternal pursuits. The stake president asked the council to address root causes and solutions, not just the symptoms. A plan was developed, and every individual on the stake council had a role in its implementation.

The stake presidency worked with the bishops, emphasizing their role in shepherding the Aaronic priesthood through the challenging teen years, with a major focus on teaching the doctrines of sacrifice and consecration.

High councilors worked with Melchizedek priesthood leaders, emphasizing their role in teaching fathers the skills of righteous leadership in the home.

The stake Relief Society worked with ward Relief Society leaders, emphasizing their role in strengthening the mothers of Zion and admonishing them to teach faith and obedience to their children.

Stake Young Men and Young Women leaders worked with local youth leaders to ensure that weekly activities as well as special programs such as community clean-up days appropriately emphasized the principles of sacrifice and service.

Stake Primary leaders worked with their local counterparts to ensure that the hearts and minds of young children were prepared for what they would learn and experience in the Young Men and Young Women programs.

Stake missionaries collaborated with ward leaders to ensure that young men and young women had frequent opportunity to go on team-ups with the full-time missionaries.

Every Aaronic priesthood boy was assigned as a junior companion to a carefully selected home teacher who would serve as his mentor. Activities people worked to ensure that every stake and ward activity had a service component.

Stake clerks worked with ward clerks to make best use of member information systems, ensuring that no baptized member could accidentally "fall through the cracks."

You get the idea. All the "infrastructure" at the stake president's disposal was brought to bear on the issue of missionary service.

Can you see the potential power of the priesthood and auxiliaries working together to systematically reach out to families and individuals? I believe that the answers to the activity problems facing our wards and stakes can be found in the priesthood and auxiliary councils.
—**M. Russell Ballard**[14]

If the stake president had simply "announced" a solution, it likely would have disappeared into a black hole. This is not to suggest that Latter-day Saints don't listen to their leaders. It is simply to acknowledge the reality of how leadership and communication work. Leadership is in a way like electrical circuitry. Over a period of time, the stake president wanted to "turn on a light" in the hearts and souls of young men. If he had simply "flipped the switch," ignoring the leadership circuitry between him and the young men (bishops, Scout leaders, parents, and many others) his leadership would have been short circuited and the light would have shown only briefly before flickering out.

Invest the time to build a coalition. Constantly engage in CPR (*Converse—Practice—Reinforce*). Create a sort of "key role map." Make sure everyone on your team understands the linkage between his or her responsibility and the success of the mission. Be clear about what you expect from others. Encourage them constantly. Coach them. Teach them. Listen to them. You and they will delight in the result. (Oh, yes . . . four years after it increased its focus, the stake described here had more than five dozen missionaries in the field. In fact, the vision was contagious. Even missionary couples from the stake were serving in greater numbers than ever.)

> Repetition is an important procedure in all teaching.
> —**Boyd K. Packer**[15]

5. Stay on Message. Inexperienced leaders often make the mistake of communicating a message once or twice, then assuming that it got through. Seasoned leaders know that effective communication requires repetition, repetition, repetition.

We must prioritize our teachings to emphasize that which is of the greatest worth.

—**Gordon B. Hinckley**[16]

Here's an example. More than six years before this chapter was written, the General Authorities of the Church embarked on what they called the "Leadership Training Emphasis." In a statement to all stake presidents, bishops, and other local leaders, they wrote: "To accomplish the mission of the Church, leaders should encourage every member to receive all essential priesthood ordinances, keep the associated covenants, and qualify for exaltation and eternal life. Church leaders should use priesthood quorums, auxiliaries, and stake and ward councils to help produce the following results." Listed were specific instruction and services to be provided for "Families," "Adults," "Youth," and "All Members." The brethren referred to this as a "balanced effort" to help convert, retain, and activate Heavenly Father's children.

Now, here's the clincher. At the bottom of the written statement was a telling sentence: *"This emphasis will continue until steady improvement is apparent."*

Now, six and a half years later, as this chapter is written, that same emphasis is part of the message carried around the world by Apostles and the Seventy. There definitely is virtue in redundancy. As leaders, we must carefully and prayerfully decide what we will emphasize, what "message" we will carry. Then we must "stay on message." This is done by repeating the message at every opportunity and in every venue. That doesn't mean you give the very same talk every time you stand before your people. It means that you continue to teach the core principles and doctrines. You may use different stories and scriptures and metaphors to illustrate your points, but you *stay on message.* You enlist the aid of your team (your counselors, your council, etc.), and you stay on message. You consistently reinforce good performance and you promptly correct poor performance. Great leaders understand that the main thing is to keep the main thing the main thing.

6. Calibrate for Result. Even in this age of sophisticated aviation, an airplane flying from, say, New York to London is slightly off course much of the time. Yet it can safely cross the Atlantic and land in London within seconds of its scheduled arrival time. Why? Because the pilots and navigators work hard to calibrate for result. They constantly examine wind direction and velocity and other weather conditions. They constantly monitor the airplane's instruments, its speed, the sounds of its engines, and the tilt of the wing and tail flaps. As a leader, you will do well to calibrate for result. Listen and watch for evidence that the "case for action" is firmly embraced by your people. Make adjustments as necessary. Listen and watch for signs of new speed bumps or other points of resistance. Make adjustments as necessary. Listen and watch for problems people may have in making transitions. Look for signs that commitment may be eroding. Make adjustments as necessary. Be on the alert for opportunities to reinforce the cascading sponsorship. Make adjustments as necessary. Solicit candid, reliable feedback on the effectiveness of leadership messages. Then make adjustments as necessary.

Great leadership is more of an art than a science. To be successful you must be constantly

> Knowledge is the basis of all his successful adjustments, . . . An adequate knowledge means the elimination of error and success in making adjustments.
> —**David O. McKay**[17]

alert. You must be ready to make adjustments along the way. You must calibrate for result.

Creating an atmosphere of hope and encouragement is one of the most important things you can do for your people. Don't rely on pep talks, although plenty of enthusiasm is a welcome ingredient in great teaching. Try the CPR (*Converse—Practice—Reinforce*) process we're discussed in this chapter. And use the six steps we've suggested to aid implementation. You'll find that they make a big contribution to a performance climate where success is contagious.

QUESTIONS OF CONSCIENCE
1. Have I carefully considered the "unwritten rules" that seem to be at play in my organization?
2. Am I working with my people to ensure that our "unwritten rules" are helping us get the results we want?
3. Do I personally *practice* the same principles and values I profess to embrace?
4. Do I utilize the Spirit in consistently and promptly reinforcing good performance? Do I consistently and promptly utilize the Spirit in correcting poor performance?
5. Am I carefully working to "make a case" for the journey I ask my people to travel?
6. Do I carefully scan for speed bumps of resistance or misunderstanding?
7. Am I deliberate and attentive in leading people through their transitions and helping them build commitment?
8. Do I invest the necessary energy in building a coalition, in making sure our goals have sufficient cascading sponsor-

ship? Do my people and I stay on message
so the sponsorship remains solid?

9. Do I seek candid feedback to find opportunities to make adjustments, to calibrate
for results?

10. As a leader, do I constantly remember that
I am a servant?

APPLYING THE PRINCIPLES

1. Look for specific ways to create and maintain a climate of hope and energy in your
leadership setting.

2. Become more conscious of the CPR
elements in your own leadership style. Be
aware of the principles and values you
Converse about. Be sure that you *Practice*
the behaviors you wish to model for
those you lead. And deliberately *Reinforce*
positive behavior and performance in
others as you sincerely affirm and
compliment.

3. In any change that you are called upon to
lead, consider how you can use the six
steps outlined in this chapter: (1) Validate
the Journey, (2) Scan for Speed Bumps,
(3) Chart the Course, (4) Build a
Coalition, (5) Stay on Message, and (6)
Calibrate for Result.

YOU CAN DO IT!

Great leaders understand their roles as
encouragers. They build strong individuals.
They build strong teams. They inspire faith.
They build commitment. They create an environment in which their people accept any
challenge with confidence and enthusiasm.
Great leaders get results.

The results that matter are always measured in the lives of our people. Were they loved and nurtured? Were they listened to? Were they praised and encouraged? Were their standards elevated? Did their capacity increase? Did their performance improve? Are they firmer in their faith? And most of all, are they closer to the Savior? Are they now better able to help *others* come to Christ?

Remember, you can do it!—in the strength of the Lord.

ENDNOTES FOR SIDEBARS

1. Neal A. Maxwell, *But for a Small Moment* (Salt Lake City: Bookcraft, 1986), 121.

2. Thomas S. Monson, comp., *Favorite Quotations from the Collection of Thomas S. Monson* (Salt Lake City: Deseret Book Co., 1985), 65.

3. Howard W. Hunter April 26, 1961, *BYU Speeches of the Year,* 1961, 3.

4. Neal A. Maxwell, "The Pathway of Discipleship," *Ensign,* September 1998, 10.

5. Editorial: "Unity in Diversity," *Ensign,* August 1971, 89.

6. Joseph B. Wirthlin, "Guided by His Exemplary Life," *Ensign,* September 1995, 38.

7. Joseph Smith, *History of The Church of Jesus Christ of Latter-day Saints,* 7 vols., introduction and notes by B. H. Roberts (Salt Lake City: The Church of Jesus Christ of Latter-day Saints, 1932–1951), 4: 475.

8. George C. Lambert (George Q. Cannon), *Treasures in Heaven: Faith-Promoting Series,* no. 15 (Salt Lake City: Juvenile Instructor Office, 1914), 22.

9. Thomas S. Monson, *Pathways to Perfection* (Salt Lake City: Deseret Book Co., 1973), 90.

10. Thomas S. Monson, *Be Your Best Self* (Salt Lake City: Deseret Book Co., 1979), 168.

11. Harold B. Lee, *Ye Are the Light of the World: Selected Sermons and Writings of Harold B. Lee* (Salt Lake City: Deseret Book, 1974), 348.

12. Alexander B. Morrison, *Feed My Sheep: Leadership Ideas for Latter-day Shepherds* (Salt Lake City: Deseret Book Co., 1992), 78.

13. Russell M. Nelson, *Perfection Pending, and Other Favorite Discourses* (Salt Lake City: Deseret Book Co., 1998), 184–185.

14. M. Russell Ballard, *Counseling with Our Councils: Learning to Minister Together in the Church and in the Family* (Salt Lake City: Deseret Book Co., 1997), 7.

15. Boyd K. Packer, *Teach Ye Diligently* (Salt Lake City: Deseret Book Co., 1975), 354–355.

16. Gordon B. Hinckley, *Teachings of Gordon B. Hinckley* (Salt Lake City: Deseret Book Co., 1997), 316.

17. David O. McKay, *Man May Know for Himself: Teachings of President David O. McKay,* compiled by Clare Middlemiss (Salt Lake City: Deseret Book Co., 1967), 195.

SECTION 3

SKILLS THAT
HELP YOU SLEEP
AT NIGHT

8

COMMUNICATION:BUILDING BRIDGES TO THEIR HEARTS

Great leaders know that communication is much more than issuing directions or giving talks. They know that communication is the lubricant of all relationships. It is about connecting with people, about understanding them, about building bridges to their hearts.

Jesus always honored people's agency, always respected their God-given freedom to choose. He was the ultimate communicator—not just because of His profound oratory, but also because of His great love and empathy for the people He served.

Nowhere in the scriptures will you find the Savior saying "As I have fixed you, fix one another." The Savior's leadership style was all about loving and inviting, not about forcing or fixing. He told parables that helped His followers understand eternal principles. He asked questions that caused even His critics to challenge their own thinking. He exhibited humility and kindness in every setting. He carefully listened and observed. He diagnosed before He prescribed. He taught life-saving doctrine with great clarity and without apology. His communication style was surely one of divine humanity.

In all our communication, Jesus must be our model.

In an atmosphere of sincere love . . . communication is pleasant, and adjustment is easy. But when this relation is impaired and one lives primarily for his own likes and self-interest, communication fails and real difficulties arise.
—**Carlos E. Asay**[1]

... the famous words attributed to St. Francis of Assisi ("O divine Master, grant that I may not so much seek ... to be understood as to understand . . . ") lies at the heart of true communication. Seeking for understanding is the product of a wise and loving heart, of humility and commitment to service.

—**Alexander B. Morrison**[2]

... in communication, we want to use our ears and our hearts so we can listen in order to know and to understand.

—**Ed J. Pinegar**[3]

As leaders we have an opportunity to "communicate" in a wide range of situations—in conducting meetings, in leading councils, in interviews, in teaching lessons, at the family dinner table, in formal settings as well as in casual conversations. In fact, we communicate at virtually all times, including those times when we're not saying a word or when we're not directly involved in the moment.

An excellent example is Elder Russell M. Nelson of the Quorum of the Twelve. We've noticed him in leadership meetings and in General Conference literally sitting on the edge of his chair as though he can't wait to absorb the speaker's next word. Even when Elder Nelson is "in the background" he communicates connection and caring for those around him. He obviously understands that much of communication (and leadership) is nonverbal.

In this chapter we will discuss some of the rudiments of effective communication. Then we will focus on a communication type of special importance to leaders at various levels in the Church: interviews.

The primary purpose of communication is to connect. In fact, part of the root word means to create a common-ness. This does not mean that communication happens only when we agree with someone. In the vernacular, it means that two people are effectively communicating when both parties "understand where the other is coming from." Communication is about understanding.

Communication is much more than verbalization. Many different studies have been done on how people communicate. Most of the studies agree that only about 10 percent of meaning comes from the actual words spoken. About 40 percent of meaning comes from how we say the words, the sounds we make. And about 50 percent of meaning comes from nonverbal cues like a raised eyebrow or other "body language."

It's hard to demonstrate this on a written page, but let's try it anyway. With the use of italics, here's a simple eight-word sentence that emphasizes a different word each time.

I didn't say you have a teaching problem. (Did someone else say it?)

I *didn't* say you have a teaching problem. (Is this just a denial?)

I didn't *say* you have a teaching problem. (Did I just think it?)

I didn't say *you* have a teaching problem. (Did I say someone else does?)

I didn't say you *have* a teaching problem. (Am I saying you had a problem earlier?)

I didn't say you have *a* teaching problem. (Am I saying you have more than one problem?)

I didn't say you have a *teaching* problem. (Am I suggesting you have some other kind of problem?)

Notice how simply emphasizing a different word implies a different meaning? Language, both verbal and nonverbal, has many nuances. Effective communication is much less about having a large vocabulary and more about making a deliberate effort to connect with the other person's heart. You've heard the expression about communicating spirit to spirit? That's precisely what good communication is about. You've perhaps been touched by a returned missionary bearing his testimony in a language different from your own. You didn't literally understand the words, but you nevertheless felt the sweet tenderness of the moment. That's because the language of the spirit is a universal language.

The best of both worlds is to communicate in the same spoken language as the other person *and* to employ the language of the spirit. Here are some ideas to help you.

First, learn to listen. Oh, we realize you may think you're already a good listener. You give others plenty of chance to talk, and maybe you've even overcome an earlier habit of interrupting. But just allowing others a chance to talk is not all there is to good listening.

Have you ever talked with someone who gave you the impression that his "silence" was really just the time he was preparing his reply to what *you* were saying? Good communication requires good listening, and good listening is all about understanding. A critical component of understanding is empathy. This involves identifying with the other person's perspective and feelings. Again, *empathy* is not necessarily about agreement. It is about understanding. We cannot effectively communicate with another person unless and until we *understand* that person's perspective and feelings.

Many of us believe we're quick to understand. Sometimes we're actually *too* quick, and we miss the opportunity to invite the other person to explore his own feelings in a way that's helpful to both parties.

There are a number of empathic listening responses that can be useful. Consider these:

Repeat verbatim the content of the communication—words only, not feelings.

> Good communication begins with listening. But more people seem to want to be heard than want to hear.
> —**Brent A Barlow**[4]

Rephrase content—summarize the person's meaning in your own words.

Reflect feelings—look more deeply and begin to capture feelings in your own words. Look beyond words for body language and tone that indicate the other person's feelings.

Rephrase content *and* reflect feelings—express in your own words the other person's words *and* feelings.

Discern when empathy is not necessary or appropriate. There are a number of phrases that can be helpful in acknowledging and enhancing understanding:

As I get it, you felt that . . .

I'm picking up that you . . .

So, as you see it . . .

What I'm hearing is . . .

I'm not sure I'm with you, but . . .

You place a high value on . . .

As I hear it, you . . .

Your feeling now is that . . .

You must have felt . . .

Your message seems to be "I . . ."

Empathic listening is useful in a number of situations:

- when you are not sure you understand
- when you are not sure the other person feels understood
- when the interaction has an emotional or spiritual component

If you're a seasoned leader with lots of experience under your belt, you may find empathic listening especially challenging.

What? Did you read that right? Someone with lots of experience might find something harder than a beginner? Yes. The reason is that in our "experience" we can make dangerous

You must learn to listen and to *empathize* (to see the world from another person's point of view). This involves *accepting* people as they are, *appreciating* their every effort, *recognizing* work well done, and *affirming* their right to be individuals, to feel and think differently.

—**Stephen R. Covey**[5]

assumptions. For example, the typical parent certainly has more experience than a teenager. But if that parent simply tries to impose his "wisdom" on the youth, more damage than good can occur. Good parenting, like any brand of good leadership, requires understanding. That comes only with patient, empathic listening. A key with empathic listening is charity. It is a spiritual approach to understanding, not some technique for manipulation or control. For empathic listening to produce the understanding you seek, your motives must be pure. You must genuinely *want* to understand the other person. Consider this experience by one of the authors:

My son Baylor was about to turn 16 and we were having a conversation. Actually, we were exchanging monologues. I said something like "When I was 16 . . ." and I saw Baylor's eyes instantly start to glaze over. It was as if he were silently saying, "Here Dad goes again, playing his home movies for me and telling me how things were in the old days." I stopped myself in mid sentence. Then I said, "I was 16 a long time ago. The world must be very different now. Tell me what it's like for you." My son looked at me carefully, studying my eyes as if to inquire "Are you serious, Dad? Do you really want to know what I think and what I'm feeling? Or is this just some kind of technique to get me talking?" In my eyes he saw that I was being genuine, that I really cared about what he was thinking and feeling, and that I longed to 'connect' with him. He started talking and I started listening. I listened not just with my ears, but with my eyes and with my heart. Our relationship was already pretty good, and that moment opened up new opportunities to make it better. For once I resisted the temptation to be autobiograpical, and instead invested myself in genuinely trying to understand what my son was feeling. Such precious moments are fleeting—sparkling like a star, then melting like a snowflake. We must use them before it's too late.

—Rodger Dean Duncan

Another reason "experience" can sometimes get in the way of effective communication is that "experienced" people are often very good at solving problems, at fixing things. Under the right circumstances, that ability is a major advantage. Applied prematurely, it can be a major roadblock to understanding.

Consider this example. Let's say you are feeling ill and you go to a doctor for help. As soon as you walk into the doctor's office, he begins to write out a prescription for you. He doesn't ask any questions. He doesn't take any medical history. He doesn't take samples of body fluids. He doesn't take your pulse or listen to your heart. He doesn't inquire about your symptoms, let alone try to identify the root cause of your ailment. You don't even get a perfunctory tongue depressor and a request to say "ahh." All you get is a prescription.

How much confidence would you have in such a diagnosis? How much confidence would you have in the prescription? Of course you would have no confidence at all, and rightly so.

That metaphor applies perfectly to communication. We should always diagnose *before* we prescribe. And effective diagnosis requires patient, empathic listening. And sometimes, no prescription is the right prescription—just effective, empathic listening.

Again, for the sake of emphasis, we remind you that empathic listening is much more than just waiting for the other person to "say his piece."

When another person is speaking, we're often "listening" at one of four levels.

We may be *ignoring* the other person, not really tending to the communication at all.

We may practice *pretend* listening. That's when we give the appearance of listening (possibly even including an occasional nod or "uh-huh"), but we're really not doing much to make a connection.

We may practice *selective listening* where we hear only those parts of the conversation that interest us or that help advance *our* agenda.

We might even practice *attentive listening* where we're paying attention to what the other person is saying and comparing it to our own experience.

But the highest level of listening—*empathic listening*—requires a deeper level of caring. It requires a special brand of unconditional love: not just the generic "I love everyone" kind of universal love, but genuine unconditional love for the *individual* you're seeking to understand and lead.

So, knowing that you care very much about the people you serve and lead, and given that caring, what can you do to be a better empathic listener?

For one thing, you can practice resisting the urge to be autobiographical. We are autobiographical when we project our own history or experience or perspective on the other person's situation.

Four of the most common autobiographical responses are advising, probing, interpreting and evaluating.

When we *advise,* we give counsel that's based on our own experience or values.

When we *probe,* we ask questions from our own frame of reference, perspective or agenda.

When we *interpret,* we try to figure something out based on our own history and perspective.

When we *evaluate,* we pass judgment on something. We either agree or disagree.

On the surface, all of these responses seem innocent enough. And they are. The point is that, offered *prematurely,* any of these responses can get in the way of understanding.

To illustrate the point, let's say Joe comes to you and with great sadness tells you that his family dog died this morning. You are well intentioned and want to help. You're also autobiographical. Here are four versions of a brief exchange:

Joe: "Oh, our family dog died today!"
You: "You know, you can get another dog at the animal shelter—and they're free!" (advising!)

In our attempts to influence others, we commonly make . . . mistakes, all related to either ignoring or shortcutting . . . influence. . . . we try to tell or advise others before we have established any understanding relationship, any real communication. Our advice, . . . will generally not be received until the feeling is good . . . the supreme skill needed here is empathy. . . . we try to build or rebuild a relationship without making any fundamental change in our conduct or attitude. If our example is pockmarked with inconsistency and insincerity, no amount of win-friends-influence-people technique will work. As Emerson so aptly put it, "What you are shouts so loudly in my ears I can't hear what you say."
—Stephen R. Covey[6]

Joe: "Oh, our family dog died today!"

You: "Don't dogs bother your allergies? Why don't you get a goldfish?" (probing!)

Joe: "Oh, our family dog died today!"

You: "Yeah, I lost a dog once. But I got over it." (interpreting!)

Joe: "Oh, our family dog died today!"

You: "That's a bummer." (evaluating!)

Sometimes the best service is to listen with love and concern.
—Jaroldeen Edwards[7]

This may seem like a silly example, but you can see how none of the autobiographical responses would help facilitate understanding. In fact, it's safe to say that such responses would provide no comfort at all to the bereaved dog owner and might in fact be hurtful.

Of course autobiographical responses are not always harmful. In fact, they can be very helpful. The key is to avoid offering them prematurely. The challenge with autobiographical responses is that—because we're viewing someone else's experience through *our* lens and not theirs—we can miss the opportunity to understand. A natural tendency for many people is to diagnose hastily, to jump to conclusions and to offer their perspective prematurely. Even when this is done with good intentions, it shuts down communication.

Context and timing are the keys. Depending on the context and timing of the interaction, as well as the amount of trust in the relationship, autobiographical responses may or may not be effective.

AUTOBIOGRAPHICAL RESPONSES *MIGHT* BE
APPROPRIATE WHEN
- the other person's communication is logical and without emotion.
- the other person specifically requests your perspective and assistance. the other
- person has a high level of trust in you.

AUTOBIOGRAPHICAL RESPONSES *MIGHT NOT* BE APPROPRIATE WHEN
- the other person wants only a listening ear, someone to talk to.
- the other person wants to express and explore his own feelings without feeling threatened or rushed.
- the other person is communicating about something emotional in nature.

Empathic listening is one of the most critical skills of a great leader. Empathic listening fills one of the most basic of human needs—the need for "psychological air"—having the opportunity to explore one's own thinking, to express feelings, to vent emotions and simply to feel understood without being judged.

Empathic listening is also a character trait because it is rooted in love and genuine caring. As the old saying goes, "I don't care how much you know until I know how much you care."

Let's say a teacher you lead expresses frustration with the irreverence of the children in her class. Rather than immediately jumping in with suggestions and other autobiographical responses, you might say something like "That must be a challenge," or "Reverence is important to you." This acknowledges the teacher's feelings and gives her psychological elbow room to

We interview with the spirit of love, and this should be the entire purpose of every interview—love. This should be the underlying factor. There should be no other source but love as we talk . . .
—**Robert L. Simpson**[8]

explore them with you. You may still offer suggestions, but you first allow the teacher to "talk through" her feelings. In doing so, you might well discover a good approach for herself. And even if she doesn't, she'll be in a better frame of mind to consider suggestions you may offer.

INTERVIEWING

So we turn to interviewing.

As with all other subjects in this book, we esteem ourselves no better than anyone else (see Alma 1:26). The principles and practices we teach here we have learned from General Authorities and other seasoned mentors. Interviewing is perhaps the most personal—and powerful—form of communication in a church setting. We would not be so presumptuous to claim exhaustive expertise on the subject, but we gladly share what we have learned.

For most leaders in the Church, interviewing is a more common form of communication than, say, giving a talk or making a presentation. We conduct interviews that involve advancement in the priesthood, extending calls to serve, extending release from duty, determining eligibility for temple blessings, reporting on stewardship performance, offering comfort and counsel, and a range of other matters. Some interviews, such as those for a temple recommend, are more "formal" in the sense that the questions are prescribed. Other interviews allow for much more latitude. In every instance, two things should prevail: (1) a spirit of love and (2) a spirit of caring.

Whether you're a bishop interviewing a ward member or a parent interviewing one of your children, your first responsibility is to exhibit a genuine spirit of love. Interviews in the kingdom of God are all about love and ministering by the Spirit. Love for God. Love for the Savior. Love for the person. Love for the gospel. Love for the plan of salvation. Love for the work that we're all asked to do, and letting God use us to minister one-on-one.

Everyone Is a Volunteer. All the people who accept callings in the ward and stake are volunteers. All the children in your home are volunteers. All of us volunteered to come to earth to be tested. As interviewers, we represent Heavenly Father in doing His work. The people we interview are His precious children. They deserve our best. Each should be treated with the utmost courtesy and respect. The people we interview don't work for us. As leader/servants, we work for them.

Unlike some interviews in secular settings, all interviews in the kingdom of God are about caring. A bishop's interview is really a "conversation with a purpose." A quorum leader's interview is really a "conversation with a purpose." A parent's interview with a child is really a "conversation with a purpose." In fact, the very best interviews don't really feel like "interviews" at all. They feel like a comfortable visit with a trusted friend.

Here we will focus on the three most common interviews in the Church: the *call to serve* interview, the *release from service* interview, and the *stewardship reporting* interview.

The *Call to Serve* Interview. The *call to serve* interview is done by stake presidency members, stake high counselors (when the stake president delegates the responsibility in certain instances), bishopric members, and, in the case of home teaching and visiting teaching,

> The ideal model is straightforward and simple: call good people to serve with you, listen carefully to their counsel and consider their input, and then listen to the whisperings of the Holy Spirit as it leads you to make good decisions.
>
> —**M. Russell Ballard**[9]

priesthood quorum and Relief Society leaders.

Many of us have heard stories about, or even experienced, the so-called "water fountain" interview. That's when someone is approached in a meetinghouse hallway and asked to accept a calling or assignment. Such a method violates every principle of dignity and respect that should accompany a call to serve in the kingdom of God. When we extend a call to serve, we are representing the Lord. The interview, and everything that precedes and follows it, should be done with that reality in mind.

Here are a few things worth remembering when extending a call to serve:

Consider the person's talents, gifts, qualifications, and needs. Not only is the work to be done an issue here, but so is the growth and development of the person receiving the calling. Prayerfully consider the "match" between the assignment and the person.

We're impressed by the story of the selection of Mormon to care for the sacred plates. He said, "And about the time that Ammaron hid up the records unto the Lord, he came to me (I being about ten years of age, and I began to be learned somewhat after the manner of the learning of my people), and Ammaron said unto me: I perceive that thou art a sober child, and art quick to observe." (see Mormon 1:2) And then Ammaron speaks of Mormon's virtues and gives him a charge in terms of his talents and qualifications.

Does the person you're calling have the talents and gifts needed to bless the lives of others? Does the person you're calling have needs that can be filled by service in this capacity? To the extent possible, there should be a good "match," and the person you're calling should be aware that you recognize that match. This is further validation of the person as well as of the calling.

Dignify the calling and the person. Gordon B. Hinckley fondly recalled the day that President David O. McKay called him to service as a General Authority. Rather than invite him to sit across the table, President McKay invited Brother Hinckley to sit beside him, thereby using physical proximity to help emphasize the importance of both the calling and the person. "He [President McKay] looked into my eyes, and I felt he was seeing my very soul," President Hinckley later reported. "I never will forget that."[1]

Elder David B. Haight recalled being invited by President Spencer W. Kimball to a room in the Salt Lake Temple. Elder Haight said President Kimball first interviewed him for worthiness. "And then he motioned for us to stand, and as I was standing with that wonderful man and he's holding my hands, he said to me, 'With all the love that I possess, I'm calling you to fill the vacancy in the Quorum of the Twelve Apostles.' . . . He did not say, 'As the President of the Church' or 'As the prophet' or 'By my authority.' He said, in that humble, humble way of his, 'With all the love that I possess.' He was teaching me that love is essential—the love that the Savior hopes that we will acquire—that we must show, that we must demonstrate, we must feel in our hearts and souls in order to teach the gospel properly."[2]

A calling to serve in the Lord's Church is a calling from the Lord. Such an invitation

The calling to serve the Lord places a tremendous, ennobling responsibility upon each of us.
—David B. Haight[10]

should be accorded all the dignity and respect that divine stewardship deserves. It is inconceivable that an Apostle would receive his calling in a casual hallway or sidewalk chat. The same reverence and decorum should characterize the interviews in which a Primary teacher, a ward Relief Society worker, an Aaronic Priesthood advisor or any other person is called to service in the Church. The interview should not be stuffy and need not be overly formal, but it should definitely be dignified and unhurried.

Explain the responsibility. As we discuss in Chapter 12 (Stewardship Delegation), it is critical that the person called to service clearly understands the responsibility he's being asked to shoulder. Although the interviewer may or may not be the person who will directly supervise the work (for example, a bishop's counselor might extend a calling to a new Primary teacher, while it is the Primary presidency who will oversee the teacher's work), the calling interview is the time to discuss at least the parameters of the stewardship. The interviewer should at least understand and explain the general expectations. The person receiving the calling should be told about meetings to attend, training to be received, materials to be obtained, and all other aspects of the assignment. It is during the calling interview that the interviewer facilitates a clear, up-front mutual understanding and commitment regarding expectations for performance (see Chapter 12 for more detail).

When Sunday School teachers fail to attend training sessions, the problem can often be traced back to insufficient explanation and commitment during the calling interview. When quorum leaders and others fail to attend the weekly missionary correlation meeting in the ward or branch, the problem can often be traced back to a call to serve interview that lacked clarity. Doing such an interview correctly does indeed take a bit of time. It is a wonderful investment in future success.

Appropriately consult with others. When issuing a call to serve, it is important that certain people are "in the loop." When a married person is called to service, his or her spouse should at least be consulted and when possible should actually be present. If a Sunday School teacher is being called to the Primary, the Sunday School president should at least be apprised that he will be needing a replacement. A stake president certainly has the authority to extend a stake calling to anyone in the stake, and he will do well to consult first with the new workers' respective bishops or branch presidents. Consulting with appropriate parties in this way is a matter of courtesy and is a hallmark of the orderliness of Church government.

Appropriately determine worthiness. At the local level in the Church, only members of stake presidencies, bishoprics, and branch presidencies have the authority to conduct worthiness interviews. Any call to serve should be extended only after the interviewer is confident of the person's worthiness to do the Lord's work (note, above, that President Kimball reaffirmed Elder Haight's worthiness before he called him to the apostleship). In some instances, this part of the interview

The second step involved in extending a call requires the authorized leader to hold a private interview with the member to issue and explain the calling. When a wife, husband, or child is to receive a call, it is recommended that the husband, wife, or parents of the candidate be consulted regarding the calling. Support by family members of the one who is receiving a call is an important consideration.
—**Brian L. Pitcher**[11]

might be relatively brief. For example, a bishop might say to a member, "I interviewed you two months ago for your temple recommend. Are you still as worthy as you were on the day that we both signed your recommend?" And in the case of an interviewer who is not authorized to ask detailed "worthiness" questions—such as an elders quorum president or a stake high councilor—he might say something like: "Brother Udall, I know you have a current temple recommend, and that is certainly a measure of your faithfulness. If every issue related to your temple recommend is in order, I want to extend to you a call to serve. If there is anything that should be discussed, please don't give me any details but schedule a visit with the bishop."

Again, only authorized judges in Israel should conduct detailed worthiness interviews with members. Stake presidents, bishops, and branch presidents should delegate calling interviews only when they are confident that all worthiness issues are in proper order with the candidate. Even with that, the interviewer should at least invite the candidate to visit with his or her bishop or branch president if any issue needs to be discussed.

Discuss "linkages." Do you recall our discussion in Chapter 1 about "linkages"? A critical element in any call to serve interview is a dialogue on the linkage between the calling and inviting people to come unto Christ. Inviting people to embrace and love and obey the Savior is not some incidental appendage to a call to serve in the Lord's Church. It is the primary purpose of *all* service in the Church. At every opportunity, leaders should underscore our

> The bishop is the judge and the shepherd who has the power of discernment and the right to revelation and inspiration for the guidance of the flock. He is responsible for holding worthiness interviews in order to authorize attendance at the temple, callings to ward positions, ordinations to priesthood offices, and the callings of missionaries.
>
> —**Dallin H. Oaks**[12]

covenant duty to encourage one another to devoted worship of Jesus the Christ. What better venue than during an interview in which we extend, on behalf of the Lord, a call to serve?

We have wonderful examples of this. When the angel Moroni appeared to young Joseph Smith, he clearly outlined Joseph's responsibility and set forth the great purpose of the work. Joseph later wrote of the interview: "I was informed that I was chosen to be an instrument in the hands of God to bring about some of his purposes in this glorious dispensation."[3]

The interview to call a new Sunday School teacher is not as dramatic as a visit from a heavenly messenger, but it is nonetheless a part of God's plan to bring His children home. Leaders would do well to follow Moroni's example in presenting the "Big Picture" of God's work and then specifying the person's role in helping to accomplish God's purposes, thus instilling vision and testimony in the new appointee.

Pass the baton. In many instances, as noted earlier, the interviewing officer is not the one who will directly oversee the work of the person being called. For example, a councilor in the bishopric may be asked to call a person to serve as a ward missionary. The actual line authority for that calling falls on the ward mission leader. At the conclusion of the interview, the councilor in the bishopric should make arrangements for the person to visit with the ward mission leader. Ideally, such a visit should immediately follow the call to serve interview. When a bishop's counselor calls a new Sunday School teacher, the interview should be immediately followed by a visit

That is the impression I desire to impart to you good people, especially those who hold the holy priesthood, and I think it is high time that every man who is so honored of God should understand his office and calling.
—**J. Golden Kimball**[13]

with the Sunday School president who provides appropriate teaching materials, a class roster, and other details pertaining to the calling. Nothing should be left to chance.

Sustain and set apart. Part of the call to service interview is an indication of when the person will be sustained and set apart.

Most callings in the Church are subject to the law of common consent. This is a wonderful part of Church government in which members have the opportunity—publicly—to pledge their support for fellow members who accept calls to service.

Every person called to service should be sustained as soon as possible in the appropriate meeting. For most callings this is the weekly sacrament meeting. The conducting officer should say something like "It is proposed that we sustain Sister Jennifer Rodriquez as a teacher in the Primary organization. Those in favor, please indicate by the uplifted hand." The language used is important. We have heard conducting officers say things like, "We have called Sister Rodriquez to the Primary. Those who can sustain the bishopric in this action, please raise your hand." This is improper because the bishopric has already been sustained. On *this* occasion, it is Sister Rodriquez who is being sustained. The language should be precise. A proper model is the language used by the First Presidency at general conference.

Shortly after the person is sustained in the new calling, he or she should be set apart. This, again, is a wonderful element of Church government. It's the priesthood ordinance in which the person is "set apart" from the

> If we will sustain those who are called to lead us, if we will pray for and uphold those who preside in the various stakes and wards of this Church, nothing can stop our progress.
> —George Albert Smith[14]

> . . . the person to be released should be notified some time in advance, and, at the moment of release, he should be given a public vote of thanks and a statement of appreciation made for the service rendered.
> —John A. Widtsoe[15]

distractions of the world to serve in a way that blesses all involved. The setting apart should be done with appropriate dignity and caring, calling down the powers of heaven to assist in the service to be rendered.

The *Release from Service* **Interview.** At the appropriate time, every person who is called to service should receive a *release from service* interview. This interview deserves the same dignity and caring as the call to serve interview.

President Hinckley said that every member of the Church—each a child of God—has an invisible badge that says "Fragile! Handle with Care."

We must remember that all workers are volunteers. When workers are released from duty, it should be done in a quiet, generous, appreciative way. Where possible, before releasing a person, it is a good idea to determine the possibility of another assignment. That way, the *release from service* interview can transition into another *call to service* interview. Then, when the person is publicly released "with a vote of thanks," the Saints have an opportunity to sustain the person in yet another calling. This underscores the doctrine that all of us should be anxiously— and continuously—engaged in the work of the Lord.

The *Stewardship Reporting* **Interview.** The *stewardship reporting* interview is—or should be—the most common interview in the Church. The doctrine of returning to report our stewardships is an eternal principle. When the principle is faithfully embraced, mighty work is accomplished. When the principle is only casually observed or altogether ignored, the work flounders.

The Lord's way is to organize, to delegate, and to require an accounting. In a revelation to the Prophet Joseph he clarified this doctrine:

> It is wisdom in me; therefore, a commandment I give unto you, that ye shall organize yourselves and appoint every man his stewardship;
>
> That every man may give an account unto me of the stewardship which is appointed unto him (D&C 104:11–12).

When we fill a vacancy in the organizations of the Church, the members being called must be taught at least three things:

- their specific duties and specific areas of responsibility, in other words, the new stewardship responsibilities now theirs by virtue of the calling
- the level of effectiveness expected of them
- where and/or from whom they may receive help, as needed

The members being called to service also need to be informed:

- that they will be expected to "return and report" on their stewardship
- how they will do their reporting—that is, in writing, orally in public, orally in private, or a combination
- where, when, and to whom they will report

This implies a strong need for well-conducted *stewardship reporting* interviews.

... and of every one shall be demanded a strict and personal accounting for his stewardship, a report in full of service or of neglect, of use or abuse in the administration of the trust to him committed.

—James E. Talmage[16]

SOME BASICS

One element necessary to a successful

stewardship interview is that both the one reporting and the one receiving the report must have a clear understanding of the stewardship being discussed. Such clarity of understanding requires deliberate focus. Both individuals must study and understand the appropriate handbooks and guidelines.

The substance of every successful *stewardship reporting* interview includes

- a feeling of appreciation, helpfulness and learning, all guided by the influence of the Holy Spirit
- a review of past commitments
- a specific report on progress made, goals accomplished or ongoing work being done
- a formulation of future commitments and plans
- the strengthening influence of encouragement, personal faith, and testimony

The *stewardship reporting* interview is ever-present in the Church. General Authorities interview stake presidents. Stake presidents interview bishops, quorum leaders, high councilors, and stake auxiliary leaders. Bishops interview auxiliary leaders. Quorum leaders interview home teachers. Relief Society leaders interview visiting teachers. Mission leaders interview ward missionaries. Parents interview their children.

For the purpose of illustration, let's consider the case of a priesthood quorum leader conducting a stewardship interview with a home teacher. The general principles are common to every other stewardship accounting situation.

It is a reality of human nature that we perform best when we feel constantly account-

> A side benefit from talking about goals and plans is that it teaches our children principles of stewardship. They enjoy reporting back on assignments.
> —**Brent D. Cooper**[17]

able. A key to effective home teaching is constant accountability. Constancy is facilitated by frequency. Home teachers should receive a stewardship interview every month. Note: this is *not* the brief telephone conversation in which the home teacher reports that he has visited the families assigned to him. By *interview* we refer to a private, face-to-face meeting with the home teacher and his companion. This meeting should be unhurried and in a setting devoid of distractions or interruptions. The interviewer should sit eye-to-eye and knee-to-knee with the home teacher. A prayer should be offered at the beginning of the interview. This helps establish the proper tone, and it underscores mutual trust and common vision. Prayer also reinforces the feeling of brotherhood that should prevail in our work together.

In short, if we want responsible people and children, we must give them responsibility and hold them accountable.
—**Stephen R. Covey**[18]

In the interview, the home teacher reports on experiences and commitments. He reviews the current needs of the people he's assigned to serve and teach. He reviews new plans and commitments (this is a great place to use SMART goals as we discussed in Chapter 5). There is discussion of how the quorum leader can help. And there is instruction, inspiration and encouragement from the quorum leader.

The *stewardship reporting* interview is a good setting for training. Training is more than just telling. It also consists of showing, allowing the home teacher to try under supervision, commending progress, correcting mistakes, and making needed check-ups. A relatively inexperienced home teacher can benefit from being teamed up with a more seasoned worker. Where both home teachers are somewhat green, a quorum leader might accompany them on a home visit or two to model effective home teaching. The *stewardship reporting* interview is then an excellent place to review what is learned, what progress is being made, and what needs further adjustment.

HELP YOUR PEOPLE SUCCEED

Remember, a critical part of your leadership role is to provide "context" and instruction for the people you lead. They need to know how they "fit" into the big picture, and they need your help in building both confidence and competence. (See the material on situational leadership in Chapter 9.)

If your people struggle, accept your share of the situation. It is your responsibility to train and encourage them so they will know the joys of success. The Church worker (or family member) looks to his leaders as if to say:

If you want my loyalty, interest and best efforts, you must take into account that

- *I need a sense of belonging, a feeling that I'm needed and wanted.*
- *I need to feel my assignment is worthwhile and of far-reaching value.*
- *I need to feel that the assignment you give me can be achieved.*
- *I need to be kept informed.*
- *I need to have confidence in you, as a leader, based on trust and mutual loyalty.*
- *I'm depending on you to be prepared to teach me.*
- *I'm depending on you to teach me how to feel the affirmations of the Spirit.*

In brief, no matter how much sense my assignment makes to you, it must also make sense to me. I have the usual human frailties. I hear what I want to hear and I place importance on

[The people you lead and teach] deserve more than your knowledge. They deserve and hunger for your inspiration. They want the warm glow of personal relationships. This always has been the hall mark of a great teacher 'who is the student's accomplice in learning rather than his adversary.' This is the education worth striving for and the education worth providing.

—**Gordon B. Hinckley**[19]

the words that are pleasant to me. I justify my actions, but I'm willing to change if you will show me how and then make the rewards great enough for me to work for them.

When you're conducting a *stewardship reporting* interview, avoid drifting into a monologue or lecture. The steward will often have a great deal to say if he feels you're ready and willing to *listen.*

If you listen carefully to their feelings, you will find out something about the heart.
—Henry B. Eyring[20]

Learn to use *silence.* Don't feel obligated to jump in to fill a brief void in the conversation. Allow the steward to explore—and think through—his relationship with the people he serves.

Help the steward move from an *external* to an *internal* frame of reference. Let him tell you how he genuinely feels about his assignment, how things truly look to *him.* As the interviewer, you should be primarily concerned with what is central to the steward, not what is central to you. If the steward says, "I hope for your sake that the people you home teach are more willing to have visitors than the ones I'm assigned," and you reply, "It so happens that the people on my list welcome visitors," you shift the frame of reference from *his* situation to *yours.* But if you remark, "Tell me about the interests of the people you're assigned to visit," you confine the discussion to his frame of reference and help him explore ways to get closer to his people.

The value of the question consists, in part, in backing away after you have asked it. By asking the question, you have invited them to turn their attention to an issue . . .
—R. Lanier Britsch and Terrance D. Olson[21]

Carefully consider what we said earlier in this chapter about empathic listening.

THE USE OF QUESTIONS

Sometimes the straight question-answer pattern fails to create the atmosphere in which a warm, positive exchange can evolve. This doesn't necessarily mean we should eliminate questions. But we should consider alternatives to the asking of questions, and we should be sensitive to the questions the steward is asking (even if he's not asking them outright).

The ultimate test is this: Will the flow of the conversation be enhanced or inhibited by the question I'm about to ask?

When you do ask questions, consider the difference between "closed" questions and "open" questions.

Here are some examples:

(closed) Do you enjoy your home teaching assignment?

(open)　Tell me how you feel about your home teaching assignment.

(closed) Is Sister Akrami still looking for a job?

(open)　What resources can you explore to help Sister Akrami find a job?

(closed) Are you making a list of things to do for the people you serve?

(open)　Tell me about the process you're using to establish goals for your home teaching.

(closed) Have you been praying for the people you're assigned to teach?

(open)　Please tell me about your prayers in behalf of the people you serve.

CLOSED QUESTION

- limits the steward to a specific answer
- curtails the steward's perceptual field

- usually demands facts only
- discourages exploration

OPEN QUESTION
- allows the steward full scope in his response
- invites the steward to widen his perceptual field
- solicits the steward's views, opinions, feelings
- can help reveal what the steward considers important; he may then volunteer information you didn't think to request

In most instances, we should avoid asking questions that can be answered with a simple yes or no or with a nod of the head. With just a little bit of adjustment we can provoke thinking and openness. Asking good questions is a skill that can be improved with care and practice.

In our leadership work, we should avoid solving people's problems for them. As the saying goes: Give a man a fish and you feed him for a day. Teach him to fish for himself and you feed him for a lifetime. Invest your leadership energy in teaching correct principles, not in trying to "fix" problems for people. One of the primary reasons for conducting interviews is to help the individual discover for himself opportunities for improvement.

In all of our interviewing, we must remember that effective *listening* is the key to our success. That entails listening to what the other person says, listening for what the other person does not say, and listening to the promptings of the Spirit.

Note the first word of D&C 1:1: *Hearken.* That means to *listen and do.* Nearly two dozen sections of the Doctrine and Covenants begin with the word *listen* or *hearken*. Another word that is frequently used as a starter is *behold*.

There's a great deal of difference between merely being quiet and genuinely listening. Heavenly Father would not invite us to pray continuously if he were not willing to listen. He expects us to follow that same pattern of caring when we deal with his children.

The Prophet Joseph often said that one of the most distinguishing characteristics of the Latter-day Saint people is that—by virtue of our confirmation—we have the opportunity to enjoy the constant companionship of the Holy Ghost. As leaders called to serve, we must be forever vigilant in maintaining our eligibility for that constant companionship. The Spirit will help us understand and deal with situations far beyond our own capabilities. As we love and coach and nurture and teach and encourage the people we're called to serve, the Spirit will show us the way. But first, we must *listen*.

QUESTIONS OF CONSCIENCE
1. Do I communicate to bless rather than to impress?
2. Do I constantly invest in being a more effective communicator?
3. Is love for God and for His Son really the motive for everything I do and say?
4. Am I genuinely worthy of the promptings of the Spirit? Am I submissive to the Spirit?
5. Do I prayerfully petition the Lord for the gift of charity which will enable me to listen empathetically?
6. Do I resist the urge to be autobiographical when it's not appropriate?

They will use open-ended questions that require more than a one-word reply and "what," "how," and "why" questions that lend themselves to more discovery and explanation. Good listeners "play back" feelings or rephrase what someone is telling them. They also pause to make sure that they understand what someone has been saying.
—Lloyd D. Newell[22]

I saw clearly that listening is a key. It is analogous to the hugs we give our young children. It is one of the ways we show affection for those who are embarrassed to be hugged or who feel too old to be cradled in our arms. By listening, we also show respect and love.
—Ted Hindmarsh[23]

7. Do I conduct interviews in an unhurried way?
8. Am I careful to "cover all the bases" in my interviews?
9. Am I sensitive to the communication needs of others?
10. As a leader, do I constantly remember that I am a servant?

Applying the Principles

1. Identify the two or three settings in which your communication is especially critical to your leadership success. This may include conducting meetings, teaching, interviewing or other circumstances.
2. Over the next couple of weeks, keep a simple journal on your own communication. Identify two things that seem to go well with your communication, and two things that are not going as well as you would like.
3. Review this chapter's ideas on empathic listening. Faithfully and deliberately practice empathic listening in every communication situation over the subsequent two weeks. (Be careful not to regard empathic listening as a "technique." Remember that it involves a genuine desire to "connect" with and understand others.) Continue to keep your journal.
4. Note the improvement in your communication. Make adjustments as necessary. Build new habits. Enjoy the results!

You Can Do It!

Great communication is not about oratory. It's about "connecting" with people.

It's about understanding the desires of their hearts and responding to their needs. It is imperative in your role as a great leader. Whether you are teaching, counseling, interviewing or visiting with those you serve, the real test is this: Do people know God is aware of them individually and cares? Are you allowing the Lord to minister to them through you? When you connect with people's hearts, wonderful things happen. You help them come unto Christ. There is no contention or misunderstanding because you have paid the price. Remember that the Lord will bless you. With the aid of the Spirit you *can* communicate well.

You can do it!—in the strength of the Lord.

ENDNOTES FOR MAIN BODY TEXT

1. Gordon B. Hinckley, "How to Call and How to Release," General Priesthood Board Meeting, December 6, 1967, 3.

2. Text from a video presentation by the First Presidency and Quorum of the Twelve Apostles of The Church of Jesus Christ of Latter-day Saints. Broadcast by satellite between general conference sessions on April 1 and 2, 2000.

3. Joseph Smith, *History of The Church of Jesus Christ of Latter-day Saints* (Salt Lake City: 1950), IV: 537.

ENDNOTES FOR SIDEBARS

1. Carlos E. Asay, *In the Lord's Service: A Guide to Spiritual Development* (Salt Lake City: Deseret Book Co., 1990), 94.

2. Alexander B. Morrison, *Feed My Sheep: Leadership Ideas for Latter-day Shepherds* (Salt Lake City: Deseret Book Co., 1992), 70.

3. Ed J. Pinegar, *Especially for Missionaries,* 4 vols. (American Fork, Utah: Covenant Communications, 1997), 2.

4. Brent A. Barlow, *What Wives Expect of Husbands* (Salt Lake City: Deseret Book Co., 1982), 5.

5. Stephen R. Covey, *Spiritual Roots of Human Relations* (Salt Lake City: Deseret Book Co., 1970), 256.

6. Stephen R. Covey, *How to Succeed with People* (Salt Lake City: Deseret Book Co., 1971), 36–37.

7. Jaroldeen Edwards, *Celebration! Ten Principles of More Joyous Living* (Salt Lake City: Deseret Book Co., 1995), 136.

8. Robert L. Simpson, *Conference Report, April 1962*, General Priesthood Meeting, 80.

9. M. Russell Ballard, *Counseling with Our Councils: Learning to Minister Together in the Church and in the Family* (Salt Lake City: Deseret Book Co., 1997), 68.

10. David B. Haight, *A Light unto the World* (Salt Lake City: Deseret Book Co., 1997), 68.

11. Daniel H. Ludlow, *Encyclopedia of Mormonism,* 1–4 vols., edited by Daniel H. Ludlow (New York: Macmillan, 1992), 250.

12. Dallin H. Oaks, "Bishop, Help!" *Ensign*, May 1997, 22.

13. J. Golden Kimball, *Conference Report, April 1931*, Second Day, Morning Meeting, 88.

14. George Albert Smith, *Conference Report, October* 1929, First Day—Morning Meeting, 25.

15. John A. Widtsoe, *Priesthood and Church Government* (Salt Lake City: Deseret Book Co., 1939), 327–328.

16. James E. Talmage, "The Honor and Dignity of Priesthood," *Improvement Era*, 1914, Vol. XVII, January, 1914, no. 3.

17. Brent D. Cooper, "Rock Me, Daddy," *Ensign*, October 1980, 41.

18. Stephen R. Covey, *How to Succeed with People* (Salt Lake City: Deseret Book Co., 1971), 103.

19. *Conference Report*, October 1965, 52.

20. Henry B. Eyring, *To Draw Closer to God: A Collection of Discourses* (Salt Lake City: Deseret Book Co., 1997), 138.

21. R. Lanier Britsch and Terrance D. Olson, eds., *Counseling: A Guide to Helping Others,* 2 vols. (Salt Lake City: Deseret Book Co., 1983-1985), 1: 109–110.

22. Lloyd D. Newell, *The Divine Connection: Understanding Your Inherent Worth* (Salt Lake City: Deseret Book Co., 1992), 243.

23. Ted Hindmarsh, "A Listening Ear," *Ensign*, September 1994, 45.

9

STEWARDSHIP DELEGATION
THE GREAT MULTIPLIER

Great leaders delegate effectively because they have a clear vision of two things: accomplishing the work and helping their people grow.

Delegation is a core principle of Heavenly Father's plan. Delegation was used in every step of the creation. Delegation was used in every phase of the Savior's earthly ministry. Delegation is the principle through which the restoration occurred. Delegation is the leadership principle used to accomplish the Lord's purposes throughout the Church today. And yet delegation is frequently misunderstood and often misapplied.

In observing a servant who is overloaded with work, most of us have heard (or even made) comments such as "He should delegate more" or "Why doesn't she learn to delegate?" The assumption seems to be that the trick to delegation is simply turning work over to someone else and suddenly being free of that responsibility. But it's a mistake to regard delegation as simply the ability to get someone else to do your job. When we treat delegation as no more than shifting responsibility, we communicate to the other person a dangerous message: "You'll be doing me a big favor if you'll complete this assignment." Then your coworker feels free either to carry out the task

Church leaders must delegate responsibility or perish under a mountain of administrative detail that no mortal man can bear.

—**Bruce R. McConkie**[1]

or to leave it incomplete. Where there's no sense of psychological ownership of a task, there's little incentive to get it done.

As any good leader can attest, delegation won't necessarily give you more time immediately. Especially at the start, delegation requires careful thought, communication, commitment and focus. At the very beginning, delegation may require even more of your time than if you had done the delegated task yourself. In the long run, however, you should expect delegation to give you time for other matters. And, of course, in addition to facilitating the accomplishment of work, effective delegation develops others by giving them the opportunity to serve, to learn new skills, to stretch their wings, to build their confidence, and broaden their competence.

Any good leader knows, however, that delegation won't necessarily give him more free time immediately. In the long run, effective delegation *should* give the leader more time for other matters, but in the short time frame, it may involve an even greater time commitment.
—**William G. Dyer**[2]

DELEGATION IMPLIES TRUST

With delegation comes stewardship. A stewardship is a job with a trust. When an assignment is delegated to us, we are entrusted with that assignment. With every delegated stewardship, certain authority, power, and trust are bestowed. When the principle of delegation is properly practiced, everyone benefits: the person who delegates the task or assignment, the person who receives the delegated stewardship, and the people who are blessed by the service rendered.

. . . in order to have the fruits of organized effort, we must have leadership; and in order to have leadership we must delegate some authority, because leadership without authority is ineffective.
—**Richard L. Evans**[3]

KNOWING WHEN TO "LET GO"

Even if he or she is clearly the most qualified for a task, a good leader must be disciplined enough to "let go." For example, one bishop we know, by virtue of his previous callings and experience, is an excellent administrator. He is exceptionally strong with organizational details, familiar with nearly every computer program used in the Church and able to put together statistical reports quickly and efficiently. Yet he understands that in his new role as bishop he is president of the Aaronic Priesthood in his ward. Today his stewardship focus is on increasing the spiritual strength and resilience of the ward's youth. Administrative details, which he loved in previous assignments, must now be delegated to his executive secretary and clerks. Those "detail" assignments are no less important than they were when he had them, but the bishop shares those burdens with people who are properly qualified and authorized to help carry the load. Regardless of the assignment, this same principle of delegation applies.

Why, then, do many leaders *not* delegate? Here are what seem to be the most common excuses given:

- "I just can't rely on my people to do the job the way I want it done."
- "It's easier and faster to do the job myself than to delegate it."
- "It's frustrating not to have something done the right way the first time."

On the other hand, most of us have observed leaders who are always calm and collected, who seem to be in control of every situation, who manage to involve their people in nearly every phase of the work, and whose team members seem fulfilled and energized by their labor. These are the leaders who understand and practice effective delegation.

If you find it difficult to "let go," you're in good company. Some of the best leaders in

> They (the Bishops) cannot do it all themselves. They have counselors to whom they can and must delegate. In so doing, they will bless themselves and their people.
>
> —**Gordon B. Hinckley**[4]

> In the final analysis, effective delegation takes the emotional courage to allow, to one degree or another, others to make some mistakes . . . This courage consists of patience, self-control, faith in others and in their potential, and respect for individual differences.
>
> —**Stephen R. Covey**[5]

history had to learn to practice the principle of delegation.

A classic case involved Moses and Jethro. Moses was exhausting himself trying to do everything for the children of Israel. He was serving as judge in all matters, both large and small. His father-in-law, Jethro, saw this and offered wise advice: "The thing that thou doest is not good. Thou wilt surely wear away, both thou, and this people that is with thee: for this thing is too heavy for thee; thou art not able to perform it thyself alone" (see Exodus 18:17–18).

Jethro then counseled Moses to do two things. First, Moses was to teach the people principles that embodied his judgments so they wouldn't have to come to him to judge every matter. They could use the principles as guidelines in addressing problems on their own. This is a powerful form of delegation—teaching true principles and trusting people to apply them.

Next, Moses was to choose faithful followers and delegate all smaller matters to them, retaining to himself only matters of major importance.

Notice that both of Jethro's recommendations required Moses to invest more time at the beginning in setting things up. This required risk. Instead of rendering judgment directly, Moses carefully selected and trained other judges. He put his faith in them, knowing that they might do things differently than he would. They might even make mistakes.

As we see, the elements of time and risk made even Moses at first reluctant to delegate. Yet learning to delegate effectively helped him become one of history's greatest leaders.

Effective delegation is the result of serious planning, a clear explanation of what is involved, proper training, follow-through, and a willingness to let go.
—William G. Dyer[6]

To work through others involves the risk of doing things differently.
—Stephen R. Covey[7]

FOUR IMPORTANT QUESTIONS

For the leader who is determined to avoid being a one-person show and who wants to bless others with opportunities to serve, at least four questions should be carefully addressed:

1. What is the task or assignment?
2. Who is available to fulfill it?
3. Whom does the Lord want?
4. How do I train and inspire this individual to accept and carry out this stewardship with excellence?

> Wise delegation requires prayerful preparation, as does effective teaching or preaching.
> —**Ezra Taft Benson**[8]

You cannot effectively delegate a task or assignment until you understand at least the general parameters. Does the task require special skills or experience? What training is needed and available? What sort of time commitments must be made by the person accepting the assignment? What meetings are involved?

Closely related to your careful assessment of the task or assignment itself is your appraisal of the people who might be available to fill it. Depending on your own role— whether you are offering counsel to the leader who must make the final selection decision or whether you are the leader making the final decision—some obvious questions must be considered.

For instance, who in your resource pool (the branch, ward, or stake) is now available or could be available for the assignment? Which of these people has the requisite skills or experience? Which of them is most likely to be reliable in fulfilling the stewardship? Do your homework on these issues and carefully seek confirmation from the Spirit.

The fourth question to be addressed— How do I train and inspire this individual to

If you treat a man as he is, he will remain as he is, but if you treat him as if he were what he ought to be, and could be, he will become what he ought to be, and should be.

—Goethe[9]

accept and carry out this stewardship with excellence?—is especially crucial. Why? Because, frankly, too often Church assignments are given with the false assumption that the task will somehow be done properly and promptly through the goodwill of the worker. In reality, the worker may have the very best of intentions but simply lack the competence and confidence to carry out the assignment.

That's where clarity of expectations enters into the delegation formula.

AN AGREEMENT ON EXPECTATIONS

Effective delegation involves expectations—the expectations of the person doing the delegating as well as the expectations of the person who's given the task or assignment. Giving an assignment is not a monologue. If done effectively, it requires a dialogue between both parties.

The high expectations of others may even help motivate us or encourage us to reach heights we otherwise would not even attempt to strive for.

—*Church News*[10]

In fact, the entire process may be defined in this way: *Effective stewardship delegation requires a clear, up-front, mutual understanding and commitment regarding expectations* about:

• desired results or outcomes
• guidelines
• resources
• accountability, and
• linkages

Now let's consider each part of that definition, because each is crucial.

The communication between the two parties must be *clear*. Without clarity, misunderstanding is inevitable. A Relief Society leader was in charge of a ward supper and enlisted the help of nearly two dozen other sisters. To each of five of those sisters, the leader gave a simple assignment: "Please bring a salad." What the leader envisioned was a variety—perhaps a bean salad, a fruit salad, a spinach salad and so on. What she got, however, was five nearly identical gelatin salads. Why? Because she failed to specify what she had in mind. Those receiving the assignment were left to guess, and their arrival at the ward supper with five gelatin salads provided a humorous lesson in the importance of clarity.

The communication between the two parties must be *up-front*. It is frustrating to a person to receive an assignment without an exchange of expectations. But it is even more frustrating to be well on your way toward accomplishing a task, only to be told that your leader had something altogether different in mind. The time to agree on the particulars of an assignment is at the beginning. Yes, this requires an investment of time and focus at a moment when both parties may feel rushed. But the investment now will pay rich dividends later.

The *understanding* and *commitment* regarding the assignment must be *mutual*. When delegating, the effective leader carefully listens to the feelings and hopes and expectations of the person receiving the assignment. The leader expresses his own vision of the assignment. When the two parties come to an agreement on all of the elements, they are well on their way to success.

The scope of Brigham's prophetic insight and understanding stood behind every act of his life. With masterful feeling and language he endeavored to share the depth of this understanding and commitment with those whom he loved and led.

—Susan Evans McCloud[11]

A REAL-LIFE EXAMPLE

To illustrate how this process works, let's take the case of Bishop Wilson and Brother Gray. As presiding high priest in the ward, Bishop Wilson is responsible for the work of sharing the gospel, retention and reactivation. The ward mission leader works under the direction of the bishop. Bishop Wilson has invited Brother Gray to an interview. The interview has begun, and Brother Gray has reconfirmed his willingness to serve wherever he's called. Bishop Wilson tells him his new assignment is that of ward mission leader.

In the "how *not* to do it" scenario, the interview might end there. The bishop would simply shake Brother Gray's hand and wish him luck. Fortunately, Bishop Wilson knows better. He is determined to do everything possible to help ensure Brother Gray's success. He does this by engaging Brother Gray in a specific discussion of the key expectations: desired results or outcomes, guidelines, resources, accountability, and linkages.

For each of these five elements, Bishop Wilson solicits Brother Gray's ideas and opinions. Then he shares his vision of the assignment that's reinforced by instruction from the stake president, pertinent handbooks and manuals, general Church authorities, and the Lord himself.

Under "desired results," for instance, Bishop Wilson discusses such items as the ward's past performance in missionary activity, the number of new members baptized during the past two years and the activity rate of those new members. He and Brother Gray then come to an agreement regarding—at least directionally—how the ward's missionary work will progress in terms of referrals, baptisms, fellowshipping and other success indicators. (After he's had a chance to get a feel for his new calling and develop a sense of

> One purpose of Church callings is to benefit individual members by letting them do the work of the Church. . . . Through service, members learn their responsibility and their capacity, enlarge their understanding, and increase their commitment to the gospel (D&C 58:26-28; Matt. 10:39).
> —**Brian L. Pitcher**[12]

vision himself, Brother Gray will no doubt seek further direction from the bishop.)

In this initial stewardship interview, "guidelines" to be discussed include such things as the approved policies and procedures to be followed by ward mission leaders. Bishop Wilson points out that these are outlined in various publications such as the *Church Handbook of Instructions.* He instructs Brother Gray in the proper correlation of the ward's missionary activities with the bishopric, Melchizedek Priesthood leaders, other ward leaders and full-time missionaries. He explains his reporting relationship to the bishop. In this portion of the initial stewardship interview, Bishop Wilson also discusses the levels of initiative expected of Brother Gray (more on that later).

With every Church assignment come certain resources. In the case of this new ward mission leader, these include human resources, financial resources, technical resources, organizational resources and even "access" resources.

The human resources include individual home teachers and visiting teachers with whom Brother Gray may coordinate missionary activities through appropriate members of the ward council.

Organizational resources include the ward council and the priesthood executive committee through which he correlates his missionary efforts.

The technical resources may include assistance from ward clerks and auxiliary secretaries who are aware of missionary opportunities within the ward family, as well as priesthood quorum members and Relief Society sisters

Think what a bishop *or anyone for that matter* (italics portion added by authors) can do if he puts all of his resources to work.
—**Henry D. Moyle**[13]

who can alert him to potential investigators.

Access is another resource that should be clarified. Brother Gray needs to know what he can expect in terms of access to the ward bishopric and others who assist him in fulfilling his assignment.

ACCOUNTABILITY IS AT THE CORE

By definition, accountability is at the core of stewardship delegation. The bishop is still accountable for missionary work in the ward. But Brother Gray now shares a portion of that accountability through his role and performance as ward mission leader. His primary accountability is to the Lord, with whom he has made sacred covenants as a member of the Church and as a holder of the priesthood. And in this instance, he gives an accounting of his performance to his priesthood leader—the bishop. Bishop Wilson and Brother Gray should now come to a clear, mutual understanding and commitment regarding when those periodic stewardship interviews will occur, what specific information will be discussed and evaluated, and what standards will be used to measure success.

Linkages constitute the element of stewardship delegation that's perhaps most often ignored in a Church setting. Yet linkages are what leadership vision and individual service are all about (see Chapter 1, "What Great Leadership Is," and Chapter 3, "What Great Leaders See"). Bishop Wilson bears his thoughtful testimony of the divinity of the Church's missionary efforts and promises Brother Gray that effective missionary work with just one family can have a soul-saving impact on countless generations of Heavenly

> Responsibility involves stewardship and accountability.
> —**Richard J. Marshall**[14]

> Each is to stand firm within his designated stewardship, for therein lies accountability.
> —**Hoyt W. Brewster**[15]

Father's children. (Brother Gray, as with every Church worker, is sure to be interested in such linkages.) The brethren then exchange stories of their own conversions to the gospel and their gratitude for the members who welcomed them into the Church.

You'll notice here that these steps to stewardship delegation involve delegating the assignment, *not* delegating the methods.

It's important to come to agreement on the desired outcomes and to share a common understanding and commitment regarding the linkages between the work and its effect on bringing souls to Christ. But if you then begin to get too specific about the actual methods of getting the agreed upon results, you risk short circuiting the steward's own ingenuity. That's called micromanaging, tending to the small details of another person's stewardship.

Remember that we suggest reaching a *clear, up-front mutual understanding and commitment* regarding (1) desired results or outcomes, (2) guidelines, (3) resources, (4) accountability, and (5) linkages. In doing this, you enter into a kind of psychological contract with the steward. Then the temptation to "Micromanage" (regardless of how you might define it) greatly diminishes. That's because "micromanaging" often takes the form of *belatedly* trying to clarify expectations. When you do it in advance and there is a *clear, up-front mutual understanding and commitment* regarding expectations, your comfort level rises and the other person's comfort *and* competence are enhanced.

Unrealized expectations often cause a negative response.
—**William G. Dyer**[16]

By the way, note that we continue to use the word *mutual.* Expectations and understandings should be shared. This implies that you can and should initiate a discussion on these five items even when you are the person who is receiving an assignment. It is not disrespectful to ask for clarity on an assignment. This is the Lord's work we're talking about, and it deserves the very best of us all.

LEVELS OF INITIATIVE

We mentioned earlier that the expected levels of initiative should be discussed in the initial stewardship interview. Stewardship delegation actually helps people develop initiative. Ideally, this development process moves them through six levels or stages:

It is true that Nephi received much instruction from the Lord in building the ship, but Nephi was also prepared to exercise personal initiative in the project from the beginning. . . . . the Lord tells him to build a ship. Nephi's response is instructive. . . . "Lord, whither shall I go that I may find ore to molten, that I may make tools to construct the ship after the manner which thou has shown unto me?" (1 Ne. 17:9). He asks for guidance in finding ore so that he can make tools.
—Anderson, Green, Dalton[17]

1. The first level of initiative is when the worker *waits for instruction.*
2. At the next level of initiative, the worker *asks what to do.*
3. As the worker gains competence and confidence, he or she *recommends* what should be done.
4. Upon gaining additional experience, the worker *acts independently* but reports *immediately* to the supervising leader.
5. The next level is when the worker *acts independently* and reports routinely.
6. Finally, the worker simply *does it* and moves on to another part of his assignment.

At which level of initiative should Brother Gray operate in his new assignment as ward mission leader? In reality, he will operate at all six levels of initiative, depending on which part of his assignment is addressed. For example, he does not have the authority to call someone in his ward to serve as a ward missionary. But as ward mission leader, he certainly has the authority and responsibility to *recommend* to his bishop that someone receive such a call. He does not need to wait for instruction to meet weekly with the full-time missionaries assigned to his ward. In that part of his assignment, he should merely *act independently but report routinely.*

Lack of mutual understanding on the expected levels of initiative is probably the most common cause for failure in a steward-ship assignment. For many people, a natural inclination (because of humility or lack of confidence or a fear of overstepping their authority) is to adopt a lower level of initiative than is necessary.

Remember: The effective leader takes the time to *teach* the steward and to *clarify* expectations. The leader should encourage the steward to lean toward initiative rather than toward inertia. After all, it's easier to tame a tiger than to motivate a turtle. And if the leader does not initiate an early and specific discussion leading to an agreement on mutual expectations, the person receiving the assignment should initiate the discussion.

With this careful attention to mutual expectations, can you see how Brother Gray is placed on a path to success? At the very beginning, he is given the opportunity to ask questions and to express himself regarding expectations for his new assignment. He is given much, much more than a handshake and good wishes. He receives a motivating mission, complete with specifics on (1) desired results, (2) guidelines, (3) resources, (4) accountability, (5) linkages and (6) levels of initiative. He can now proceed with confidence.

> A point of mutual understanding is reached in the training process when the assignee commits him- or herself to do the job. If the training is well done and the communication is two-way, this commit-ment will be honest, deep, and realistic and will internalize the source of motivation or supervision from then on.
> —Stephen R. Covey[18]

"But wait a minute," you may be thinking. "These are helpful principles and they certainly apply in some cases. But I'm working with people who have a wide range of experience. They have many different sets of skills. Some of them are already highly committed, while others clearly need motivating. Their testimonies of the gospel are at different levels of maturity. How can I lead such people with one set of principles?"

That's the very point! True principles of delegation apply to every situation.

> It is time for us to reflect and to think upon our situation, and to consider our ways and be wise. What do you want to do?
> —John Taylor[19]

Please note: We are not suggesting that you apply the principles in a "cookie cutter" fashion, treating every individual precisely the same. In fact, an important principle to remember is that *there is nothing as unequal as the equal treatment of unequals*. One of the practices that made the Savior so successful in His earthly ministry is that He "taught the one." He carefully considered the individual needs of the person he was teaching. So must we use true principles to address the individual and personal needs of each person we are charged to lead. This principle of delegation combined with trust is vital in raising responsible and accountable children.

SITUATIONAL LEADERSHIP

Like any good physician, the effective leader diagnoses before he prescribes. He carefully and prayerfully considers the situation at hand—the situation regarding the challenges of the work to be accomplished and the situation regarding the ability and readiness of the person being asked to do the work. In this sense, one size does *not* fit all.

Situational leadership[1] honors the differences in people and accelerates the learning and growth of everyone involved. It also helps ensure that the work is accomplished in a way that meets expectations.

As an example of what we mean, take the case of Sister Ramos and Brother Walters. Sister Ramos, baptized only 18 months ago, is called as a Primary teacher. She is full of faith and enthusiasm and is eager to bless the children in her class. Brother Walters, a less-active high priest, is called to serve in the Young Men organization. He is very experienced in Scouting (his new assignment), though his reliability in following through has been a bit shaky in the past. So here we have two children of God called to do God's work. They are the same in that both are precious in the Lord's sight. But their circumstances and needs are different, so *situational* leadership is required.

Most people have peak performance potential. You just need to know "where they're coming from" and meet them there. With situational leadership you are able to "teach the one" by applying a leadership style that meets the current needs of the person you want to bless.

One such leadership style is **Directing**. This means you provide specific instructions and closely supervise task accomplishment.

With a **Coaching** leadership style, you continue to direct and closely supervise task accomplishment. You also explain your reasons for suggesting certain things, you solicit suggestions from the person you're leading, and you honestly compliment progress.

President Spencer W. Kimball was one of the kindest and most courageous men I have ever met. . . . How sweet, how humble and sincere was his leadership style. His whispering voice pierced every heart that would listen. He was courteous, friendly, and willing to be the servant of all. It was his leadership style to never demand or use the influence of his mighty calling to take the lead in what people would do or how they would respond to him. He had the kind of approach, humility, mildness, and love that would inspire all of us to sustain and support him and love him under all conditions.
—Marvin J. Ashton[20]

In the **Supporting** leadership style, you help and support the steward's efforts and you share responsibility for decision making.

Finally, in the **Delegating** leadership style, you turn over to the steward the responsibility for decision making and problem solving.

Bear in mind, there is no one best leadership style. The issue here is *situational* leadership. In other words, deciding which style is most appropriate for a given situation.

Another important thing to remember about situational leadership is that a person's performance or achievement involves two key ingredients: *competence* and *commitment*. *Competence* is a combination of knowledge and skills. These can be gained from education, training, coaching, and/or experience. *Commitment* is a combination of conversion, confidence, and motivation. Confidence is a measure of a person's self-assuredness, a feeling of being able to do something well without much supervision. Motivation is a person's interest in and enthusiasm for doing something well.

DEVELOPMENT LEVEL
Low Competence • High Commitment
Some Competence • Low Commitment
High Competence • Variable Commitment
High Competence • Variable Commitment

As you can see, people who are at different development levels need to be treated differently. There's nothing negative about being at a lower level of development. In reality, all of us have been at a low level of development at some time or another.

So, given these two ideas—leadership styles and development levels—consider these graphics.

Figure 1 will help you determine the leadership needs of the steward you want to bless. With the examples given earlier, it would seem that Sister Ramos is likely at the lowest development level—Low Competence and High

In light of this doctrine developmental discipleship assumes genuine significance, inasmuch as our individual spiritual growth is so vital to our happiness and salvation.

—Neal A. Maxwell[21]

Commitment. She has lots of faith and enthusiasm and little experience. Brother Walters is at the High Competence and Variable Commitment level. Again, different people with different needs. If you try to apply precisely the same leadership style to both situations, neither you nor they will be satisfied by the results.

Figure 2 shows the leadership style that most appropriately helps people at the different development level. Note, for example, that the Directing style is most appropriate for Sister Ramos. Her enthusiasm (commitment) is high while her teaching skill (competence) is low. So she will benefit most from structure and close supervision. For Brother Walters, who is experienced (high competence) but sometimes not reliable (variable commitment), the Supporting style is most appropriate.

DEVELOPMENT LEVEL	APPROPRIATE STYLE
Low Competence • High Commitment	DIRECTING Structure, control and supervise
Some Competence • Low Commitment	COACHING Direct and support
High Competence • Variable Commitment	SUPPORTING Praise, listen and facilitate
High Competence • Variable Commitment	DELEGATING Give responsibility *and* accountability

An important purpose of your leadership, of course, is to help Sister Ramos and Brother Walters progress to a higher level of development. When they do, they will need a different leadership style. Again, that's what *situational* means. As Sister Ramos and Brother Walters grow in the gospel, they will receive other opportunities to serve. And every situation will be, well, situational, and will require a leadership style suited to the circumstance.

I have learned that leadership is facilitating and delegating, providing the environment for decision making and letting groups of people make decisions.

—Cornwall and
Howe[22]

Stewardship delegation is the key to multiplying yourself. It is the law of growth, both for individuals and for the kingdom. As with a child learning to walk, missteps are an inevitable part of the growing process. Stewardship delegation requires your courage to allow—to one degree or another—mistakes. This courage consists of your patience, self-control, faith in others and in their potential, and respect for individual differences. In the end, more good work can be accomplished and more people can enjoy the blessings of personal development. It begins when you practice the delegation principles modeled by the greatest leader of all, our Lord and Savior Jesus Christ.

QUESTIONS OF CONSCIENCE

1. Do I genuinely try to "teach the one" with every individual I lead?
2. Do I prayerfully and carefully consider individual differences so I can provide the most appropriate and timely assistance?
3. Am I willing to "let go" and appropriately allow others to take on responsibilities that I'm tempted to keep for myself?
4. Do I reach clear, up-front mutual understanding and commitment regarding expectations on assignments I delegate?
5. Do I give people sufficient "elbow room" to make decisions required by their callings?
6. Do I provide praise and affirmation to help people increase in desire to do better?
7. Do I establish appropriate check points and follow-up procedures so people will return and report?

8. Am I careful to use stewardship delegation to bless people rather than merely to load them up with work?

9. Do I constantly consult with the Lord in delegating to others?

10. As a leader, do I constantly remember that I am a servant?

APPLYING THE PRINCIPLES

1. Consider one of the stewardship delegations situations in which you are involved—either as the person delegating or as the person receiving an assignment. Now consider the definition of effective stewardship delegation: *A clear, up-front, mutual understanding and commitment regarding expectations.* To what extent can your stewardship delegation situation(s) benefit from operationalizing this definition? Try it. You'll like the result.

2. Review this chapter's ideas on situational leadership. How can you use these ideas to bless the people you're asked to lead?

YOU CAN DO IT!

Great leaders realize that everyone is part of the body of Christ—each with a duty and responsibility to work together in building up the kingdom of God. This requires the principle of delegation—the principle that God the Father employs. This multiplies your effort. This involves many that all might be edified, that all have a responsibility. Helping people do their duty requires careful instruction, adequate training, and inspiring motivation. Time invested in proper delegation ensures a greater amount of good in building up the Kingdom. At first, delegation may seem to require too much time and effort. But with careful accountability and follow up, in the end more work is completed and more lives are blessed. Make delegation a part of family life, a useful tool in the workplace and a guiding principle in your Church service. It is an eternal verity. It is exciting. It is so productive. Once you apply the principle, you will want to use it at every opportunity.

You can do it!—in the strength of the Lord.

ENDNOTES FOR MAIN BODY TEXT

1. For an excellent treatment of increasing effectiveness through situational leadership, see Kenneth Blanchard, Patricia Zigarmi and Drea Zigarmi, *Leadership and the One Minute Manager* (New York: William Morrow and Company, Inc., 1985). Some of the illustrations used here are adapted from that work.

ENDNOTES FOR SIDEBARS

1. Bruce R. McConkie, *Doctrinal New Testament Commentary*, 3 vols. (Salt Lake City: Bookcraft, 1965–1973), 2: 65.

2. William G. Dyer, "Why, How, and How Not to Delegate: Some Hints for Home and Church ," *Ensign*, August 1979, 12.

3. The Spoken Word from Temple Square by Richard L. Evans, *Improvement Era*, 1945, Vol. XLVIII. October, 1945. no. 10.

4. Gordon B. Hinckley, *Teachings of Gordon B. Hinckley* (Salt Lake City: Deseret Book Co., 1997), 92.

5. Stephen R. Covey, *How to Succeed with People* (Salt Lake City: Deseret Book Co., 1971), 103.

6. William G. Dyer, "Why, How, and How Not to Delegate: Some Hints for Home and Church," *Ensign*, August 1979, 15.

7. Stephen R. Covey, *How to Succeed with People* (Salt Lake City: Deseret Book Co., 1971), 101.

8. Ezra Taft Benson, *God, Family, Country: Our Three Great Loyalties* (Salt Lake City: Deseret Book Co., 1974), 131.

9. Stephen R. Covey, *The 7 Habits of Highly Effective People,* as quoted by Goethe (New York: Simon & Schuster, 1989), 301.

10. "What Other People Think," *LDS Church News,* May 19, 1990.

11. Susan Evans McCloud, *Brigham Young, A Personal Portrait* (American Fork, Utah: Covenant Communications, 1996), 271.

12. Daniel Ludlow, *Encyclopedia of Mormonism*, 1-4 vols., edited by Daniel H. Ludlow (New York: Macmillan, 1992), 249.

13. Henry D. Moyle, *Conference Report,* October 1961, General Priesthood Meeting, 89.

14. Richard J. Marshall, *Home Teaching with Purpose and Power* (Salt Lake City: Deseret Book Co., 1990), 117.

15. Hoyt W. Brewster, Jr., *Doctrine and Covenants Encyclopedia* (Salt Lake City: Bookcraft, 1988), 25.

16. William G. Dyer, (personal conversation).

17. Dawn Hall Anderson, Susette Fletcher Green, and Dlora Hall Dalton, eds., *Clothed with Charity: Talks from the 1996 Women's Conference* (Salt Lake City: Deseret Book Co., 1997), 281.

18. Stephen R. Covey, *Spiritual Roots of Human Relations* (Salt Lake City: Deseret Book Co., 1970), 133–134.

19. John Taylor, *Journal of Discourses,* 26 vols. (London: Latter-day Saints' Book Depot, 1854–1886), 18:143.

20. Marvin J. Ashton, *The Measure of Our Hearts* (Salt Lake City: Deseret Book Co., 1991), 93.

21. Neal A. Maxwell, *But for a Small Moment* (Salt Lake City: Bookcraft, 1986), 95.

22. Marie Cornwall and Susan Howe, eds., *Women of Wisdom and Knowledge: Talks Selected from the BYU Women's Conferences* (Salt Lake City: Deseret Book Co., 1990), 75.

10

THE POWER OF INFLUENCE

Some of the best leaders we know are not formally trained teachers or business people and are not necessarily skilled in the nuances of management. Their organizing and planning skills are only average. They don't rely on their position or title. It would never occur to them to "pull rank" in any way. Yet they get exceptional results with the people they serve.

How do they do it? They *influence*. They wisely understand that a leader's key purpose is to *influence* others to have a desire to be better and to do better.

By "influence" we do *not* mean "manipulation" in any form. Manipulation consists of actions that are unrighteous. *Influence*, in this context, denotes unconditional love and an open, transparent desire to be helpful. It honors individual agency and it is based on trust and authenticity. In this context, the leader's whole purpose is to help people be worthy of, receptive to, and eager for the Holy Spirit.

> It is the duty of a Saint of God to gain all the influence he can on this earth, and to use every particle of that influence to do good. If this is not his duty, I do not understand what the duty of man is. 12:376.
> —**Brigham Young**[1]

Great leaders lift and inspire. They teach and nurture. And they *influence*. They are ministers. They feed their sheep. They are true shepherds, to the individual lamb as well as to the entire flock.

This teaching, nurturing, and influencing are part of Heavenly Father's plan. When people come into the Church, they are to be numbered, they are to be named, and they are to be nourished by the good word of God (see Moroni 6:4).

When the Savior asked Peter, "Lovest thou me?" Peter answered, "Yea, Lord, thou knowest I love thee." Three times the Lord repeated the words, "Feed my lambs" or sheep (see John 21:15-17). When our love is Godlike and unconditional, we can feed (teach, nurture and influence) in a way that's worthy of our people's confidence.

Leaders spend much of their time trying to strengthen and increase the performance of those they lead and serve. Mission presidents exhort, plead, admonish and simply try almost anything to encourage young missionaries to be obedient, to work harder, to open their mouths . . . and on and on the list goes. Bishops plead with the priesthood brethren to do their home teaching.

Leaders often entreat people, but no one really "motivates" anyone. Real motivation comes from within. It's a product of internal commitment and desire, not external poking or prodding. Great leaders build commitment and desire with praise, encouragement, and Spirit-directed instruction. They are sincere and genuine. They affirm and express appreciation at every opportunity.

They *influence*.

THE POWER OF DOCTRINE

Great leaders never send people on guilt trips. Rather, they allow the Spirit to guide and they allow the doctrines to distill upon their souls. When people understand doctrine and when they embrace true principles for

We cannot hope to influence others in the direction of virtue unless we live lives of virtue. The example of our living will carry a greater influence than will all the preaching in which we might indulge. We cannot expect to lift others unless we stand on higher ground ourselves.

—Gordon B. Hinckley[2]

themselves, *then* they change. *Then* they increase in desire to be diligent in their duty.

Before you can influence them, the people you lead must know that you have a personal concern for their welfare. When they know you truly care they are more likely to listen to your message as well as follow your instructions. Your influence is enhanced when they know they are understood and appreciated.

Your responsibility is to provide a climate to help people *choose* to do well. Agency is always the test. As leaders, we of course want to help people make correct choices. External pressures may be effective for short-term or momentary change, but lasting performance comes only through a change of heart. That change of heart must be rooted in Jesus Christ and in His infinite Atonement.

A man's living determines his personality and his personality is the greatest power he possesses to influence others.

—Stephen L. Richards[3]

When people internalize doctrines and principles, their hearts are changed and they literally become new creatures. When their hearts are right (prepared to receive the will of God) they are easily entreated, they are righteously submissive and they have a desire to do good.

Sometimes, of course, people simply are not prepared to change. They may not yet be at a level of knowledge or understanding to bring about change. Or they may have inadequate faith or they may lack the vision necessary to receive inspiration at that particular time. We must always work at the level people are to raise them one step at a time—line upon line and precept upon precept.

Sometimes the situation is not conducive to inspiration. It simply is not the right time. When people have competing concerns or priorities, it's difficult for them to receive instruction or even encouragement that can make a difference in their feelings or their behavior.

Change or improvement can occur only when the person you hope to influence is ready.

Great leaders use correct principles to inspire and encourage those they serve. They teach and inspire by example, precept, coaching and mentoring in groups or in one-on-one settings. The principles and doctrines they teach are like the roots of a magnificent tree—in a sense like the tree of life. Remember that the fruit of the tree of life is the Love of God. Love is the pure motive for every righteous attempt to influence.

> Do not underestimate the profound influence—politically and socially—of the principles of the restored gospel upon all of mankind.
> —**David B. Haight**[4]

Effective leaders use doctrine, principles, covenants and concepts to help people understand and appreciate to a point where they are filled with gratitude. This gratitude works within them and provides the impetus to move forward. They literally change. Their attitudes and behavior become more Christlike. They become instruments in the hands of God—willing, able, and eager to do right things for the right reasons.

How conscientious should we be as we teach and influence? As a model, consider the report of Jacob, the younger brother of Nephi:

> And we did magnify our office unto the Lord, taking upon us the responsibility, answering the sins of the people upon our own heads if we did not teach them the word of God with all diligence; wherefore, by laboring with our might their blood might not come upon our garments; otherwise their blood would come upon our garments, and we would not be found spotless at the last day (Jacob 1:19).

As parents, we must recognize our responsibilities as well (see D&C 68:25-28). We must be worthy of the trust of all those we teach (see Mosiah 23:14). If we are not humble, full of faith, love, hope and charity, we cannot assist in the Lord's work of strengthening souls (D&C 12:8).

THINGS TO REMEMBER AS YOU TEACH FOR INFLUENCE

1. A good leader/teacher is inspired by love and respect.

The key ingredient is love. Above all other qualities, an effective leader/teacher has a generous measure of love for the learner. Love those you lead and teach. Truly care for them so they *know* you care. Righteous influence does not occur in the absence of love.

2. A leader/teacher is visionary.

Focus on the potential. A leader/teacher sees less what is, and more what can be. A leader/teacher has faith, confidence and hope in the outcome of the leading and teaching process. Only where you clearly see the potential of the people you're leading and teaching can they be taught to catch the vision of their own possibilities.
Open their eyes. A leader/teacher illuminates new pathways and helps people practice the art of the possible.
Illuminate their understanding. A key to change and continuous improvement is helping your people understand and appreciate pertinent information and see

. . . when he feels that the teacher loves him, is trying to do him good and to teach him that which will be for his everlasting welfare, then the teacher has an influence over the child, that when he studies he will study with a purpose and with an earnest desire to be benefited and to please the teacher; because he knows and feels in his little heart that the teacher loves him and is seeking to do him good.
—Joseph F. Smith[5]

its value. This improves their attitude and improves their behavior.

3. A leader/teacher exemplifies the learning process.

Be a model. Demonstrate the qualities of hard work, persistence, and the determination to excel so you can be an example.

Know those you lead. Know their needs, concerns, strengths, desires, etc. When you understand them you can better teach them. Influence does not occur in a vacuum. Seek revelation to discern the people's hearts and to learn of their needs. God can make known in an instant what we may never discover on our own.

Earn their trust. Establish a relationship of trust based on dependability, love, and respect.

Be humble. A master teacher is humble, ever willing to acknowledge that he or she likewise is in the growing process. All learning depends on the courage and willingness to learn and improve.

4. A leader/teacher builds an atmosphere for optimal growth.

Create a climate for learning. Create an appealing atmosphere for learning and change. This does not refer to the "classroom" or to the physical space as much as to the framework for learning—the vision, the relationships, the opportunities, the excitement, the energy, and the encouragement.

Focus on desire. When you create the desire to learn, the biggest part of hurdle to learning is overcome. In reality it is the

. . . try the best you can to think of them individually, to let them feel something personal and special in the concern of you, their teacher. Pray to know which student needs what kind of help, and remain sensitive to those promptings when they then come.

—Howard W. Hunter[6]

learner who makes the difference. Desire is the fuel for learning. Without desire, the learner does not give you "permission" to influence him.

Listen. Then listen some more. A master teacher listens. This skill nourishes the understanding and enables you to discern the needs, prospects, strengths, vulnerabilities, and potential of the individual. Only through understanding can genuine teaching and influence occur.

Master the techniques that foster learning. Teach efficiently and effectively by the Spirit. When the heart is touched there is greater change.

Involve your people in the process. Discovery learning is very powerful.

Use high energy. Make learning fun and exciting. It truly can be the adventure of life.

Encourage reach. Help them stretch beyond their level. It inspires creativity and discovery.

Be honest and candid. A teacher is honest. When any of your people head into false byways and unproductive pathways, you must be willing to set forth with clarity the consequences so they can make wiser choices on the directions to go.

Be gracious. Never embarrass anyone.

Use praise. Praise them for work well done.

Be creative. A teacher is resourceful and innovative. No legitimate option for learning is left unattended and unapplied where it might assist the individual to have the "ah hahs" needed for true discovery.

> Teachers should be generous in their praise and encouragement. They can do more to govern behavior through that channel than in any other way.
>
> —**Boyd K. Packer**[7]

5. A leader/teacher has endless patience.

How patient Jesus was as the Master Teacher —with how very good but far less than perfect students. Is this example of patient persistence not one that we, whether as pupil or teacher, are to contemplate and to implement, time and again, in our lives? Will we be sufficiently trusting and patient as we teach others, or as we must wait upon the Lord for fullness of understanding concerning that which we too have been taught but do not yet comprehend?
—**Neal A. Maxwell**[8]

Never give up. A master teacher is patient. Some people grasp immediately, others take more time. What makes the difference in the outcome? Patience, longsuffering, gentleness, and meekness (sound familiar?). You cannot force a young tree to grow up any faster than nature has provided for its growth. But you can continually nourish it, prune it in wisdom and provide an environment where it can rise to fulfill its destiny.

Watch for the straggler. Encourage those who struggle and fall behind. Look for the signs of discouragement. Shore up the weak and instill hope in the fearful. Your attentiveness can in itself be a great influence for good (see D&C 81:5).

Have relentlessly high expectations. Always expect the best and treat your people like they *are* the best. You, and they, will like the result.

Remember that presentation counts. The way you "serve" the message makes all the difference in your influence. The way you present doctrines, principles, concepts and covenants often makes the difference as to the acceptance of your teaching. In his classic story entitled "A Piece of Cake," Boyd K. Packer describes his experience with a group of missionaries.

We scheduled zone conferences. For each one, Sister Packer baked a three-tiered cake, which she . . . decorated beautifully with thick, colorful layers of frosting, trimmed beautifully, and with "The Gospel" inscribed across the top. When the missionaries were assembled, with some ceremony we brought the cake in. It was something to behold!

As we pointed out that the cake represented the gospel, we asked, "Who would like to have some?" There was always a hungry elder who eagerly volunteered. We called him forward and said, "We will serve you first." I then sank my fingers into the top of the cake and tore out a large piece. I was careful to clench my fist after tearing it out so that the frosting would ooze through my fingers, and then as the elders sat in total disbelief, I threw the piece of cake to the elder, splattering some frosting down the front of his suit. "Would anyone else like some cake?" I inquired. For some reason, there were no takers.

Then we produced a crystal dish, a silver fork, a linen napkin, and a beautiful silver serving knife. With great dignity I carefully cut a slice of the cake from the other side, gently set it on the crystal dish, and asked, "Would anyone like a piece of cake?"

The lesson was obvious. It was the same cake in both cases, the same flavor, the same nourishment. The manner of serving either made it inviting, even enticing, or uninviting, even revolting. The cake, we reminded the missionaries, represented the gospel. How were they serving it?[1]

Cultivate a low, persuasive voice. How you say it often counts more than what you say.
—**Thomas S. Monson**[9]

One should constantly remember that all leaders are teachers. Your influence often reflects the power of your teaching. In your own self development as a leader, make excellent teaching a priority. Then, as you teach to influence others to be and do better, encourage them to:

- **Recognize and Remember God's Goodness, Mercy, and Covenants**

People change when they recognize and remember the goodness of God. Until they recognize, until they acknowledge, until they recall and appreciate, until they respect and understand the things that God has done for them, they will not begin the process of growing and becoming like unto Christ and doing the will of our Heavenly Father. Until this recognition and remembrance are internalized, their performance will be mercurial at best. We discover in the Book of Mormon that the first step the prophets and leaders took to help a wayward people was to call to their minds the great things the Lord had done for them. Nephi tried to inspire Laman and Lemuel. "Yea, and how is it that ye have forgotten what great things the Lord hath done for us, in delivering us out of the hands of Laban, and also that we should obtain the record?" (1 Nephi 7:11).

The first thing a person in this condition should remember, or be taught, is the tender mercies and goodness of God. The key is to *remember*. There are many ways to remember. You can select your own way—personal prayers, a note on your mirror or even a penny in your shoe—to remind you. "I must keep Heavenly Father's commandments." "I must remember the goodness of God." "I must stay on the straight and narrow path." "I must do my duty." Remembering is the key.

When your testimony sags or appears to stumble along the way, why not remember the goodness of the Lord? In the process of positive recall, perhaps you can experience the spiritual healing that King Lamoni and his father expressed. How exhilarating it is to ponder the merciful nature of God, and how healing it is to remember the eternal gifts of Christ!
—**Carlos E. Asay**[10]

All the covenants we have entered into with the Lord, whether baptism, priesthood or temple, are linked to the sacrament and the commitment we make at that time. And in that prayer, the word *remembrance* or *remember* is mentioned twice. Remembrance becomes a key. At the sacrament table we not only recognize the goodness of God, but we remember it. Why? That we might have his spirit with us. We learn that when the Spirit is upon us, we are nurtured by the power of God and it will show us all things to do (see 2 Nephi 32:5) as well as inspire us to do them.

It is difficult, if not impossible, to influence people for righteousness if they are in a state of spiritual amnesia. Work to help your people remember who they are, remember what they have promised, and remember what has been promised to them.

• **Realize the Power of Love**

As we recognize, remember, and feel the tender mercies of God in our lives, our love for God increases. Our affection toward God, our concern for His will and our desire to serve Him begin to grow. As we love Him, we will do His will, we will keep His commandments (see John 14:15), we will do our duty, and we will be happy. In other words, happiness lies in keeping the commandments of God (see Mosiah 2:41).

We might describe our *love* for God like this: ultimate concern and devotion, to such an extent that we desire to serve Him. Likewise, love for our fellowmen becomes a primary concern; we have a righteous desire to serve them. This love, this concern, begets righteous service. God loved us first through

> How do we take upon us the name of the Son? The Church is called by his name, and we are to remember that by partaking of the sacrament, we acknowledge his hand in our redemption from death, which is the gift to all men, and in the remission of our individual sins which comes through our obedience in keeping his commandments.
>
> —**Joseph Fielding Smith**[11]

the gift of his Only Begotten Son. His work and his glory are in and for us. When we understand this, we appreciate Father's goodness for all he has done. Then we can *love*. Then we will serve with all the heart, might, mind and soul.

Yes, love is the binding power, the stimulus, for all that is good, both from God and from man. A person is genuinely different when he truly and deeply loves God. He seeks to do Father's will. Duty becomes a pleasure and an honor.

We learn from the sad story of some of Adam and Eve's posterity that when love is not complete and total, we become carnal, sensual and devilish to one degree or another (see Moses 5:13). We cannot love both the world and God. Remember, " No man can serve two masters: for either he will hate the one, and love the other; or else he will hold to the one, and despise the other. Ye cannot serve God and mammon" (Matthew 6:24).

It is difficult, if not impossible, to influence people for righteousness if their love for God is superficial. Work to help your people develop a deep and abiding love for God and a desire to become like him.

- **Gain Appreciation and Gratitude for the Atonement**

Understanding the atonement of Christ and its relationship to our eternal existence is the greatest knowledge we can have. This knowledge is an absolute imperative in our eligibility to return to God our Eternal Father. The atonement is the supreme center of the gospel of Jesus Christ. When we apply the atonement's principles to our lives, through

> Each of us can, with effort, successfully root the principle of love deep in our being so that we may be nourished by its great power all of our lives. For as we tap into the power of love, we will come to understand the great truth written by John: "God is love; and he that dwelleth in love dwelleth in God" (1 John 4:16).
>
> —**Gordon B. Hinckley**[12]

faith unto repentance, baptism, and receiving the Holy Ghost, we become liberated from the fallen state we are in. We become free through Christ by obedience. Yet it is by the grace of God that we are saved, after all we can do (2 Nephi 25:23). This knowledge draws us to Christ and inspires us to do His will.

When people genuinely appreciate the atonement, they are more receptive to your righteous teaching.

- **Seek to Understand the Doctrines and Principles of the Gospel**

The doctrines of the Kingdom of God are in the Word of God. Alma taught this so plainly and simply in Alma 31:5. "And now, as the preaching of the word had a great tendency to lead the people to do that which was just—yea, it had had more powerful effect upon the minds of the people than the sword, or anything else, which had happened unto them—therefore Alma thought it was expedient that they should try the virtue of the word of God."

Nothing does more to prepare people for your righteous influence than a love for the word of God. Use the scriptures as the launch pad for all your teaching. Why? Because the Word has the power to change lives.

- **Acknowledge the Power of True Conversion**

When we have faith unto repentance and apply the atoning sacrifice of the Lord to our souls we become truly converted. We have a testimony of the doctrines of the Gospel of Jesus Christ and the Kingdom of God. We act differently because we *are* different. We are the sons and daughters of Jesus Christ (see Mosiah

There is no more wonderful doctrine in all of Christianity than the doctrine of the Atonement. I think about it—and thank God for it—every day of my life.
—**M. Russell Ballard**[13]

Remembering the voice of the angel who had spoken to him and the sons of Mosiah, he knew the power of conversion that accompanied that visitation. Now he and the sons of Mosiah were all in the ministry. The voice of the angel had done its work.
—**Mark E. Petersen**[14]

5:7). Look what happened to the behavior and actions of Enos, Alma, and the sons of Mosiah. Help your people understand that conversion is a continuous process, not a momentary event. Your teaching for influence can play a valuable role.

• **Understand the Worth of Souls**

Heavenly Father and our Savior care about us. Their purpose is our immortality and eternal life. The Savior describes his joy when we change and repent: "And how great is (my) joy in the soul that repenteth"(D&C 18:13).

This is the joy that we can feel when we realize the precious worth of souls. The three-fold mission of the Church is to proclaim the gospel, redeem the dead, and perfect the Saints. By helping in the proclaiming, redeeming, and perfecting, the children of God are blessed and many souls are saved. When we truly understand the worth of souls we do the Lord's work more gladly and more effectively. We bless the lives of our eternal brothers and sisters . . . for this is of most worth unto us (see D&C 15:6).

Help your people understand the worth of souls, especially their own. Then they will be even more receptive to your teaching.

• **Recognize the Power of Self-Image**

When people truly know who they are and their potential, they can do the will of God. They can excel in their own lives. They can become . . . even as He is (3 Nephi 27:27).

Leaders who can teach and inspire people to come to this realization will empower all they serve. Heavenly Father has created us in His image. He has promised us a life like His life if only we keep the commandments and

> Oh, my brothers and sisters, do not be weary in well-doing. If we feel that our contribution is small or insignificant, remember that the worth of souls is precious in the sight of God.
>
> —Thomas S. Monson[15]

> One of the root social problems of our day concerns the lack of self-esteem. A shallow self-image is not reinforced by always letting others establish our standards or by habitually succumbing to peer pressure. Young people too often depend upon someone else's image rather than their own.
>
> —James E. Faust[16]

honor our covenants. He has given us principles and commandments to live by that continually build us up to become as He is. All of the doctrines of the gospel and Kingdom of God increase our self-esteem, self-worth, self-image and help us gain self-confidence as we apply them to our lives.

As leaders, we should do all we can to help people come to this knowledge. They need to accept this information not just intellectually or academically, but they must feel it and act upon it.

As leaders, we need to encourage those we serve to have eyes to see and hearts to feel this tender teaching of their divine birth, their eternal destiny and their capacity not only to return to God, but to live Godlike lives.

• **Increase Their Faith in the Savior**

All things can be done through faith in the Lord Jesus Christ (see Moroni 7:33). Faith is belief and hope, the moving cause of all action. The early apostles pleaded for more faith as described in Luke 17:5—"And the apostles said unto the Lord, increase our faith," and the power to do all things.

Faith increases by hearing the Word of God (see Romans 10:17) and through prayer (see Helaman 3:35) and works through love, the motivating cause of all righteous deeds (see Galatians 5:6). Not only is love the great commandment (see Matthew 22:36-40), it motivates faith, which is a gift from God through righteousness (see 1 Corinthians 12:9). Faith is the power to act, the power to do our best.

How does this happen? The Prophet Joseph Smith said that faith is exercised through mental exertion. In mentally thinking

All members and leaders must come to the realization that the greatest force multiplier within the Church is the converted and motivated member. So long as only a few serve and share with all their "heart, might, mind and strength" (D&C 4:2), the productivity of the group is limited. But when all increase their faith and labor with throbs in the heart, the power of the missionary force of the Church is multiplied many, many times over.
—**Carlos E. Asay**[17]

Prayer has been the great undergirding strength of my life. On many occasions the Lord has answered my prayers, and I bear testimony that nothing brings us more strength and more peace and more answers to today's vexing problems than to speak with the Lord humbly in sacred prayer.

—Joseph B. Wirthlin[18]

[Speaking of Moriancumer] his knowledge of the things of God must have given him wonderful power and influence in teaching his people the righteous truths which are fundamental and universal. This confidence and strength must also have been imparted to others, for certain it is that the Jaredites had prophets of great power sent to them from time to time to teach and reprove them; and even some of their monarchs were shining examples of spiritual power and righteousness.

— B. H. Roberts[19]

on these things, exerting the power of our minds, acting with every fiber of our being, we exert so much power that when we speak, things come to pass. The power of God is exercised by our words.[2] We literally are at a high level of performance due to our faith.

A critical part of your teaching is your work to increase your people's faith in the Savior.

- **Improve Their Prayer Habits**

Is there anything too hard for the Lord to do? As we seek to help others improve and do better, are we not praying in mighty prayer for them—individually—to be instruments in the hands of the Lord? Are not these following phrases heartfelt and offered throughout the world to Heavenly Father:

- *Please help them catch the vision.*
- *Bless them to be obedient.*
- *Help them change so they will want to do better.*
- *Bless the missionaries to find the honest in heart.*
- *Bless our children so they will . . .*

The list goes on. One might ask, is this part of teaching, nurturing and influence? The scriptures would answer a resounding *yes*! "Ask and ye shall receive; knock and it shall be opened unto you"(see D&C 4:7). Words similar to these occur throughout our standard works.

Prayer is a power to bless, strengthen and change lives. This is what we try to do as we attempt to nurture and inspire others. We seek to bless, strengthen and change lives through the grace and power of God through prayer.

Teach your people to pray. Work to increase their faith and confidence that righteous prayers are answered. Teaching for influence is always more powerful in an atmosphere of prayer.

Righteous teaching—leading your people to partake of the Spirit—is more about character than curriculum. It is more a matter of tone than of technique. It is borne of your love for the Lord and for the people you serve. Naturally, you want to help your people develop a passion for the Gospel and for keeping commandments and honoring covenants. To do so, you must honor their agency. You must avoid even a hint of manipulation. You must love them unconditionally. You must nurture their confidence patiently. You must "let virtue garnish (your) thoughts unceasingly" (see D&C 121: 45).

Teaching to influence could be the most difficult thing you'll do as a leader. But it is completely possible with the enabling powers of the Atonement. And it certainly has the highest reward.

QUESTIONS OF CONSCIENCE
1. Do I really understand the principles of influence?
2. Do I carefully avoid sending people on guilt trips? Do I honor their agency? Do I avoid all forms of manipulation?
3. Do I demonstrate love and respect in all my dealings with the people I serve?
4. Am I genuinely humble as I teach and lead?
5. Do I work to maintain the appropriate climate for learning? Do I give plenty of encouragement? Do I frequently affirm my people by accentuating the positive?
6. Do I carefully watch for stragglers, then find ways to help them with their

unique needs?

7. Do I help my people understand and appreciate the blessings of the Savior's Atonement?

8. Do I teach that commandments provide liberation, not constraint? Do I teach that covenants open the doors to heaven?

9. Do I personally model faith in the Lord by praying *with* my people as well as *for* my people?

10. As a leader, do I constantly remember that I am a servant and that others are depending on me?

APPLYING THE PRINCIPLES

1. As you seek to have righteous influence with the people you're asked to lead, list some of the specific spiritual doctrines that are most pertinent to your (and their) assignments. Find opportunities to teach those doctrines in a non-preachy way.

2. Review Boyd K. Packer's story about the piece of cake. How can the principles inherent in that story be applied to the way you teach and lead?

3. Take three of the main principles taught in this chapter (such as realizing the power of love, understanding the worth of souls, etc.) and write a brief "action plan" around each one. List specific ways you can apply the principles in your own stewardships. Make commitments. Follow through. Enjoy the results.

YOU CAN DO IT!

The Lord is on your side. He needs you to nurture and teach and influence His children.

Mothers and fathers, visiting teachers and home teachers, Relief Society and Young Women presidencies, quorum leaders and presidencies, bishops, high councilors, and stake presidencies—we are all leaders/teachers. You have a covenant to nurture, teach and influence those you love and serve. You cannot forget the one or ninety and nine—each needs you. Cultivate a sweet, caring demeanor and people will respond to your influence. Help them see their own possibilities and you will be a partner with God in helping them reach their potential.

You can do it!—in the strength of the Lord.

ENDNOTES FOR MAIN BODY TEXT

1. Boyd K. Packer, *Teach Ye Diligently* (Salt Lake City: Deseret Book Co., 1975), 270.

2. *Lectures on Faith*, (Salt Lake City: Deseret Book Co., 1985), 7:3.

ENDNOTES FOR SIDEBARS

1. Brigham Young, *Discourses of Brigham Young,* selected and arranged by John A. Widtsoe (Salt Lake City: Deseret Book Co., 1954), 285.

2. Gordon B. Hinckley, *Be Thou an Example* (Salt Lake City: Deseret Book Co., 1981), 55.

3. Stephen L Richards, *The Church in War and Peace* (Independence, Mo.: Zion's Printing and Publishing Co., 1943), 187.

4. David B. Haight, *A Light unto the World* (Salt Lake City: Deseret Book Co., 1997), 71.

5. Joseph F. Smith, *Gospel Doctrine: Selections from the Sermons and Writings of Joseph F. Smith,* compiled by John A. Widtsoe (Salt Lake City: Deseret Book Co., 1939), 388.

6. Howard W. Hunter, *The Teachings of Howard W. Hunter,* ed. Clyde J. Williams (Salt Lake City: Bookcraft, 1997), 209.

7. Boyd K. Packer, *Teach Ye Diligently* (Salt Lake City: Deseret Book Co., 1975), 109.

8. Neal A. Maxwell, *Even As I Am* (Salt Lake City: Deseret Book Co., 1982), 53.

9. Thomas S. Monson, comp., *Favorite Quotations from the*

Collection of Thomas S. Monson (Salt Lake City: Deseret Book Co., 1985), 142.

10. Carlos E. Asay, *Family Pecan Trees: Planting a Legacy of Faith at Home* (Salt Lake City: Deseret Book Co., 1992), 90.

11. Joseph Fielding Smith, *Answers to Gospel Questions,* 5 vols. (Salt Lake City: Deseret Book Co., 1957–1966), 3:3.

12. Gordon B. Hinckley, *Faith: The Essence of True Religion* (Salt Lake City: Deseret Book Co., 1989), 49.

13. M. Russell Ballard, *Our Search for Happiness: An Invitation to Understand The Church of Jesus Christ of Latter-day Saints* (Salt Lake City: Deseret Book Co., 1993), 88.

14. Mark E. Petersen, *Alma and Abinadi* (Salt Lake City: Deseret Book Co., 1983), 88.

15. Thomas S. Monson, *Pathways to Perfection* (Salt Lake City: Deseret Book Co., 1973), 53.

16. James E. Faust, *Reach up for the Light* (Salt Lake City: Deseret Book Co., 1990), 4.

17. Carlos E. Asay, *The Seven M's of Missionary Service: Proclaiming the Gospel as a Member or Full-time Missionary* (Salt Lake City: Bookcraft, 1996), 113.

18. Joseph B. Wirthlin, *Finding Peace in Our Lives* (Salt Lake City: Deseret Book Co., 1995), 145.

19. B. H. Roberts, *New Witnesses for God,* 3 vols. (Salt Lake City: Deseret News, 1909), 2:179–181.

11

GATHERING OF THE SAINTS
THINK *PURPOSE*, NOT MEETING

Great leaders focus constantly on a central vision. Everything they do and say is aimed with laser beam precision on a deliberate, premeditated core purpose. In the Church (and of course in the family), our core purpose is inviting people to come unto Christ.

The doctrine of meetings is stated clearly in D&C 43:8–10:

> And now, behold, I give unto you a commandment, that when ye are assembled together, ye shall instruct and edify each other, that ye may know how to act and direct my church, how to act upon the points of my law and commandments which I have given. And thus ye shall become instructed in the law of my church, and be sanctified by that which ye have received, and ye shall bind yourselves to act in all holiness before me—that inasmuch as ye do this, glory shall be added to the kingdom which ye have received. Inasmuch as ye do it not, it shall be taken, even that which ye have received.

A commandment is given that when we assemble together (have a meeting) we shall:

At the opening session President Young outlined the purpose of the meetings.

" . . . giving them such instructions and advice as we have for them, trusting that each and every heart may possess a due portion of the Spirit of God, so that the Saints may be strengthened, and that the truth may be taught in simplicity, and may commend itself to those who are as yet unacquainted with it."

At the closing session he fervently expressed the hope that the Saints would give their hearts to God and yield obedience to His principles.

—Preston Nibley[1]

- be instructed (by the Spirit)
- be edified (by the Spirit)

So that we may know:

- how to act (by the Spirit)
- how to direct the Church (by the Spirit)
- how to act upon the points of the law and commandments (by the Spirit) so we will become instructed in the law of the Church—so that we may be sanctified by the things we receive. Then we will bind ourselves (make covenants and commitments) to act in holiness and righteousness before the Lord.

Now, when we do this in our meetings, the results are wonderful. Glory is added to the Kingdom (lives are blessed, people come unto Christ and souls are saved). And if we don't do these things in our meetings, the results are sad: "it shall be taken, even that which ye have received."

As we just learned, all meetings are to be directed by the Spirit.

> And their meetings were conducted by the church after the manner of the workings of the Spirit, and by the power of the Holy Ghost; for as the power of the Holy Ghost led them whether to preach, or to exhort, or to pray, or to supplicate, or to sing, even so it was done (Moroni 6:9).

By definition, Latter-day Saints are busy people. In a typical week we have sacrament meeting, priesthood meeting, Relief Society meeting, Sunday School classes, Primary activities, instruction for youth and many other meetings pertaining to planning, coordination,

It is most delightful to be in meetings where the Spirit of God reigns, controlling the speaker and softening the hearts of the hearers. I do not take any pleasure in meetings where this is not present. It is a blessed thing to know that God is with us, and that He condescends to pour out His Spirit and give unto us a testimony that He is with us.

—George Q. Cannon[2]

leadership and shepherding. In addition, during the same week we may have social activities, sporting events, Scouting campouts and many other gatherings. In every single instance, the underlying purpose is to invite people to Christ.

The question begs: Do our meetings fit the format designed by the Lord?

By covenant and by commandment, members of the Church meet together often to teach the doctrines of the kingdom and to strengthen one another. This camaraderie and fellowship is a wonderful thing, and yet many of our meetings are not what they could or should be.

None of our meetings needs to be (or should be) boring or repetitious or lacking in clear achievement of desired outcomes. None of us who lead meetings or participate in them should regard anything less than excellence as "just the way things are." Time—in increments of minutes, hours and years—is one of our greatest blessings. There is no thief of time like a poor meeting.

So what can you do? Plenty.

As a leader of meetings, you can personally manage all the components that result in success. As a participant in meetings you do not actually lead, you can exert influence in ways that bless everyone present and significantly advance the causes for which you are gathered. Great meetings are not terribly complicated, and they are certainly not accidental.

First, let's consider how great leaders help produce great meetings.

Do you recall our discussion in Chapter 3 about the difference between *transactional* lead-

We need to strengthen our sacrament meetings and make them hours of worship in very deed. Cultivate a spirit of reverence, an attitude in which people come into the chapel and are quiet and reverent and thoughtful.

—Gordon B. Hinckley[3]

ership and *transformational* leadership? *Transactional* leadership involves administrative things, sort of like making sure the train runs on time. *Transformational* leadership involves influencing positive change, sort of like making sure the train is headed in the right direction and everyone who wants to travel has a ticket. Great meetings require both kinds of leadership.

Every great meeting begins with smart planning. Ask yourself a series of simple questions. For example:

- Why are we having this ward council or presidency meeting? Is it only because it's eight o'clock on Sunday morning and that's just what we do on Sunday mornings?
- What is the core purpose of our meeting? If inviting people to come unto Christ is our purpose, specifically what are we trying to do that will help advance that cause?
- What are the desired outcomes of our meeting? As a direct result of the gathering, what do we want people to know, to feel and to do?
- What can we do to ensure that the Spirit is an active participant in our meeting?
- What can we do to generate sincere energy in what we're doing? How can we breathe life into the "routine" and be reminded of its linkage to soul development?
- How can we ensure that this meeting provides spiritual enlightenment and causes participants to have a great desire to live their religion, to come unto Christ, and to want to *be* like Christ?
- What can we do to ensure that every person who attends the meeting is inspired, edified, and strengthened? How

It is only when we get beyond the administrative details of our callings and focus our attention on the principles of ministering to God's children and bringing the blessings of the gospel into their lives that our Church offices take on their full meaning, and we experience the fulfilling joy and satisfaction to be found in rendering significant service in the kingdom.

—M. Russell Ballard[4]

can we manage the meeting so that all participants are glad they came and are eager to attend next time?

If great meetings result from great planning—and they *do*—it makes sense that the planning has structure. A good way to ensure structure is to use an agenda.

We suggest that every meeting should have an agenda. Where possible, the agenda should be given to each participant in advance, even if it's only at the beginning of the meeting. An agenda doesn't need to be an elaborate document. In fact, it should be relatively simple with the appropriate "guideposts" to keep the participants (and the leader) on track. The agenda can be typed and printed. It can be handwritten on a chalkboard or flip chart. If there are only two or three items to be covered, it can be communicated orally.

As the leader of a meeting, you need more agenda detail than the other participants. For instance, you should have a rough time allocation for each item. This helps you gauge the progress of the meeting and know when it's time to come to closure on a particular item.

Regularly scheduled meetings seem to be the most common violator of the agenda requirement. One way to overcome this is to take five minutes at the beginning of the meeting to develop and post an agenda. If your agenda contains several items, prioritize them so you can deal with the most important ones in the time available.

It's best, of course, to be so focused on purpose and desired outcomes that you can produce an appropriate agenda in advance. A good agenda helps participants funnel their

One of the most effective means by which any leadership accomplishment can be brought about is the habitual use of a good, well-planned agenda. . . . if those conducting an important meeting do not have a well worked-out agenda in writing, the meeting may not be nearly as productive. Those present may then have to guess at the pertinent facts and depend upon their memories, which may not be very dependable.

—**Sterling W. Sill**[5]

... you should see that the written agenda for each executive meeting, especially on the ward or quorum level, focuses mainly on people rather than programs—and then make sure that you follow your agenda.
—**M. Russell Ballard**[6]

thinking and energy. It emphasizes unity of purpose over division of labor. It underscores accountability for results. It helps us make the best use of that precious commodity called time.

A common challenge for our meetings is that the right subject is sometimes addressed in the wrong forum. For instance, the appropriate forum for planning the details of a ward social is the ward activities committee, *not* the ward correlation council. The ward council members may be asked to provide general guidance and assistance, but the nitty-gritty details of the planning and preparation should fall on the shoulders of the activities committee. Likewise, a discussion on helping Brother Wilson upgrade his employment is more appropriate for welfare meeting or a quorum presidency meeting or in an interview with Brother Wilson's home teacher than it is for a meeting of the activities committee.

A well-conceived agenda helps us ensure that the right subject is addressed in the right forum to produce the right results and outcomes.

The following ideas will help you plan and lead great meetings.

TIMING

Time is a precious, finite resource. We all have the same amount of it and we are rightfully protective about how it is used. In planning and leading our meetings, we must be constantly sensitive to the amount of time we ask people to invest.

In terms of time, your first decision is "when" the meeting should occur. Considerations in selecting a meeting time include your availability, the availability of other participants, the availability of an appropriate meeting place, and the preparation time required.

After the "when" decision has been made, you might consider using an odd time strategy to encourage promptness.

Here's what we mean.

If you were driving along a highway and saw this sign, "Speed Limit, 24.5," you would likely think something like "Hmmm . . . that's odd. The police must really mean business. That's an awfully specific speed limit. They must mean '24.5.' I think I'll slow down."

In the same way this sign catches attention and encourages compliance, announcing meetings that have unusual and very specific start—and finish—times can help tighten up your meetings and reduce time wasted.

Let's say your regular meeting has been scheduled for eight o'clock. It's probably a safe guess that some of the participants have regarded that time as "eight-ish" and have routinely straggled in at 8:05, 8:10 or even later. This is disruptive to the meeting as well as disrespectful of the underlying purpose (inviting people to come unto Christ).

If you have sometimes delayed the start of the meeting beyond the eight o'clock announced time—so that the stragglers can be present for the beginning—your misplaced courtesy has actually penalized the people who arrived on time and reinforced the behavior of those who are tardy.

Try announcing the starting time of your meeting as, say, 7:58, and then absolutely start the meeting at that time even if several people are missing. They will eventually come, and

When the secretary of President George Washington tried to excuse his lateness by saying his watch was slow, Washington replied, "Then you must get a new watch or I another secretary." Isn't it quite likely that God may feel the same way about us when we continously and habitually violate this first law of order, which is punctuality?
—**Sterling W. Sill**[7]

The question is not one of managing the clock, but one of managing ourselves with respect to the time we have. As Peter Drucker, the distinguished management consultant, has said, time is "man's most perishable resource," and unless it is managed, nothing else can be managed. (Peter F. Drucker, *Management* (New York: Harper and Row, 1974), p. 70.) Each minute is a little thing and yet, with respect to our personal productivity, to manage the minute is the secret of success.

—Joseph B. Wirthlin[8]

they will quickly learn that the meeting starts promptly at 7:58 rather than at some imprecise "eight-ish" time.

Also, be sure to *end* your meeting promptly at a pre-announced time. Meetings that drag on and on are usually lacking in good organization, preparation, and management. This is another point in favor of having a well-conceived agenda. It helps keep meeting participants on track and on time.

Speaking of your agenda, be sure that it helps you maintain a good "pace" in the meeting. Avoid placing all the "administrative stuff" in one block of time on the agenda. Sprinkle throughout the agenda items requiring decisions or specific action assignments. Pre-assign a spiritual thought. Given at the beginning of the meeting, a spiritual thought lends context and perspective to all that follows. Given at the end of a meeting, a spiritual thought energizes people for action and sends them off on a definite high note

Beginning on time, managing on pace, and ending on time is a great way to demonstrate respect for your meeting participants and to produce great results for the people you serve.

ROOM ARRANGEMENTS

The meeting room environment can significantly contribute to or detract from the effectiveness of your meeting. Never take this for granted. Even if you delegate the actual physical setup, taking a personal interest in the details will pay rich dividends. Ignoring the details can results in unpleasant surprises.

Plan far in advance. Especially in a meetinghouse used by more than one Church unit, be sure to reserve the room as early as possible.

Use a room suitable for the occasion. A classroom would be adequate for an auxiliary presidency meeting, while a ward council meeting would be more comfortable in the Relief Society room or another more spacious setting.

Arrange for audio-visual needs. If you need an overhead projector, be sure it's there at the appointed time and that it has an extra lightbulb. If a chalkboard or white board is adequate, be sure they are clean and that you have suitable writing instruments.

Use a seating arrangement appropriate for your purpose. If you want lots of face-to-face interaction, a circular or U-shaped seating arrangement works best. For a training session, you might consider a classroom effect with rows of chairs. (Most participants appreciate having a table for a writing surface.) If you are eager to create an atmosphere of collaboration (in a missionary correlation meeting, for instance), you might consider a room and seating arrangement that bring people closer together physically.

Be sure the ventilation is adequate. Nothing stifles a meeting's effectiveness like a lack of free-flowing fresh air.

Check the temperature. Where possible, keep the room temperature fairly cool—65 to 70. Set it near the low end to stimulate the group (remember, the room automatically grows warmer when the people arrive). Avoid going over 75 unless you want your group to nap.

Check the lighting. To stimulate creative thinking, open the curtains and let in the view and the sunlight.

Consider amenities. Relief Society sisters are great about using simple items—like a table cloth, a centerpiece or a framed picture—to enhance the meeting space and contribute to the "message" of the meeting. The rest of us would do well to follow suit.

Greeters and ushers. Any gathering like sacrament meeting or larger should have greeters assigned to welcome people. Greeters—stake missionaries or full-time missionaries are an excellent choice for this assignment—should cheerfully and reverently welcome each person entering the meeting room. A firm handshake and good eye contact contribute to effect. For especially large meetings like stake conferences, ushers (wearing "Usher" badges) should escort people to their seats. This contributes to reverence and helps fill the seats in an orderly fashion.

STIMULATING PARTICIPATION

Our planning, coordination, leadership, and shepherding meetings depend heavily on participation. An atmosphere of free exchange is created only when participants sense that mutual sharing of opinions and ideas is welcome. If you're the leader of the meeting, be careful not to "pull rank." As always, lead by love and influence, not by position or authority.

One good way to encourage participation and discussion is by the skillful use of questions. Stay alert for cues from the group that suggest problems. If participants begin to fidget, seem bored or show by their expressions that they either disagree with or don't understand, consider asking questions to discover what's going on.

> As members participate in councils, they learn about larger organizational issues. They see leadership in action, learning how to plan, analyze problems, make decisions, and coordinate across subunit boundaries. Participation in councils helps prepare members for future leadership responsibilities.
> —Daniel Ludlow[9]

Four basic question types can help.
- **General**, which invite a broad range of potential responses
- **Specific**, which focus on a particular idea, leaving a limited range of responses
- **Overhead**, which are asked of the entire group and invite volunteer responses
- **Direct**, which are asked of a specific individual

General and *overhead* questions are better for starting a discussion. *Specific* and *direct* questions are best used after participants are "warmed up" and are comfortable with group discussion.

Here are some useful guidelines for generating discussion.

1. **Solicit feelings and opinions**

    Ask questions that draw people out and invite them to express their ideas:
    - What is your reaction to . . . ?
    - How do you feel about . . . ?
    - What are some other ways to . . . ?
    - What is your thinking on . . . ?

2. **Paraphrase**

    To help people reach mutual understanding, paraphrase what one person said and state what you believe that person meant:
    - Let me see if I understand your point. Are you saying that . . . ?
    - Let me restate your last point to see if I understand.
    - What I'm hearing is . . . Is that right?

3. **Encourage involvement**

    Sometimes people hold back in meetings. They may lack confidence, they may feel overwhelmed, they may be distracted, or they may simply be content to let others

It is just as important to focus on gospel fundamentals and on people (rather than programs) in stake councils as it is in ward councils, and it is just as important that those who participate in stake councils be able to do so in a spirit of free and open discussion.
—**M. Russell Ballard**[10]

Sometimes we discount useful communications, perhaps unintentionally, because of their source. Most are familiar with the marvelous episode in 2 Kings 5 wherein the leprous Naaman gets feedback not from the prophet, but from his servants. But he was man enough to receive correction from his servants and thereby was aided in finally being obedient to the prophet's direction.

—Neal A. Maxwell[11]

carry the load. You can encourage their involvement in the meeting by asking such questions as:

- Before we go on, can we hear from Brother Hoffman?
- Sister Sanchez, how would you respond to Brother Fuller's question?
- We've heard from everyone but John. John, what's your feeling on this?

4. **Request a summary**
- We've heard a lot of good ideas the past few minutes. Before we go on, would someone please summarize the main points?
- These are some great proposals. Brother Tyler, would you please summarize what you regard as the advantage of each one?

Note: When the participants in your meetings realize that you sometimes ask "summary questions," they will tend to listen more carefully.

5. **Ask for examples**
- Could you offer some examples of what you have in mind for quorum social activities?
- Brother Zenk, could you expand on that? I'm not sure I understand.

6. **Initiate action**
- Sister Thorne, how would you suggest we proceed with this?
- I'd like some suggestions on ways to move forward. Brother Grady, how would you propose we get started?

7. **Explore an idea in more detail**
- What are some other ways to approach this issue?
- What other factors should we consider?
- Sister Sanford, what would you add to what has been said?

8. **Suggest a procedure**
   - I notice that two or three have done most of the talking on this issue. Let's go around the table to see how others feel.
   - Would it help if we distilled our discussion into bullet points on the chalkboard?

9. **Offer support**
   - Let's give Brother Howard a chance to share with us his views.
   - Sister Randall, you've been listening carefully. What would you say about this issue?

10. **Question assumptions**
    - This approach assumes that our missionaries are getting plenty of member referrals. Is that right?
    - Your concern seems to assume that not enough workers will accept the assignment? Has that been your actual experience?

11. **Role reversal**
    - Brother Nixon, why don't you take the role of a home teacher for a moment? Now, as a home teacher, how would you approach this situation?
    - Sister Ames, if you were in the Laurel class, what kind of activity would be most useful in teaching that principle?
    - If you were Mom and Dad, what would *you* do?

12. **Look into the future**
    - If this plan works the way we hope it will, in what ways will it bless the widows in the ward?
    - What do you envision as the specific advantages of doing it this way?

As you work to stimulate participation, be careful to maintain a friendly and inviting tone. In the interest of clarification you may need to ask questions, but remember that you're not out to prove anything. Your purpose is to build a sense of unity in moving the Lord's work forward. Your questions should feel conversational and gracious, not like a courtroom cross-examination. Great leaders are affirming. While bringing out the best in others, they help people around them feel welcome, accepted and comfortable.

SPECIAL THOUGHTS FOR SACRAMENT MEETING

Sacrament meeting is the week's only gathering of Saints that is for every member of the local congregation. By definition, it is the time and place to partake of the sacred emblems representing the Savior's sacrifice and atonement. It is where we gather to sing hymns of praise and anthems that proclaim the divinity of our Creator and the reality of the restoration. It is where we "seek diligently and teach one another words of wisdom" (D&C 88:118). Moreover, sacrament meeting is where local priesthood leaders model meeting behavior.

Priesthood leaders: When you plan and conduct your next sacrament meeting, think of Cheerios. Yes, Cheerios. You know, that breakfast cereal that is sometimes crunched into the carpet in the chapel. It's there because that sweet young mother wrestling four preschoolers (you know the one; her husband is probably in the foyer comforting the baby) is devotedly attending all her meetings. She feeds the Cheerios to her toddlers to help keep them quiet. She faithfully listens to the Spirit, and she is depending on you to help provide a meeting experience of edification, not just endurance.

. . . a carefully planned sacrament meeting should be a spiritual feast in which we worship and learn of our Heavenly Father and His Beloved Son, our Lord and Savior, Jesus Christ. . . . it would be wise to invite suggestions from counselors and ward council members on ways to make every sacrament meeting a more reverent, spiritual experience. Let the councils also help teach our members that the chapel is a special place . . . the auxiliary presidents could teach in their meetings the need to improve reverence in sacrament meeting.
—M. Russell Ballard[12]

The tone and feel of sacrament meeting should be reverent, welcoming and comfortable. And every detail should be "buttoned down" so that the emphasis is on ministering rather than administering. Announcements should be kept at a minimum (the printed bulletin is an appropriate place for such information). All participants should be prepared and in their places several minutes before the meeting begins.

One bishopric used the following written instructions when inviting members of the congregation to speak in sacrament meeting.

SO YOU'RE GIVING A TALK . . .

The scriptures tell us that the Saints should meet together often and teach one another the doctrines of the kingdom.

We appreciate your accepting the assignment to speak in the Moorestown Ward's sacrament meeting on September 19. We ask that you speak for approximately 12–14 minutes on a topic discussed with a member of the bishopric.

This informal brochure is designed to help you in preparing for your talk.

Bear in mind that sacrament meeting is precious time. The Saints come—through faith—to be taught and inspired. Consider this: If you address a congregation of 150 people for 15 minutes, you have used a total of 37.5 hours! (15 min x 150 = 2,250 min. or 37.5 hrs.)

Please prepare your talk carefully and prayerfully. The Lord will bless you as well as those who hear your message.

"Assemble yourselves together, and organize yourselves . . . Continue in prayer and fasting . . . Teach one another the doctrine of the kingdom. . . . And my grace shall attend you, that you may be instructed more perfectly in theory, in principle, in doctrine, in the law of the gospel, in all things that pertain unto the kingdom of God, that are expedient for you to understand." (D&C 88:74-78.) Spiritually, we teach gospel principles, bear fervent testimony, and exercise spiritual gifts to bless the lives of others. Any who have received blessings of earth life have a moral responsibility to share them with others.
—**Victor L. Ludlow**[13]

When you teach with power, you teach the mind and the will of God. . . . You speak by the Spirit, and the Spirit speaks the word of Christ, which is the mind and the will of God.

—Ed J. Pinegar[14]

SOME THOUGHTS ON TALKING IN CHURCH

A talk is not a dramatic performance. The good speaker is not acting a part. He is being himself.

A talk is not a public reading, either.

In brief, effective speaking starts from within *you*, arising from your sincere desire to communicate a gospel message and including an attitude of respect for your listeners.

With rare exception, talks in sacrament meeting should be scripture-based treatments of gospel principles.

Cite authorities without boring the congregation by reading long quotes. Relate stories and anecdotes—in your own words—that underscore the main points of your message.

If appropriate, bear specific personal testimony regarding the gospel principle you are addressing. For instance, if your topic is *prayer*, the congregation would likely benefit from a specific example of *how* prayer has helped you, *what* prayer has done to enhance your relationship with the Savior, etc. This is more interesting and instructive than a general statement like "I've been blessed by prayer."

Practice your talk. Using a tape recorder can often be helpful. Edit your notes. Unless a story or a scripture or a quote or an observation contributes directly to your main message, it should be omitted. (A good rule is "when in doubt, leave it out.")

Relax. Most all of your listeners have been behind the pulpit themselves. They know how it feels. They aren't expecting a "professional" lecture. What they want is a simple, sincere treatment of a gospel principle, with some specific ideas on how it can contribute to their happiness.

You can do it!

PREPARING A TALK

1. Plan: Determine the best approach to your topic. Plan to address this topic in a way that will benefit the entire congregation. (Remember that your listeners have widely different backgrounds in terms of gospel scholarship, education, age, Church experience, etc.)

2. Organize: List the points you want to cover. Then sift and re-arrange these into no more than three or four main ideas, putting all the rest under these as sub-ideas. Effective introductory material usually (a) establishes a bond of common interest with your listeners, (b) identifies your topic and purpose and their importance to the congregation, and (c) mentions the main points to be discussed in the talk. The effective conclusion is usually a brief summary of what you've said, with a final statement of the basic message you want your listeners to retain . . . or the belief you want them to have . . . or the action you want them to take.

3. Develop: Read and pray. Pray and read. Make notes. Gather material. Then select the necessary "evidence"—scriptures, quotations, comparisons, anecdotes, etc.—to support and develop your points throughout the talk.

4. Practice: Condense your material to a simple outline. Practice delivering your talk *aloud*. Keep your delivery conversational and

How do you prepare an interesting and informative talk? First, decide on the *purpose* or *problem* of your talk by deciding what you want to accomplish . . . Next, ask yourself, "If I could say only three or four things about this topic, what would I say?" . . . After you have identified your main ideas, look for inspirational stories, appropriate scriptures, and personal examples to expand each of the main ideas . . . The final part of your talk is your testimony.

—**Randy L. Bott**[15]

Nor will he be organized so mechanically as to miss inspiration. He will have read this verse: "But notwithstanding those things which are written, it always has been given to the elders of my church from the beginning, and ever shall be, to conduct all meetings as they are directed and guided by the Holy Spirit" (D&C 46:2).
    —**Boyd K. Packer**[16]

natural. (You're talking to friends.) Time yourself. If you've been asked to talk for 12 minutes and your outline requires 15, trim it by at least three or four minutes. Then practice some more. The more you practice (a little bit every day over a period of several days), the more comfortable you'll be.

Some bishoprics even provide a list of specific scriptures and other materials that they ask speakers to use in their talks. When this kind of guidance is provided lovingly and with a supportive demeanor, it comes across as helpful rather than as micromanagement.

Rate Yourself as a Meeting Leader

Instructions: Check Yes or No beside each of the following questions based on how you act (or would act) as a meeting leader. Be candid.

Yes   No

1. Do I have clear objectives for the meeting?
2. Do I arrive early enough to check arrangements?
3. Do I start the meeting promptly regardless of who is present?
4. Do I prayerfully prepare an agenda and make sure each participant gets a copy?
5 Do I actually use the agenda as a map in leading the meeting?
6. Do I work to ensure that we stay on track?
7. Do I use the meeting to help people "catch the vision" of the Lord's work?
8. Do I use righteous influence rather than position to lead the meeting?
9. Do I try to help every participant feel included and involved?

10. Do I frequently summarize so we know where we've been, where we are and where we're going?
11. Do I hold people accountable for following through on action items?
12. Do I hold myself accountable for following through on action items?
13. Do I conduct the meeting in a way that causes participants to feel their time is well invested?
14. Do I affirm participants for their contributions?
15. Do I model Christlike behavior in all I do and say?

RATE YOURSELF AS A MEETING PARTICIPANT

Each of us is a meeting participant. A Relief Society president attends ward council and welfare meetings as a participant. A bishop or a priesthood president attends stake leadership meetings as a participant. When you attend a meeting as a participant you have yet another opportunity to model effective meeting behavior.

Great meetings depend on effective and involved participants. As a participant, you are often in a position to make a significant contribution to the meeting's success. A productive participant demonstrates many of the same behaviors recommended for meeting leaders. This includes promptness, avoiding side conversations, being willing to ask pertinent questions, staying alert and attentive, listening carefully, and staying engaged.

Instructions: Check Yes or No beside each of the following questions based on how you participate in meetings. Be candid.

If we are called to positions of leadership, we are accountable to the Savior for the acts we perform in that office.
—**Russell M. Nelson**[17]

We attend sacrament meetings to worship the Lord. If the meeting is conducted or if we attend with any other thought, we have missed the spirit of the occasion.
—**Dallin H. Oaks**[18]

Yes   No

1. Do I typically know the purpose of the meetings I attend?
2. Do I clearly understand my role in these meetings?
3. Do I confirm my attendance in advance of the meetings?
4. Do I complete any "homework" in advance of the meetings?
5. Do I arrive at meetings before they are scheduled to begin?
6. Do I avoid side conversations while the meeting is in progress?
7. Do I ask appropriate questions to ensure that I understand?
8. Do I stay open and respectful to the ideas of others?
9. Do I listen to understand rather than to judge or criticize?
10. Do I actively participate when I feel I can add real value?
11. Do I speak to bless rather than to impress?
12. Do I help the group (including myself) stay on track and on time?
13. Do I promptly follow through on action items assigned to me?
14. Do I appropriately inform people who did not attend the meeting about what was discussed and the outcomes?
15. Do I model Christlike behavior in all I do and say?

God help us to do our duty, to be equal to our task, and when we say, "I go," let us be true to the promise that is

Most of our interaction with other Latter-day Saints is in one meeting or another. Depending on our own leadership behaviors, those meetings can be boring or inspiring, burdensome or uplifting, tiring or energizing, redundant or refreshing. The Lord Himself asks us to meet together often to carry out His work and to bless us, His children. Surely He doesn't want our meetings to be anything but positive, strengthening experiences. The charge to "endure to the end" is about keeping commandments, not about suffering through meetings.

Remember, great leaders focus constantly on a central vision. Their ministry is about inviting souls to come unto Christ. Their meetings, characterized by clear purpose, are carefully and prayerfully planned. Your meetings can be that way, too. And everyone who attends will be all the better for it.

QUESTIONS OF CONSCIENCE

1. When I plan a gathering of Saints, do I carefully and prayerfully consider the purpose?
2. Do I specifically consider what I want the participants to "take away" from the meeting?
3. Do I ensure that gospel doctrine is taught?
4. Do I ensure that the meetings I plan—even when some of the agenda items are "administrative"—are spiritual in nature?
5. Are gifts and blessings of the Spirit evident?
6. Do I ensure that participants feel involved and have a chance to contribute value?
7. Do I effectively summarize meetings and clearly indicate delegated action items and expected results?
8. Do I maintain a cheerful, positive, and affirming tone?
9. Do I aim to bless, not to impress?
10. As a meeting leader, do I constantly

implied and stay until the end of the day, that when the time shall come that we shall be released from this part of our labors and we go on to greater labors, we may be able to say with the Apostle Paul, "I have fought a good fight, I have finished the course, I have kept the faith."
—**Hugh B. Brown**[19]

Everything discussed, every plan made, every activity coordinated should have as its central focus bringing souls to Christ by either proclaiming the gospel, perfecting the Saints, or redeeming the dead—or a combination of the three.
—**M. Russell Ballard**[20]

remember that I am a servant?

APPLYING THE PRINCIPLES

This chapter contains several checklists and questions related to effective meetings. Apply these to the meetings you lead as well as to the meetings in which you are a participant but not the designated leader.

YOU CAN DO IT!

Great leaders can make the meetings they hold edifying and sanctifying to the souls of all who attend. When you take the time to plan well, your meetings can not only be productive, but exciting. As people become engaged in the purpose, a meeting can and should be enjoyable to attend. The overriding principle of holding meetings is to bless Heavenly Father's children and to ensure they are fed and nurtured. In planning meetings we should ask the question: "Will this provide an experience to strengthen their faith, maximize the commitment to their covenants and nurture them with the word of God?" You can make Church meetings simply wonderful by investing just a few minutes more in planning. You will be blessed and your meetings will be absolutely inspiring.

You can do it!—in the strength of the Lord.

Endnotes for Sidebars

1. Preston Nibley, *Brigham Young: The Man and His Work*, 4th ed.(Salt Lake City: Deseret Book Co., 1960), 518.

2. Brian H. Stuy, ed., *Collected Discourses*, 5 vols. (Burbank, Calif., and Woodland Hills, Utah: B.H.S. Publishing, 1987–1992), 4.

3. Gordon B. Hinckley, *Teachings of Gordon B. Hinckley* (Salt Lake City: Deseret Book Co., 1997), 558.

4. M. Russell Ballard, *Counseling with Our Councils: Learning to Minister Together in the Church and in the Family* (Salt Lake City: Deseret Book Co., 1997), 72.

5. Sterling W. Sill, *Principles, Promises, and Powers* (Salt Lake City: Deseret Book Co., 1973), 40–41.

6. M. Russell Ballard, *Counseling with Our Councils: Learning to Minister Together in the Church and in the Family* (Salt Lake City: Deseret Book Co., 1997), 124–125.

7. Thomas S. Monson, comp., *Favorite Quotations from the Collection of Thomas S. Monson* (Salt Lake City: Deseret Book Co., 1985), 163.

8. Joseph B. Wirthlin, *Finding Peace in Our Lives* (Salt Lake City: Deseret Book Co., 1995), 60.

9. Daniel H. Ludlow, ed., *Encyclopedia of Mormonism*, 4 vols., (New York: Macmillan, 1992), 1141.

10. M. Russell Ballard, *Counseling with Our Councils: Learning to Minister Together in the Church and in the Family* (Salt Lake City: Deseret Book Co., 1997), 80.

11. Neal A. Maxwell, *All These Things Shall Give Thee Experience* (Salt Lake City: Deseret Book Co., 1979), 77.

12. M. Russell Ballard, *Counseling with Our Councils: Learning to Minister Together in the Church and in the Family* (Salt Lake City: Deseret Book Co., 1997), 72–73.

13. Victor L. Ludlow, *Principles and Practices of the Restored Gospel* (Salt Lake City: Deseret Book Co., 1992), 176.

14. Ed J. Pinegar, *Especially for Missionaries,* 4 vols. (American Fork, Utah: Covenant Communications, 1997), 3.

15. Randy L. Bott, *Prepare with Honor: Helps for Future Missionaries* (Salt Lake City: Deseret Book Co., 1995), 17.

16. Boyd K. Packer, *Things of the Soul* (Salt Lake City: Bookcraft, 1996), 68.

17. Russell M. Nelson, *Perfection Pending, and Other Favorite Discourses* (Salt Lake City: Deseret Book Co., 1998), 91.

18. Dallin H. Oaks, *Pure in Heart* (Salt Lake City: Bookcraft, 1988), 133.

19. Hugh B. Brown, *The Abundant Life* (Salt Lake City: Bookcraft, 1965), 38.

20. M. Russell Ballard, *Counseling with Our Councils: Learning to Minister Together in the Church and in the Family* (Salt Lake City: Deseret Book Co., 1997), 70.

SECTION 4

SPECIAL
CHALLENGES AND
OPPORTUNITIES

12

DISCERNMENT:
THE GIFT OF GREAT PRICE

When you were confirmed as a member of The Church of Jesus Christ of Latter-day Saints, hands were placed on your head and by the power and authority of the priesthood of God you were invited to "receive the Holy Ghost."

This priesthood ordinance is remarkable in its elegant simplicity. In that moment—fresh from the baptismal font—you were given one of the greatest teachers and comforters in all eternity.

And as long as you honor your covenants, this companionship remains constant through all of your days.

Great leaders rely on the Spirit for direction, insight and courage. In seeking help, they listen to the Spirit. Then, in working to help others, they listen by the Spirit. They teach by the Spirit. They plan and counsel by the Spirit. They affirm and encourage by the Spirit. They coach and correct by the Spirit. Everything they do is accomplished by and through the Spirit.

By worldly standards, you may regard yourself as simple or even pedestrian. But the scriptures promise that, with the Holy Ghost, you can "speak with the tongue of angels."[1] When you're in doubt about how to handle your leadership role, the Holy Ghost "will show unto you all things what ye should do."[2] The Holy Ghost will "teach you . . . what ye ought to

> Leaders need the spirit of their calling. . . . We may study and work hard, yet there will be a deficiency unless we have the spirit of our calling. You may possess a wealth of ideas and information—you may know the program perfectly—you may have the ability to teach and direct and to show others how, but the great attribute which will make you successful as a leader is to have the spirit of your calling.
>
> —Howard W. Hunter[1]

say."[3] As you sort through mountains of information and choices, the Holy Ghost is right there beside you, helping you "know the truth of all things."[4] When you get discouraged or disheartened, the Holy Ghost is available to fill you with hope and perfect love.[5] When you search for appropriate words of counsel, the Holy Ghost will give you utterance and enable you to stand as a credible witness to wonderful truths that you will both hear and see.[6] The Holy Ghost will even prompt you when to reprove in righteousness.[7] The Holy Ghost is a counselor beyond compare.

OBTAINING THE SPIRIT

To be successful, we must have the Spirit of the Lord. We have been taught that the Spirit will not dwell in unclean tabernacles. Therefore, one of our first priorities is to make sure our own personal lives are in order.

—**Ezra Taft Benson**[2]

To receive and act with the Spirit in all we do, we must exercise our faith,[8] we must be full of love and purity before God,[9] and we must live in obedience.[10] The first great principle of *faith* allows us to receive the direction of the Holy Ghost. The first great commandment of *love* makes possible the gift and blessings of the Spirit. And *obedience*, the first law of heaven, enables us to maintain the Spirit "always."

But we must be ever vigilant.

In his unforgettable book about the rabbits of *Watership Down*,[11] Richard Adams describes an affliction that the rabbits call "tharn." "Tharn" occurs when a rabbit that is crossing a road at night is suddenly caught in the glare of the headlights of an oncoming car . . . and held transfixed until tragedy strikes.

The author might well have been referring to Latter-day Saints who allow themselves to be caught in the glitter and clatter of the world's distractions. These aren't always just the marginal Church members. They can include—and often do include—active, tithe-paying, recommend-holding, testimony-bearing Latter-day Saints, well-intentioned people, certainly, but dangerously indifferent to the powers of the adversary. It's an indifference that can render us captivated by a kind of spiritual "tharn"—a potentially tragic condition.

"THARN" OF A DIFFERENT KIND

The scriptures warn that "there are many . . . who are blinded by the subtle craftiness of men, whereby they lie in wait to deceive."[12]

What kind of subtle craftiness is involved? Priestcrafts?

Not often. Although tools of the devil, priestcrafts are generally so obvious that only the most untutored and gullible fall victim.

Blatant wickedness?

No. Most of us are wise to the damage inflicted by whoredoms and pornography, drug abuse and the many other practices that defile and debase.

The "subtle craftiness" comes in many forms and disguises—each one ready to exploit our inattention, all designed to lull us into complacency and blind us from our potential as children of God.

Fortunately, the great plan of salvation provides us with the special companionship of the Holy Ghost to help us focus on the path that leads back to our Father.

The gift is given. It's up to us be worthy to accept—and maintain—the gift. The Holy Ghost will not dwell in *unclean* or disobedient or unready tabernacles.

> You get your mind on the things of the world and you lose the Spirit of the Lord in your work.
>
> —**Gordon B. Hinckley**[3]

Satan has had great success with the gullible generation. As a consequence, he and his angels have victimized literally hosts of people. There is, however, an ample shield against their power. This protection lies in the spirit of discernment through the gift of the Holy Ghost.

—James E. Faust[4]

We must nourish the gifts of the spirit on the same daily basis as we feed our physical bodies.

—Russell M. Nelson[5]

Everyone who earnestly seeks the Holy Ghost can be lifted and guided. As Elder James E. Talmage taught, "The special office of the Holy Ghost is to enlighten and ennoble the mind, to purify and sanctify the soul, to incite to good works, and to reveal the things of God."

—L. Tom Perry[6]

It is through the power of the Holy Ghost that we can seek out the truth and gain testimonies of the gospel.

It is the power of the Holy Ghost that can defend us from the deceit and craftiness of false teachers.

The scriptures—in 1 Cor. 12, Moroni 10, D&C 46, and elsewhere—clearly enumerate some of the ways the Holy Ghost blesses us.

For example, in D&C 46:13–26 we are taught:

To some it is given by the Holy Ghost to know that Jesus Christ is the Son of God, and that he was crucified for the sins of the world.

To others it is given to believe on their words, that they also might have eternal life if they continue faithful.

And again, to some it is given by the Holy Ghost to know the differences of administration, as it will be pleasing unto the same Lord, according as the Lord will, suiting his mercies according to the conditions of the children of men.

And again, it is given by the Holy Ghost to some to know the diversities of operations, whether they be of God, that the manifestations of the Spirit may be given to every man to profit withal.

And again, verily I say unto you, to some is given, by the Spirit of God, the word of wisdom.

To another is given the word of knowledge, that all may be taught to be wise
and to have knowledge.

And again, to some it is given to have
faith to be healed;

And to others it is given to have faith to
heal.

And again, to some is given the working
of miracles;

And to others it is given to prophesy;

And to others the discerning of spirits.

And again, it is given to some to speak
with tongues;

And to another is given the interpretation
of tongues.

And all these gifts come from God, for
the benefit of the children of God.

The Holy Ghost can make us more effective teachers, helping us "reach the one" instead
of resorting to an instructional scattergun that
reaches no one.

The Holy Ghost can make us more effective parents—calming us when our children
act like, well, like children; offering counsel
when we're confused or frustrated by the fine
line between discipline and punishment,
filling our hearts with love and gratitude as

we glimpse the eternal possibilities of the human family.

The Holy Ghost can make us more effective leaders—holding our tongues as we encourage the slothful, quickening our minds as we teach and preach, opening our ears and hearts to the unspoken needs of those whom we serve.

PERSONAL REVELATION

It's through the power of the Holy Ghost that we receive personal revelation.[13]

In a 1981 address,[14] Dallin Oaks discussed revelation by identifying and expounding on eight different purposes served by communication from God:

- to testify
- to prophesy
- to comfort
- to uplift
- to inform
- to restrain
- to confirm
- to impel

Here we touch on a ninth purpose served by personal revelation: to *clarify*.

In our various roles in life, how often do we feel that somehow we've been slighted, that the economy of heaven has short-changed us?

Let us recall a story.

The year was 1970. The two authors served together as officers in one of the Brigham Young University stakes. One of our student wards was blessed to have an excellent bishop—let's call him Bishop Brown—who, in turn, was blessed with a lovely, supporting wife. The members of this particular ward were all single, and they dearly loved this good

Men and women should pray in the same way. They both have the same privilege of receiving answers to their prayers and thereby obtaining personal revelation for their own spiritual benefit.
—M. Russell Ballard[7]

bishop and his wife—regarding them as their away-from-home parents.

Naturally, the ward members were thrilled when it was announced that Sister Brown was expecting a baby.

The Browns already had five children—the youngest was about ten years of age—and this baby was a surprise bonus. For nine months the excitement grew among the ward members. A new baby is always a big event in a ward—but it's especially so in a ward where only one woman is married!

When the long-awaited day finally came, it turned out to be a soul-wrenching, faith-testing event. The Browns' little baby boy was born with a severe physical handicap that was sure to make his life very difficult.

Ten days later, at the ward's fast and testimony meeting, Sister Brown was the first one to the microphone. There was stone silence in the congregation. Nobody moved. Two hundred sets of eyes were riveted on this sweet woman's face.

"Why?" she asked rhetorically. "Why *me*? Why did the Lord decide to bless me with this little spirit who has such special needs? Why did the Lord deem *me* worthy to assume this responsibility? I feel so honored and so humble," she said, "that the Lord has confidence that *I* can measure up to the challenge of raising a child who has such a difficult road ahead. But I'm determined to prove myself worthy of this blessing. I'm determined to be worthy of the love and faith and trust that will emanate from our little boy."

Many of us might have perceived that experience differently. But through the power

> Answers to prayers come in a quiet way. The scriptures describe that voice of inspiration as a still small voice.
> —**Boyd K. Packer**[8]

of the Holy Ghost, this good sister had received a personal revelation—a revelation that clarified the meaning of her circumstance.

LEMON OR LEMONADE

As our dear friend Elaine Cannon taught, it's often a matter of the lemon and the lemonade:

> In adversity we can complain bitterly, 'Why me? Why now?' and wallow in self-pity, thus denouncing God. Or we can find our way by asking that all-important question: 'Which of my Heavenly Father's principles will help me now?' And when we find that appropriate principle, the next step is to live that law 'irrevocably degreed' upon which the particular blessing is predicated.[15]

Does God help those who seek him? Yes, but all blessings are predicated upon obedience to law. Man must therefore live up to divine principles to claim the blessings of God. Only those who seek him and seek to do his will have claim upon him.
—**Gordon B. Hinckley**[9]

We testify that our loving Father—through the influence of the Holy Ghost—can teach and comfort us by *clarifying* the real meaning of our circumstance.

If we are worthy.

THE PRICE OF THE GIFT

What can we do to increase our susceptibility to the ministrations of the Holy Ghost?

The steps are clear.

First, we must be humble and obedient, living the Lord's gospel on the Lord's terms. "Selective" obedience is a cop-out. "Partial" commitment is really no commitment at all.

The Lord doesn't expect us to be perfect, yet. But he *does* expect us to be making definite and deliberate progress *toward* perfection.

. . . we must be worthy of the companionship of the Holy Ghost to aid us in the work of righteousness all the day long, to enable us to sacrifice our own will to the will of the Father . . .
—**Lorenzo Snow**[10]

Obedience is the result of faith and love. "Line upon line, precept upon precept" can be roughly translated to read: "Yard by yard it's hard, but inch by inch it's a cinch." To make it so, our hearts must undergo the "mighty change" discussed in the fifth chapter of Alma. Our loving Father shows us the way.

Second, we must study the scriptures.

How can we *obey* the law if we don't *know* the law? Gospel scholarship cannot be acquired through osmosis or by proxy. We can't be saved through someone else's understanding of the scriptures. The plan of salvation is not a piggy-back proposition. It's a personal, *individual* opportunity. We must read and study and internalize the richness of the scriptures for ourselves. That includes the standard works and the words of the living prophets.

Third, we must pray.

The most repeated command that we've received from our Father is to pray. Prayer is the principal means by which the Spirit is obtained and felt. The scriptures admonish us to "pray unto the Father will all the energy of heart."[16]

You've likely found that the most productive prayers are personal, private prayers—when you're not fashioning words for the ears of any mortal person.

And it's clear that productive prayers—especially those in which we are asking for specific guidance—require preparation. "Behold, you have not understood," we are taught in D&C 9:7–8, "You have supposed that I would give it unto you, when you took no thought save it was to ask me. But, behold, I say unto you, that you must study it out in your mind; then you must ask me if it be right."

> The mechanism of the spirit is so delicate that even our thought may interfere with good reception and unguarded actions may create such static as to make reception impossible.
> —**Hugh B. Brown**[11]

A fourth step that will make us more susceptible to the influence of the Holy Ghost is clearing the static from our spiritual airwaves. Static comes from interference. Interference is all around us. Certain kinds of literature, television programming and movies can clog our minds with debris unworthy of a child of God. If we're honest with ourselves, most of us can identify these. Simply follow the counsel in the Doctrine & Covenants: ". . . that which doth not edify is not of God, and is darkness" (See D&C 50:23).

Interference can come from music. Many of us enjoy a wide range of musical fare, and different kinds of music can be appropriate for different circumstances. The kind of music that might be just right when you're doing aerobic exercise is terribly out of sync with invitations to the Spirit.

The kind of music that helps prepare us for inspiration is *soothing* music. Music that promotes quiet introspection. For many of us, the kind of music often sung by our Young Women is a perfect spiritual conditioner.

Interference can come from poor health.

When we talk about the Word of Wisdom, we often confine our meaning to the abstinence from substances known to harm us. But how many of us who wouldn't dream of drinking a cup of coffee have allowed our bodies—the tabernacles of our spirits—to get woefully out of shape? From personal experience, we know that when we're in good physical condition we think more clearly, we listen more carefully, we learn more surely.

To quote President Boyd K. Packer, "As valuable as the Word of Wisdom is as a law of

health, it may be much more valuable . . .
spiritually than it is physically."[17]

HOW INSPIRATION IS RECEIVED

Just how is inspiration from the Holy Ghost
received? One thing is for sure. The Holy Ghost
does not shout. He is one messenger who
requires that we be alert, attentive, and willing.
His counsel comes in a whisper. The people in
the Book of Mormon heard His voice, ". . . and
beheld that it was not a voice of thunder,
neither was it a voice of great tumultuous noise,
but behold, it was a still voice of perfect mildness, as if it had been a whisper, and it did
pierce even to the very soul."[18]

May we suggest that there is not a right or
wrong answer to every question. In some
instances you may be left to your own judgment.
But when you are worthy of the whisperings of
the Holy Ghost, *you can know the difference.*

How do you discover the needs of the
people you serve? You listen by the Spirit. You
listen with empathy. You try to feel as they feel

- Look for clues as you visit with your
  people. *Focus.* Avoid the trap of listening
  only to their words. Be aware of all the
  nuances of their communication. The
  Spirit will coach you.
- Seek first to understand rather than
  thinking about what your response
  will be.
- Listen primarily to connect with the heart
  and soul of the other person, not to judge.
  If you *are* a judge, you will fill that role
  much more effectively if you first connect
  with the person who needs your help. The
  Lord's Church has no room for condem-

If we will ask for help
and then listen, the
Spirit of God will
whisper to us and tell
us what we should do
and give us the
strength to do it. Even
though the voice of
the Spirit is small and
comes from deep
within us . . .
—**John H. Groberg**[12]

The Holy Ghost can
be our constant
companion. It enlarges
our conscience. . . . It
sharpens our eyes to
see the needs of others
who would otherwise
be obscure. It quickens
our pulse of pure
passion, stirs us to
action to assist others
whom we might
otherwise pass by and
notice not.
—**Neal A. Maxwell**[13]

nation, only for love and caring. The Spirit will show you how.

DECISIONS, DECISIONS

Counseling is part of only a few leadership roles in the Church. For most leaders, the more common challenge is in making decisions.

As a general rule, decisions should be made as low as possible in the organizational hierarchy. Not every decision can or should be made by the prophet or by the local stake president. Everyone has a part in the marvelous system of Church government. Decisions should be made:

- where there is personal responsibility and competence
- where there is the necessary information on which to base sound judgment
- where there are the necessary resources to carry out the decisions

When you're faced with a decision, ask yourself a number of questions:

1. Am I the one who should make this decision, or should it be delegated to someone else?
2. Have I looked at all the issues involved in the scenario?
3. Are all the pertinent facts in front of me?
4. Do I clearly understand what the facts reveal about the objective or problem under study?
5. Have I honestly considered the issues with objectivity?
6. Am I dealing with root causes instead of just superficial symptoms?
7. Have I sought the opinions and counsel of others, as appropriate?
8. Have I listed alternative routes to the objective or alternative solutions to the problem?

> Cultivation of that faith will entitle you to the companionship of the Holy Ghost, who will help you make wise decisions.
> —Russell M. Nelson[14]

9. Have I evaluated and compared the alternatives in terms of probable effectiveness, cost, feasibility and other considerations?
10. Is my decision truly in the best interests of the people most affected?

And, most of all,

11. Have I consulted with the Lord and have I genuinely listened to the promptings of the Spirit?

That final question, of course, is by far the most critical.

And remember the Holy Ghost can not only direct us in the answers, but even inspire the right questions to be asked.

The Holy Ghost always knows what's best. The key, of course, is to listen. I've lost count of the times I was headed for an interview with someone who needed help. "Dr." Duncan or "Consultant" Duncan had it all figured out. Then—as Bishop Duncan or President Duncan—I listened to the Spirit and found myself offering counsel and insights that I would never have thought of on my own. In one ward we needed a new nursery leader. The Spirit indicated to us in the bishopric that we should call a member of the Relief Society presidency, an enormously capable woman who happened to be a physician. At first we resisted the impression because it seemed so counter-intuitive. Logic said this woman could add the greatest value as a Relief Society counselor. But the Spirit persisted and we listened. This woman was a wonderful nursery leader. A short time later, she moved from the area. Then it became even more clear why she was so well

All faithful members are entitled to the inspiration of the Holy Spirit for themselves, their families, and for those over whom they are appointed and ordained to preside.
—**Harold B. Lee**[15]

suited for the nursery calling. In the past, serving in the nursery was regarded by many ward members as a kind of penalty, something to be avoided. This great lady changed all that. From then on, serving in the nursery was seen as the choice opportunity it always was. The Spirit knew it all along.

—Rodger Dean Duncan

In your role as a leader, the Lord will provide a way for you to accomplish the work, just as He did for Nephi (see 1 Ne. 3:7). As a faithful servant of the Lord Jesus Christ, you are on the most marvelous team in all of eternity. And as a faithful keeper of your sacred covenants, you are eligible for the constant ministrations of the Holy Ghost. Those ministrations come in the form of discernment, a splendid gift of great price.

QUESTIONS OF CONSCIENCE

1. Do I really understand the implications of having the gift of the Holy Ghost in my life?
2. Am I honestly willing to pay the price of personal revelation? Do I?
3. Do I ask the Lord for guidance and then grab the steering wheel, or am I honestly prepared to follow his will?
4. Do I carefully avoid circumstances and influences that are contrary to the Spirit?
5. Do I deliberately and consistently seek out circumstances and influences that invite the Spirit into my heart?
6. Does my interaction with others seem to be "just business" or does it feel spiritual in nature?

7. When approaching decisions, do I do the appropriate "home work" before taking the matter to the Lord?
8. When I take something to the Lord, am I ready to obey if the Spirit directs me in a direction not of my choosing?
9. Do I seem to be known as a person who follows the Spirit, or am I just an administrator?
10. As a leader, do I constantly remember that I am a servant and that others are depending on me?

APPLYING THE PRINCIPLES
1. Consider the many ways in which the Holy Ghost can bless you in your various leadership roles. Carefully consider the benefits—to you and to others—of having the Holy Ghost as your partner rather than relying solely on the teachings of man.
2. Review the behaviors and mindset necessary to be eligible for the ministrations of the Spirit. Make commitments. Take responsibility. Follow through.

YOU CAN DO IT!

To live by the Spirit is not only a key to a righteous life, but a sure compass as you seek to fulfill your leadership role. You cannot fail. You are an instrument in the hands of the Lord. You were foreordained to do this work. The fruits are joy, glory, peace, love, and all the blessings of heaven. The Spirit will guide you. Believe it. Trust in it.

You can do it!—in the strength of the Lord.

ENDNOTES FOR MAIN BODY TEXT

1. See 2 Nephi 32:2.

2. See 2 Nephi 32:5.

3. See Luke 12:12.

4. See Moroni 10:5.

5. See Moroni 8:26.

6. See D&C 14:8.

7. See D&C 121:43–46.

8. See 1 Nephi 10:17.

9. See D&C 76:116.

10. See the sacramental prayers in D&C 20:77, 79.

11. Richard Adams, *Watership Down* (New York: William Morrow & Co., 1975).

12. See D&C 123:12.

13. D&C 46.

14. Dallin H. Oaks, "Revelation," *New Era*, September 1982, 38.

15. Elaine Cannon, "Reach for Joy," Women's Conference, March 27, 1982. See also D&C 130:21.

16. See Moroni 7:48.

17. Boyd K. Packer, "Prayers and Answers," *Ensign*, November 1979, 20.

18. See Helaman 5:30.

ENDNOTES FOR SIDEBARS

1. Howard W. Hunter, *The Teachings of Howard W. Hunter*, ed. clyde J. Williams (Salt Lake City: Bookcraft, 1997), 221.

2. Ezra Taft Benson, *Come Unto Christ* (Salt Lake City: Deseret Book Co., 1983), 91.

3. Gordon B. Hinckley, *Teachings of Gordon B. Hinckley* (Salt Lake City: Deseret Book Co., 1997), 708–709.

4. James E. Faust, *Reach Up for the Light* (Salt Lake City: Deseret Book Co., 1990), 107.

5. Russell M. Nelson, *The Power within Us* (Salt Lake City: Deseret Book Co., 1988), 35.

6. L. Tom Perry, *Living with Enthusiasm* (Salt Lake City: Deseret Book Co., 1996), 44.

7. M. Russell Ballard, *Counseling with Our Councils: Learning to Minister Together in the Church and in the Family* (Salt Lake City: Deseret Book Co., 1997), 55–56.

8. Boyd K. Packer, *Memorable Stories and Parables of Boyd K. Packer* (Salt Lake City: Bookcraft, 1997), 43.

9. Gordon B. Hinckley, *Teachings of Gordon B. Hinckley* (Salt Lake City: Deseret Book Co., 1997), 402.

10. Lorenzo Snow, *The Teachings of Lorenzo Snow*, ed. Clyde J. Williams (Salt Lake City: Bookcraft, 1984), 38.

11. Hugh B. Brown, *The Eternal Quest* (Salt Lake City: Bookcraft, 1956), 73.

12. John H. Groberg, *The Fire of Faith* (Salt Lake City: Bookcraft, 1996), 152.

13. Neal A. Maxwell, *Of One Heart: Look Back at Sodom* (Salt Lake City: Deseret Book Co., 1990), 36–37.

14. Russell M. Nelson, *Perfection Pending, and Other Favorite Discourses* (Salt Lake City: Deseret Book Co., 1998), 81.

15. Harold B. Lee, *The Teachings of Harold B. Lee,* ed. Clyde J. Williams (Salt Lake City: Bookcraft, 1996), 434.

13

PERSONAL BALANCE:
YOUR "BEING" VS. "DOING"

Great leaders invest enormous amounts of energy in behalf of the people they serve. They don't pamper or indulge them, they *lead* them. They challenge them. They provide vision and focus. They listen with love and empathy. They teach and nurture, coach and correct. They oversee the big picture and they note the details. When it's managed well, all this can be exhilarating. Or, as it was for the Church worker quoted in Chapter 5, it can drag you into "a chronic state of overwhelm."

While it's certainly true that the requirements of effective leadership are demanding, our service in the kingdom should feel like a blessing, not a burden. It should build us up, not wear us out. The key, in a word, is *balance*.

In this context, *balance* is about renewal. It's about refreshment. It's about tending to your own needs so you're better equipped in tending to the needs of others. As a leader, you constantly seek for results. To get results, you need resources. The Lord Himself is your primary resource. It's important that you do everything possible to preserve and enhance that resource. Some leaders regard taking time for themselves as selfish or even unrighteous. Other would-be leaders are so self-indulgent that they seem to regard stewardship as an

Wise shepherds recognize the need for physical, mental, emotional, and spiritual renewal. . . . From that renewal, positive change will flow.

—Alexander B. Morrison[1]

intrusion on their leisure pursuits. Neither extreme is appropriate. That's why we're talking about *balance*.

Replenishing or renewing your own resources is a critical part of your leadership work. In this chapter we'll address four primary dimensions of renewal: the *Physical* dimension, the *Mental* dimension, the *Spiritual* dimension, and the *Social/Emotional* dimension.

The most effective people we know *are* effective because they understand the law of he harvest. They deliberately and consistently pay the price of personal balance. They avoid the common trap of claiming they "don't have time" for the things that boost their capacity. They understand the great value of *making time* for activities that are important though not urgent (see Chapter 5: "Planning the Work, Working the Plan"). They understand that for it to benefit them over the long haul, personal renewal must become a second nature choice. It must become an ingrained habit. They understand that personal balance is an investment that pays huge dividends. They understand that while the work they accomplish is an important measure of their leadership, their "doing" is always fueled by their "being."

THE *PHYSICAL* DIMENSION

As the words imply, the physical dimension is about caring for your physical body. It's about eating the kinds of foods that promote good health and vitality. It's about getting sufficient rest and relaxation. It's about regular exercise that's appropriate for your age and circumstances.

Have you noticed that people who enjoy good physical health seem to be more upbeat

> Today, many are becoming extremists and are losing balance and effectiveness and are missing the results which they would desire to attain. Wouldn't they be far better off to align themselves with the constructive forces and attempt a slower, more peaceful way to reach the same ends?
>
> —**Spencer W. Kimball**[2]

and optimistic than others? That's because there's such a close correlation between the condition of the body and the condition of the spirit.

The Word of Wisdom, the Lord's most noted revelation regarding our physical health, is a "principle with promise." The Lord assures us that "all saints who remember to keep and do these commandments (regarding physical health) . . . shall receive health in their navel and marrow to their bones . . . and shall run and not be weary, and shall walk and not faint." (See D&C 89.) Scores of studies from the scientific community show what Church members already know: Latter-day Saints enjoy a disproportionately higher level of health than the general population.

This is not to say that faithful Latter-day Saints do not get tired. Busy people are certain to get tired. The point is that good physical health enables us to bounce back quickly so we can continue to shoulder the load of service and be alert to the blessings the Lord has in store for us.

The diet we eat should be sensible, grounded in good doctrine and good science. Grains, vegetables, fruits, fish, poultry, and a moderate amount of dairy products and red meat works well for most people. And plenty of water. The diets of many people, especially those who carry more pounds than they would like, is often too heavy with carbohydrates and sugars. Consult a good physician and consult with the Lord, and you'll know what's best. The rest is up to you.

Physical exercise is where many people falter, especially as they get busy with other things. Many people believe they don't have time to exercise.

There are basic rules of physical health that have to do with rest, nourishment, exercise, and with abstaining from those things which damage the body.
—**Boyd K. Packer**[3]

The truth is, they don't have time *not to*. Most experts agree that exercising three to six hours a week—or a minimum of about an hour every other day—can bring great benefits. We're not talking about merely speeding up your use of the TV remote. We're talking about some form of exercise that uses all your muscle groups and significantly increases your heart rate.

Again, you should consult with a good physician before starting any regular exercise regimen. People of all ages should consider the value of regular physical exercise. President Gordon B. Hinckley, well into his tenth decade as this book is written, walks on an electric treadmill every day, lifts light weights, and regularly does a series of stretching exercises. His level of vitality is a marvel, and it's no accident.

Exercise is an important part of our day, and the time spent in it will pay dividends.
—Joseph B. Wirthlin[4]

Good habits of physical exercise do not require special equipment. Brisk walking is available to almost anyone. Simple push-up exercises between two sturdy chairs can be great for upper body muscle tone. One General Authority we know travels with a piece of surgical tubing. He uses it to do a range of exercises designed to maintain his strength and flexibility.

The idea is to be imaginative, to tailor your exercise to your circumstances—and to *do it regularly*. Regular exercise increases your endurance, it increases your flexibility, it boosts your strength, and it tends to improve the quality of your sleep. Good dietary habits, combined with sensible exercise and rest, are the keys to good physical health.

Great leaders take this very seriously.

THE *MENTAL* DIMENSION

The mental dimension is about exercising and challenging the mind in ways that stretch and strengthen it. Mental dullness is the sign of a person who's in a rut. Even people who are constantly busy run the risk of becoming mentally dull unless they deliberately make time for good mental gymnastics.

The sharpest people we know are excellent readers. Their reading diets include a wide range of materials—good literature, science, biographies, history, politics, current events, as well as materials related to their occupation and Church callings. (Again, President Hinckley is a great model.)

Other ways to open and expand your mind include:

- Keeping a journal or a daybook. Jot down random ideas that you find interesting and valuable. Don't worry about rules or format. Just write. Leonardo di Vinci kept books of his ideas. So did Thomas Jefferson, Mahatma Gandhi, and Spencer W. Kimball. Very good company.

- Independent study, or formal classes. The world is full of information to stimulate your mind. Jesse Evans Smith, wife of Church President Joseph Fielding Smith, took classes in various subjects every year for more than half a century. It was her way of keeping mentally sharp.

- Listening to uplifting music. Much has been said about the value of great music. Try it. It's a great tonic.

- Limiting your television time. Much of today's television fare is intellectual junk food at best. Use the weekly television

. . . [people] will maintain a better mental balance if they understand the teachings of the gospel.
—**Harold B. Lee**[5]

guide in your newspaper as you would a restaurant menu. In a restaurant you wouldn't order a table full of fattening desserts. You'd ask for a balanced diet. Do the same with your television diet. Decide in advance what you will watch, and balance your diet with fare that genuinely nourishes your mind.

- Planning and organizing. Someone said that wars are won in the general's tent. Your own planning and organizing— regarding your personal life as well as your leadership role—can be an excellent mind-expanding activity. (See Chapter 5.)

THE *SPIRITUAL* DIMENSION

A map, a target, a course, our direction on the path of eternal life must be charted with long-range, medium-range and short-range goals and plans that will lead us back to Father and these goals must be written. The plan should bring balance in our life as well as direction in becoming like Christ.

—Ed J. Pinegar[6]

Spiritual renewal is your source of meaning and purpose. Think how grateful you are for the clarity of the doctrines of the restored gospel. Consider how much hope and encouragement you derive from the promises of God. Spiritual activities uplift and inspire us. They help us discover and rediscover our mission in life. They reinforce our commitment to do better and to be better.

Our living prophets constantly urge us to pray often and to study and ponder the scriptures. They warn us to avoid places and influences that damage or contaminate our spirits. They plead with us to form daily habits that draw us closer to God and cause us to yearn for his presence.

Here are some suggestions for maintaining good spiritual health:

- Pray early and often, every day. Avoid rushing your prayers. Take time to listen to the promptings of the Spirit.

- Study and ponder the scriptures early and often, every day. Avoid the mistake of thinking that a *weekly* dose of scriptures (studying for Sunday School, for example) is sufficient. Would you consolidate all of your food and vitamins into a single weekly meal? Of course not. Just as with physical nourishment, your spiritual nourishment needs to come in several daily doses.

- Keep a "grateful journal." Gratitude is the foundation for a powerful life. Gratitude can change the most habitual cynic into a full-fledged optimist, a worrywart into a "one day at a time" person. Gratitude is sort of like a muscle. It is developed through exercise. Gratitude helps us battle negativity, self-pity and other destructive feelings. Make a daily list of your blessings, especially the not-so-obvious ones. Corrie Ten Boom wrote of her experiences in a Nazi concentration camp during World War II. She and her sister Betsie, along with many other women, were held captive in an awful circumstance that included a terrible infestation of fleas. Corrie and Betsie found themselves thanking God for the fleas. Only later did they realize that the fleas were what kept the guards away from the women, enabling Corrie and Betsie to study the scriptures and teach Christianity to their fellow prisoners.

- Attend the temple as often as possible. The temple is sometimes called "the Lord's university" because it's there—and only there—that we can learn and participate in the highest level curriculum of our religion.

> To the extent that we are not willing to be led by the Lord, we will be driven by our appetites, or we well be greatly preoccupied with the lesser things of the day.
> —**Neal A. Maxwell**[7]

Remember the draft horse: he can't pull when he's kicking; he can't kick when he's pulling.
—**Wendall Ashton**[8]

When obedience ceases to be an irritant and becomes our quest, in that moment God will endow us with power.
—**Ezra Taft Benson**[9]

. . . peace of mind which can be [yours] with the proper balance between the spiritual and the secular.
—**Ezra Taft Benson**[10]

- Notice the miracles. It's been said that there are only two ways to live your life. One is to regard nothing as a miracle. The other is to regard everything as a miracle. Pause. Look around you. Be honest. Be humble. Be appreciative.
- Study and ponder great literature. Literature is great when the author skillfully explores timeless themes like faith, charity, unconditional love, courage and integrity.
- Periodically read and ponder your patriarchal blessing. Notice how the blessing never changes, but *you* change and grow so you're better able to enjoy and benefit from the blessing's promise and perspective.
- Recognize the difference between pleasure and happiness, then pattern your life so you will seek happiness as opposed to mere pleasure.
- When adversity strikes, avoid the temptation to counsel the Lord. Pray for strength to get you through, and for wisdom to help you understand and grow. President Harold B. Lee used to say "Never put a question mark where the Lord has put a period."
- Create, review, and refine your personal mission statement. This is your own personal constitution or declaration of interdependence with God. It should serve as a compass in keeping you constantly on course, and as a gyroscope in keeping you constantly in balance. (See Chapter 3 for detailed suggestions on mission statements.)

President David O. McKay taught that "the greatest battles of life are fought out daily in the silent chambers of the soul." It is in that venue—in the heart and the soul—that we struggle with the choices that either burden us or bless us. Great leaders do everything possible to maintain the spiritual health that makes greatness possible.

THE *SOCIAL/EMOTIONAL* DIMENSION

The quality of the relationships we have with others is vital to our personal balance. Our physical, mental and spiritual health are associated with the principles of personal vision and management (see Chapters 2, 3, and 5). Our social/emotional health are associated with the principles of empathic communication (see Chapter 8) and creative collaboration (see Chapters 6, 9, and 10).

While renewing the physical, mental, and spiritual dimensions of our lives usually requires some adjustment in our schedules, renewing our social/emotional dimension can be done in the course of our daily interactions with other people. This does not imply that it's nonchalant or haphazard. Our social/emotional health requires just as much deliberate care as the physical, mental, and spiritual.

There are fragile relationships all around you waiting to be strengthened, and good relationships waiting to be made even better. Identify a key relationship that presents a challenge for you. Maybe it's a fellow worker who never seems to see the world through the same lens as you. How can better empathic listening on your part help that relationship? Maybe you have a child or a spouse or a friend who is not quite as responsive as in the past. What can *you* do about *you* that could add value to the relationship?

. . . we do need to strike a spiritual balance in our lives where spiritual senses and sensitivity come first.
—**Spencer J. Condie**[11]

As he pondered the assignment, he saw as in a panorama the things that contribute to permanent human joy . . . He (Joseph Smith) saw among these factors lying deep in man's earthly and heavenly needs: economic sufficiency, bodily health, social contentment, educational development, joyous family life, emotional satisfactions, and an understandable spiritual program, to hold all else together . . .
—**John A. Widstoe**[12]

The most effective people we know constantly cultivate their relationships. They are affirming and encouraging to others. They look for the good. They attend to the courtesies. They listen to understand, not to judge. They honor their commitments. They are slow to take offense and quick to apologize. They look for opportunities to widen their circle of friends. They are anxiously engaged in many good causes. They value differing perspectives and look for opportunities to learn and discover and collaborate with others. They know that the key to having good friends is *being* a good friend. They tend to all the little things that build and maintain strong, trusting relationships. And their lives are the better for it.

In a nutshell, here are some summary ideas on the four dimensions we've discussed:

- *Physical*—Live your life as though you just had a heart attack.
- *Mental*—Remember that knowledge has a half-life. Assume that your education becomes obsolete every two years and it will no longer be applicable to your job or Church calling. Engage in continuous learning.
- *Spiritual*—Live your life as though you were scheduled for a quarterly, face-to-face interview with the Savior.
- *Social/Emotional*—Talk about others as though they were always within earshot.

To a large degree, personal balance is strictly a matter of choice. Although people who live balanced lives certainly plan for the future, they tend to live in the here and now.

People with balanced lives tend to keep things simple. They distill their dreams to a

> Rather than try to see through people, we should try to see people through.
> —**Wendall Ashton**[13]

handful of goals (see Chapters 3 and 5) and they frequently evaluate their activities to ensure that they're on course. They are clear about what matters most. Rather than prioritize their schedules, they schedule their priorities.

People with balanced lives are good at managing their emotions. One man described this as "unloading the cannon." Some days it seems like the world is against you. Nothing goes right. It's during times like this that some people "load the cannon" and wait for someone else to "strike the match." This is stressful and destructive behavior. Smart people maintain a sense of calm during the inevitable storms of daily living. We can learn from the archer. He stretches his bow to its full strength only at the moment he needs it. To do otherwise is to waste the energy and power required to reach his target. Why? Because if it's left tight too long, a bow loses its strength and resilience and becomes useless. The same principle applies to humans. Some people are so high-strung that they exhaust themselves just from being constantly "up tight." Truly powerful people tend to be relatively calm. They visualize what they want to accomplish, sometimes in vivid detail. They plan and organize. They marshal their resources. Then, when the timing is right, they figuratively pull back their bow to its appropriate tautness and aim for the target. By maintaining this balance, by reserving their "power" for those discreet moments when it's needed, their influence actually increases.

People with balanced lives tend to be good humored. They are especially good about laughing at themselves. They enjoy a sense of

We're not trying to balance reading the scriptures against making a casserole for the ward dinner, or visiting teaching against serving on a PTA committee, or earning money to keep a missionary son or daughter in the field against writing a family history. We're not trying to balance the Savior or our spiritual life against any other aspect of our life. The Savior is the fulcrum of the balance, the pivot point of the balance, the trunk and roots of the tree that keep the branches in balance. We're trying to keep this feeling about the Savior sweet and strong, because then, questions of priorities and how to spend our time will be easy and clear.

—Chieko N. Okazaki[14]

perspective. Any time you get discouraged, just think about Noah. He preached the gospel for nearly a thousand years, then the Lord drowned all his investigators.

People with balanced lives enjoy the journey. They avoid getting overwhelmed with the "doing" of their lives because they invest significant time in the "being" part of life. In today's world, nearly everything around us seems accelerated. In our effort to cram more and more life into the 1,440 minutes that make up each day, we risk losing out on the whole point of life. Slow down. Enjoy the journey.

People with balance make God their partner. They realize that no matter how capable they are, no matter how smart, no matter how well trained, no matter how experienced and seasoned, they can never do it all alone. Most importantly, they readily acknowledge that all their blessings and gifts come from a loving Heavenly Father who wants them to find their way back home.

Make no mistake. Great leaders are very busy with the tasks of their stewardships. They also invest plenty of deliberate energy in self-renewal. With their batteries charged, they are better able to accomplish the work to which they have been called.

QUESTIONS OF CONSCIENCE
1. Am I willing to pay the price of personal balance? Do I?
2. Do I consciously and deliberately tend to my physical, mental, spiritual, and social/emotional needs?
3. Do I avoid using my Church calling as an "excuse" for not balancing my life?

4. In all my busy-ness, do I play the part of victim or martyr or do I make proactive choices regarding balance?
5. Do I conduct myself in my calling to bless or to impress?
6. When possible, do I appropriately delegate responsibility to others?
7. Do I remember that my body is a temple that deserves careful maintenance?
8. Is personal balance an integral part of my planning and organizing activity?
9. Am I on a plateau with my personal balance, or is it improving?
10. As a leader, do I constantly remember that I am a servant and that others are depending on me?

APPLYING THE PRINCIPLES
1. Identify four or five of the "signs" you notice when your life is out of balance.
2. List some of the obstacles you face in implementing renewal activities in your busy life.
3. Brainstorm (use the mind mapping technique discussed in Chapter 6) ways to overcome these obstacles so you can properly tend to the physical, mental, spiritual and social/emotional dimensions of your life.

YOU CAN DO IT!
The Lord does not require that we run faster than we have strength (see Mosiah 4:27). Life is a myriad of activities for the family, the workplace, school, the community and in Church service. We must organize every needful thing so that all is in its proper place and time. Don't be a Church service martyr for your ego's sake. Your first duty in the Church is your

family duty. The Church supports the family in all things. Lack of balance leads to burn-out. Make the time for physical, mental, spiritual and social/emotional renewal. As you rejuvenate your spirit and body, you increase the joy here on the earth and also increase your power to accomplish good. There should be no guilt in taking time for self-renewal. *Make* the time. Balance your life and life will be more fulfilling. You can do it!—in the strength of the Lord.

ENDNOTES FOR SIDEBARS

1. Alexander B. Morrison, *Feed My Sheep: Leadership Ideas for Latter-day Shepherds* (Salt Lake City: Deseret Book Co., 1992), 67.

2. Spencer W. Kimball, *The Teachings of Spencer W. Kimball,* ed. Edward L. Kimball (Salt Lake City: Bookcraft, 1982), 410.

3. Boyd K. Packer, *That All May Be Edified* (Salt Lake City: Bookcraft, 1982), 64.

4. Joseph B. Wirthlin, *Finding Peace in Our Lives* (Salt Lake City: Deseret Book Co., 1995), 226.

5. Harold B. Lee, *The Teachings of Harold B. Lee,* ed. Clyde J. Williams (Salt Lake City: Bookcraft, 1996), 609.

6. Ed J. Pinegar, "Achieving Success in Life Through Vision," *LDS Church News,* Jul. 6, 1991.

7. Neal A. Maxwell, *If Thou Endure It Well* (Salt Lake City: Bookcraft, 1996), 50.

8. Wendall Ashton, quoted at his funeral by his missionary companion, Gordon B. Hinckley.

9. Ezra Taft Benson, quoted by Donald L. Staheli, "Obedience—Life's Great Challenge," *Ensign,* May 1998, 81.

10. Ezra Taft Benson, *The Teachings of Ezra Taft Benson* (Salt Lake City: Bookcraft, 1988), 317–318.

11. Spencer J. Condie, *In Perfect Balance* (Salt Lake City: Bookcraft, 1993), 241.

12. John A. Widtsoe, *Joseph Smith—Seeker after Truth, Prophet of God* (Salt Lake City: Bookcraft, 1951), 133.

13. Wendall Ashton, quoted at his funeral by his missionary companion, Gordon B. Hinckley.

14. Chieko N. Okazaki, *Aloha!* (Salt Lake City: Deseret Book Co., 1995), 74.

14
COMMON QUESTIONS, HUMBLE RESPONSES

Great leadership requires constant learning. Every calling you receive in the Church is a laboratory experience, the chance to observe, to listen, to learn, to try. Ordinary people can accomplish extraordinary things when they exercise faith and obedience and when they believe in and apply correct principles.

Every leadership calling offers challenges and opportunities. Adversity brings a chance to learn valuable lessons. Setbacks are often steppingstones to improvement.

In this final chapter we offer our humble responses to some of the questions we're often asked about leadership. These responses are not intended to be all-inclusive—only to demonstrate that regardless of the situation, every challenge is an opportunity to practice a correct principle.

CHALLENGE:

The people I lead aren't as reliable as they should be. How can I hold them accountable without offending them?

OPPORTUNITY:

Early in my Church membership, I was blessed with a leader who refused to play the mediocrity game. I was a freshman at

And we did magnify our office unto the Lord, taking upon us the responsibility, answering the sins of the people upon our own heads if we did not teach them the word of God with all diligence; wherefore, by laboring with our might their blood might not come upon our garments; otherwise their blood would come upon our garments, and we would not be found spotless at the last day.
—Jacob 1:19

No power or influence can or ought to be maintained by virtue of the priesthood, only by persuasion, by long-suffering, by gentleness and meekness, and by love unfeigned. By kindness and pure knowledge, which shall greatly enlarge the soul without hypocrisy, and without guile—Reproving betimes with sharpness, when moved upon by the Holy Ghost; and then showing forth afterwards an increase of love toward him whom thou hast reproved, lest he esteem thee to be his enemy.
—D&C 121: 41-43

. . . if you shall ask the Father in my name, in faith believing, you shall receive the Holy Ghost, which giveth utterance, that you may stand as a witness of the things of which you shall both hear and see, and also that you may declare repentance unto this generation.
—D&C 14:8

Baylor University, where I had enrolled only five weeks after my baptism. Bishop Roy D. Hoppie of the Waco (Texas) Ward called me to serve as deacons quorum advisor. I enjoyed working with the boys and became pretty good at preparing and presenting priesthood lessons.

One December Saturday night that first semester I stayed up very late studying for exams. When the alarm clock jolted me awake the next morning, I groggily turned it off, rolled over, and returned to sleep. In a far corner of my mind a rationalization had formed: "It's okay to miss priesthood today. I'm tired. Besides, someone else can fill in for me. I'll never be missed."

I thought nothing more of it. Until that evening.

After sacrament meeting (these were the days before the three-hour block of meetings), Bishop Hoppie asked if he could talk with me a moment in his office. I assumed he wanted to tell me again what a bright young man he thought I was and how grateful he was to have me in the ward.

But Bishop Hoppie was in no mood for chitchat: "Brother Duncan, this morning you failed the Lord!" he said.

I was startled by his abruptness. Yet the bishop had only begun. "You probably assumed you wouldn't be missed in priesthood today," he continued. "You figured that someone else would fill in for you in your assignment." It was incredible. The bishop was repeating practically the same words that had passed through my slumbering brain early that morning.

Then he softened his voice—as if to soothe my shock—and proceeded to teach me one of the most important lessons of my early Church experience. "A call to serve in the Lord's Church is sacred," he said. "Excellence is the only standard by which we have a right to measure our performance. When the Lord gives us an assignment, he is extending to us his trust and confidence. Our integrity is on the line. Integrity isn't always convenient, but true commitment to the Lord can be based on nothing less."

The blunt counsel from Bishop Hoppie—a wonderful deep-voiced Teddy Bear of a man—literally set the course for all my future service in the Church. Through scores of other assignments during the 40 years since then, I've always remembered his wise words: "When you're released 'with a vote of thanks,' be sure you've earned it. There are no slackers on the Lord's team."

Bishop Hoppie wisely understood the importance of holding people lovingly accountable for serving with "exactness."[1] He also understood how easy it is to fall into the trap of unconsciously colluding with each other and accepting less than our best. Elder Neal A. Maxwell put this in perspective. He wrote: "One wonders if the tolerance of unnecessary mediocrity in others isn't at some deep level of consciousness, a way of protecting ourselves or excusing ourselves for our own personal mediocrity. In human relationships there are too many tacit, silent deals in which one person agrees not to demand full measure, if the other person will agree to mediocrity when excellence may be possible."[2]

I'm grateful for a bishop like Roy Durlin Hoppie. He was a sensitive, loving man who knew precisely when bluntness was needed to hammer home a principle. His straight talk saved me from a dangerous habit. It's made an important difference in my life.

Even if you're not comfortable being as forthright as my bishop was, you might at least say something to your co-workers like: "This is the Lord's work, and he deserves our best. Will you give the Lord your commitment to . . ." You get the idea. Loving, straight talk. It's a correct principle, and the spirit will help you know what to say.

—Rodger Dean Duncan

CHALLENGE:
People often love their callings and become closely attached to those they serve. It's time for their release and they struggle in the situation. How can we let go of our callings upon our release?

OPPORTUNITY:
I was a young bishop, nearing the time for my release. I was sad. I loved the ward so

much and yet it was time to pass the torch of leadership. A new young man had been called—a fine man with a lovely wife and small children, and I thought to myself, "But he doesn't know the ward members like I know them. He doesn't love them like I do. He doesn't understand all their needs." And I thought, "Oh, Heavenly Father, what will happen to all these great people I love? Will they be okay? I'm their bishop and I'm the only one who's known them. How will they manage without me?" And so my mind was in turmoil.

The day of my release ended, and as night came I was visiting with the stake president's counselor. He looked at me and he said, "Brother Ed, I know how you're feeling." He was a discerning man. "You know, they're going to love the new bishop. In six months many will be moved to a new ward. Yes, they'll still remember you fondly. But you must remember that the Lord is in charge and those whom He calls will be magnified to bless them. So don't worry about the ward. They're in good hands. They're in the hands of the Lord." As he said that, peace came to me and I finally recognized as a young 34-year-old boy that the Lord truly is in charge.

Never take a calling as if you were the only one on the earth who can do it. The Lord will raise up a prophet each time a prophet is taken home. He will raise up a new leader every time. It is His kingdom and He is in charge, and our duty is merely to

That ye may be prepared in all things when I shall send you again to magnify the calling whereunto I have called you, and the mission with which I have commissioned you.

—D&C 88:80

be an instrument in his hands. The Lord will magnify those that are called.

—Ed J. Pinegar

CHALLENGE:

Some of the management techniques I've learned in my profession seem applicable to my Church work. Should I try them?

OPPORTUNITY:

. . . seek ye diligently and teach one another words of wisdom; yea, seek ye out of the best books words of wisdom; seek learning, even by study and also by faith.

—D & C 88:118

A few years ago, my wife Rean and I decided on the spur of the moment to take an October holiday in New England. We love that part of the United States, and it's especially beautiful in its autumn splendor of bright red, yellow and orange. We flew to New York City, rented a car and headed north. Somewhere in western Massachusetts we passed through a little village that had an interesting sign on its outskirts. It simply read: "Please drive carefully. We have no children to spare."

I chuckled at first, then saw a deeper meaning. It occurred to me that our Heavenly Father must surely feel the same. He has sent billions of his children to earth to experience the trials and tests of mortality. Each one of us is his literal spiritual offspring. Father loves each one of us, and he has "no children to spare." He has plans for us. He wants us—all of us—to return home to live for eternity in his presence.

Remember that your primary responsibility as a servant in the Church is to help Father's children return home by inviting them to come unto Christ. You can apply many good principles in your service, including good principles that you've learned in your professional work. But be very cautious. Many of the "management" methods used in the secular world are not grounded in correct principles. Moreover, people are not effectively led by "techniques." People respond best to loving, thoughtful care. We do not "manage" each other in the Church. We are asked to "lead" each other. Righteous leadership is characterized by prayerful attention to the individual as well as to the group.

All of us must pass the tests of mortality. Be sure that *you* are not one of the "tests" that must be passed by the people you're asked to lead. Heavenly Father has no children to spare. Everything we do as leaders should be well grounded in doctrine and totally consistent with the teachings and modeling of the living prophets.

—Rodger Dean Duncan

CHALLENGE:

My Church calling is very demanding and I work hard at it, but my leaders always seem to expect me to do more. Isn't it sometimes okay for "good" to be good enough?

OPPORTUNITY:

We can learn from a story about Dr. Henry Kissinger when he was U.S.

. . . it is necessary to distinguish between right and wrong behavior, good and bad performance, moral and immoral conduct.

—Lloyd D. Newell[1]

Secretary of State. He asked a couple of his young assistants to draft a "white paper" for him. A "white paper" is simply a document that lays out a particular problem or situation and then carefully reviews several possible courses of action and their attendant consequences. The purpose is to help the decision maker choose a course of action from a position of solid information and flawless reasoning.

A couple of days after they got the assignment, Dr. Kissinger's young assistants delivered their white paper. The next morning they were called into his office. "Does this document represent your very best thinking?" asked the Secretary of State. The two young men acknowledged that the paper could probably use a bit of fine tuning, so they took it back.

The following day they delivered the second version. Dr. Kissinger called them in for another accounting. "Are there any missing arguments or positions that could make this more valuable to me?" he asked. The two young assistants looked at each other, then one responded, "Well, sir, I suppose we could possibly sharpen the reasoning just a bit more. We would be happy to work on it again tonight." After they delivered the *third* draft, they were summoned to Secretary Kissinger's office again. "Are you absolutely certain that this is your best work?" the exhausted young assistants were asked. "Yes sir," came the reply. "We are certain that we've covered all the bases. The information is complete, the reasoning is sharp. This paper represents our very best work." To which Secretary Kissinger responded: "Thank you. *This time I will read it.*"

The story illustrates an important principle. If our employers deserve our very best effort—and they do—why wouldn't our Father in Heaven deserve our best, too? Again, we can gain insight from Elder Neal A. Maxwell. He wrote: "So often we feel, implicitly, that we are doing God a favor if we do his work, that we are helping him along when, in fact, our performance properly undertaken is for the welfare of *our* soul, not his! It is our happiness and our growth he seeks! How wonderful it could be to pray that what we do would be mind-stretching and soul-expanding. Such genuine, prayerful forethought could also reduce the less-than-necessary tasks we do that are trivial and could lessen the number of right things we do for the wrong reasons."[3]

Faithful people serve best when they (1) are thoroughly committed to the cause, (2) focus their energy on the most critical work to be done, and (3) genuinely do their best. Look at every calling as a growth and learning opportunity. And remember that your "best" is always acceptable to the Lord. The Lord always expects your best, and will bless you with energy and insight sufficient to the task.

—Rodger Dean Duncan

> As all of us blend into the programs of the Church, it behooves us to set goals for ourselves in order to reap the blessings of self-improvement and excellent performance in given assignments.
> —**Marvin J. Ashton**[2]

Challenge:

In my calling I'm expected to work with people who aren't as committed as I am. This is frustrating to me. How should I handle the situation?

Opportunity:

One of my great joys as stake president was greeting missionaries on their return home and extending to them an honorable release from their service. I'd then invite them to attend our next high council meeting and report to the brethren.

For ye have need of patience, that, after ye have done the will of God, ye might receive the promise.

—Hebrews 10:36

One young missionary returned to our stake after serving two years in Korea. He reported to us that during the first several months in Korea, his mission president assigned him to work with the so-called "problem elders"—those young men who had special struggles with immaturity or fragile testimonies or even disobedience.

For a while—this returned missionary told us—he *resented* this assignment. After all, he didn't go half way around the world to *baby sit* with boys from California and Indiana and North Carolina. He went to Korea to teach the gospel to *Koreans.* Then it finally dawned on him: He had agreed—unconditionally—to teach Father's children . . . *any* of Father's children. This wonderful young elder learned many lessons on his mission. And one of those lessons is articulated in the lyrics to Hymn #219—which he spontaneously sang *a cappella* to the high council:

Because I have been given much,
   I too must give;
   Because of thy great bounty,
   Lord, each day I live
   I shall divide my gifts from thee,
   With every brother that I see
   Who has the need of help from me.

This young man—who already understood the fatherhood of God—had come face-to-face with the reality of the brotherhood of man. And he had caught the vision of the 107th section of the Doctrine & Covenants. "Wherefore, now let every man learn his duty, and to act in the office in which he is appointed, in all diligence" (D&C 107:99).

It's true that we're sometimes asked to work with people who are not as experienced or as gifted or even as committed as we would like. It's also true that, no matter where *we* are on the experience-gifts-commitment scale, someone, somewhere was patient and loving enough to help *us* along. That's precisely what the Lord expects. He never promised that serving him and his children would always be fun or convenient or easy. He promised only that it would be worth it.

—Rodger Dean Duncan

CHALLENGE:

The people I lead have some fears and need to be trained in some skills. How can I prepare them to be more proficient in their duties?

OPPORTUNITY:

The new missionaries arrived. They were nervously anticipating the work before them. We fed them dinner, gave them a blessing, let them bear their testimonies and they prepared for their first day in the mission. The following morning my assistants spent four hours teaching them some of the procedures and proselyting skills necessary to do contacting. Then the new missionaries met their companions who told them, "Here's where we'll work and here's where we'll baptize." We sang the mission song and sent them out on the streets with their new dialogues—questions they could use to start up a gospel conversation.

The missionaries went out, then returned bubbling with enthusiasm. They had found people actually willing to listen to a discussion, actually willing to accept a copy of the Book of Mormon and read it and have a return appointment to discuss how they felt about it. It was exciting. So many missionaries would come out with fear and doubts, but once they had been taught, once they had been trained and once they had practiced the things they had been taught, their fears were overcome. They were full of love, they were prepared, they had the knowledge, and being faithful missionaries, the experience of door-to-door and street contacting caused them to overcome all fears.

In all leadership roles, we must remember that people need to participate in order to

. . . but if ye are prepared ye shall not fear.

—D&C 38:30

That they themselves may be prepared, and that my people may be taught more perfectly, and have experience, and know more perfectly concerning their duty, and the things which I require at their hands.

—D&C 105:10

overcome fears and doubts. In the gospel of Jesus Christ, many people are less active simply because of their lack of involvement, and people don't want to be involved because they're fearful. Fear can be overcome with faith, love, knowledge, preparation and an experience where they can practice the things they've been taught.

—Ed J. Pinegar

CHALLENGE:

Sometimes I'm asked to attend leadership meetings that don't seem to have anything to do with my calling. What should I do?

OPPORTUNITY:

First, you should of course attend the leadership meetings you're asked to attend. And you should prayerfully search for ways that *you* can add value to the meetings—either by active participation or by silently applying to your own calling the principles taught.

Second, you might anticipate what the future could hold. If the readers of this page were standing before me, I would ask two questions: "How many of you are currently serving in a Church assignment different from your assignment of two years ago?" and "How many of you know what Church position you'll be filling two years from today?"

A good friend of mine in the eastern part of the United States once told me how he had taken the long and tedious ride across

Indeed, the great challenge we face as we prepare for the future is to be more spiritually enlightened.

—James E. Faust[3]

two state lines—frequently using three or four different means of public transportation—to attend stake priesthood leadership meetings. He recalled wondering how meetings often devoted to topics such as youth leadership applied to him as a Seventies president, but nonetheless found them interesting because of his curiosity about and pleasure in the functioning of the Church. Later on, my friend George Downing was an outstanding bishop—the president of the Aaronic Priesthood in his ward—aided in that wonderful calling by insights gained long before in meetings not quite "relevant" to his assignment.

The Church is a wondrous tapestry. We should be interested in the whole cloth, not just our little, current patch. Faithful service in our present callings is a key element in preparing for future stewardships. Only the Lord knows what opportunities may come our way in the future. Only we can prepare.

—Rodger Dean Duncan

And he commanded them that there should be no contention one with another, but that they should look forward with one eye, having one faith and one baptism, having their hearts knit together in unity and in love one towards another.

—Mosiah 18:21

CHALLENGE:
The people I lead are filled with contention. How can I help resolve the situation?

OPPORTUNITY:
The couple called. "President Pinegar, there's a major problem. Elder So-and-So and Elder So-and-So have done something that's embarrassed everyone, and we're really upset. We even told the bishop about it and he's upset, too. We need to

meet with you and make sure that these elders get set straight right now."

"Is the zone leader aware of this?" I asked.

"Well, I think he heard about it yesterday. And we called him and he said he didn't know what he was going to do. President, we want to meet with you tomorrow morning at seven o'clock and get this resolved."

I said, "Well, let's wait a bit. Let me talk to Elder Toone. He's the zone leader. He's the one who's responsible and I'm sure he can handle it."

They retorted, "He's just a nineteen-year-old kid. What can he do about it?"

And I said, "Let's be patient. The Lord's in charge and He can handle it."

They were frustrated. Needless to say, there was concern on both sides. Elder Toone called me up and said, "President, what do I do?"

I said, "Elder Toone, let's counsel together and pray about it, and tomorrow morning before you meet with the couple, the bishop and these elders, you call me and the Lord will tell us the things we need to do."

That night we prayed. Elder Toone prayed. The next morning, he said, "President, what can I do?"

And it came to pass that there was no contention in the land, because of the love of God which did dwell in the hearts of the people.
—4 Nephi 1:15

I said, "Elder, as you get together, first of all you have a kneeling prayer. Pray for charity for all involved and ask that kindness and the spirit of love will be in the meeting. Then after you have the kneeling prayer, suggest to the people that you'd like to share some scriptures. Read Moroni 7:45 on the qualities of charity. Then read John 13:34-35 on how when we're disciples we will love one another. Then read Matthew 25:40, 'Inasmuch as you've done it unto the least of these, my brethren, you've done it unto me.'"

After we'd discussed those scriptures, he said, "Okay, I'll try, President."

He went off to his meeting. About nine o'clock that morning I received a phone call. "President, I'm so happy."

"Elder Toone, what happened?"

"Oh, it was wonderful. I cannot believe that the Lord blesses us so much. Everyone loves each other. Everyone is doing fine and there are no problems. We just need to love each other and look at the situation from each others' perspective so we can better understand. Oh, President, everyone feels fine. There's no contention, and love abounds in our district."

The Lord truly blesses us when we practice true principles in the spirit of love.
—Ed J. Pinegar

CHALLENGE:

There are a lot of people in the business and political world who seem to be good leaders. Is there anything wrong with using them as models?

OPPORTUNITY:

As a consultant to business and political people, I've come across all sorts of leadership styles. Some of them are effective, many of them are not.

In Great Britain I heard about a man who works for Scotland Yard, the British law enforcement agency. He's recognized around the world for his expertise in counterfeit currency. Officials in many different countries call on him for help in maintaining the integrity of their economic systems. Someone once asked this man, "How did you become such an expert in counterfeit currency? Was it by studying the work of counterfeiters?" The expert's answer was revealing: "No, I've spent many years carefully studying the real stuff. Then when I see a counterfeit I immediately recognize it for what it is."

That is precisely what we should do as we work to improve our service to the Lord. Study and emulate "the real stuff." The primary source of "the real stuff" is the scriptures. Consider the wonderful leadership examples of Moses, Saul, Solomon, King Hezekiah, Nephi, Jacob, Alma, King Benjamin and all the other great leaders. And of course, carefully study the example

> For I say unto you that whatsoever is good cometh from God, and whatsoever is evil cometh from the devil.
> —Alma 5:40

of the Savior Himself. Consider not only *what* He did in serving and leading people, but consider *how* he did it.

It is of course true that some of the leadership examples we see in the business and political world can be of use in our own leadership service. But be cautious. Like the counterfeit expert in Britain, focus your attention on "the real stuff."

—Rodger Dean Duncan

CHALLENGE:

People need love and to feel appreciated. What can I do that can encourage and lift them to higher heights?

OPPORTUNITY:

Genuine, honest praise is needed by everyone. Everyone needs to know that they are important, that they matter and that the work they are doing is appreciated.

Praise your children more than you correct them. Praise them for even their smallest achievement. Encourage your children . . .

—**Ezra Taft Benson**[4]

On some home evening nights, our family would have a mini lesson and then the children would stand by Daddy as I would praise them in front of all the others and then we'd have family interviews. One night I had something for each person except Cory and then I turned to my wife Pat and I said, "Honey, what has Cory done that has really been good?" She said, "Sweetheart, he's in charge of putting away the breakfast dishes and he does a wonderful job."

And so that night Cory came up and I said, "Kids, you are looking at the greatest dish putter-awayer in the whole world. No one puts them away as nicely as Cory." A big smile came on the little five-year-old face and he went back and sat down.

That following week my wife said, "Sweetheart, you can't believe what's happened to Cory. He is unrelenting. Those dishes . . . he brings them over so fast and then he says, 'Is this perfect enough? You know, I'm the best in the world. I've got to be the best. I've got to do the best.'" Oh, the power of praise in the lives of everyone.

When I was a young teenager, I played basketball in high school and I wasn't doing too well. Then we got a new coach by the name of Don Snow. Don came in and said at the beginning of my senior year, "Ed, you're going to be great this year. You're going to be our center and you're going to be the captain of the team." I was so excited. I went from not even starting to being the captain of the team. Lo and behold, things were wonderful. Everything turned out. We went to the state tournament, all the way to the championship game. I got a scholarship to BYU and played ball for the great coach Stan Watts.

Could anything be better than this as far as basketball is concerned? And it all began

Genuine praise is a stimulant even for adults; with children, if wisely administered, it is decidedly beneficial. As a result of judicious comments on his desirable behavior and his successes, a child's self-respect is built up.

—**Laura Gray**[5]

because a coach took the time to say, "Ed, you're going to be great. You will be my center. You'll be the captain of our team." The power of praise is the power to cause change.

—Ed J. Pinegar

CHALLENGE:
My life is very busy and frankly I'm tired. Isn't it okay for me to coast a bit in my leadership calling?

OPPORTUNITY:
It was October of 1978, and I was in Great Britain on a special assignment for the Church. A colleague and I drove to the London Temple to confer with President Spencer W. Kimball, who was there to install a new temple presidency.

Being content with mediocrity is not good enough for a disciple of Christ.
—**Elaine Cannon**[6]

President Kimball was his usual smiling, buoyant self as he inquired about and expressed appreciation for our work. After our brief interview we chatted for several minutes and the Prophet stood by my side with his arm locked in mine. He stayed in that pose while he talked with others, and I was of course in no rush to move away. I was especially impressed by one part of his conversation. One of the brethren there asked President Kimball if he was tired of his hectic pace. It was then 2:30 P.M. in England, 7:30 A.M. in Salt Lake City, and President Kimball had just crossed the Atlantic the night before after installing a new presidency at the Washington Temple. Later on this day he was flying to South African for an area conference. So he, especially at the age of 83, had every right to be tired. The Prophet's response to the question? "Oh, no, it's hard to get tired doing something you love!"

President Kimball survived throat cancer and suffered a wide range of other serious illnesses. But he never lost his resolve to serve.

If only all of us could feel that way about Church assignments. Surely we may get tired *from* our labors, but fatigue is usually ignored when we are truly committed to a calling.

For someone who feels a little "burn out" from serving, I would ask these questions:

- Have you developed a specific vision of what you should accomplish in your calling? (Vision brings energy.)

- Have you considered the linkages between your good service and the souls of others? (Clear linkages spawn enthusiasm.)

- Have you considered what the Lord may wish for you to learn from sacrifice? (Sacrifice literally means to "make sacred.")

- Are you organized in a way that makes the most of your time? (Good organization makes a task more "do-able.")

Trying to measure up to too many particular expectations without some sense of self-tolerance can cause spiritual and emotional "burn-out."
—**Dean L. Larsen**[7]

- Is your planning as careful as it could be? (Good planning provides perspective and pace.)

- Are you delegating tasks that can appropriately be done by others? (Delegation frees you up to do the "vision work.")

- Are your meetings as effective as they should be? (Good meetings help eliminate duplication of effort.)

- What are you doing to ensure that you are in appropriate personal balance? (Renewal is a critical key to vitality.)

- Are you asking the Lord for help, and are you genuinely *listening* for his answers? (The Lord is *always* "on duty.")

By definition, effective leadership is no holiday. It requires commitment, focus, hard work, patience and, yes, even some endurance. The scriptures don't teach us to "endure until it's no longer convenient or comfortable." We are asked to endure to the end. If it weren't possible, the Lord wouldn't expect it of us.

It's been wisely said that "service is the rent we pay for our own room on earth." We should remember that the rent is due on a daily basis and the receipt is never

stamped "paid in full" because the rent—
service in God's kingdom—is due again
today and due again tomorrow.
—Rodger Dean Duncan

CHALLENGE:

Dealing with change is one of the most diffi-cult things we do in life. How can I help myself and others deal with change?

OPPORTUNITY:

Getting out of our comfort zone is often full of fear and doubt. We struggle in new situations and callings. If we haven't done something before, there can be some anxiety.

While serving as president of the Provo Missionary Training Center, I witnessed this on a regular basis. Missionaries struggled in the new environment. Some even went home at their own insistence.

One day as I was pondering and praying about this, I was inspired to call the BYU registrar's office. I asked about the number of freshman students who left prior to completing their first semester. I was astonished. The percentage leaving BYU was the same that left the MTC. They expressed reasons like "It isn't what I thought it would be." "I really didn't want to come." "I miss home, family, friends and my girlfriend." "I wasn't prepared for this."

From this I learned the difficulty of managing change. Upon interviewing

. . . the painful changes and vicissitudes of life, instead of breaking down the orderliness and goodness of the universe and its Master-Creator, are actually stepping stones to glory, an assurance that our yearning to attain perfection may one day be satisfied.
—**David S. King**[8]

those leaving and the many thousands who stayed, I learned how people can accept and deal with change.

Preparation is key: When people have knowledge of a situation and know what to expect, they are better prepared. If they have studied and worked for this moment in life they come with confidence.

Desire to succeed is a must: Those who really want to do well simply will do well. It is the inner motivator that drives one in overcoming challenges.

Recognition of self-image and self-worth: When we know who we are and realize our divine capacity we can do all things in the strength of the Lord.

Plans and goals: If early on we write down our goals and plans to accomplish them, we are more likely to succeed. There are days that we all might give in if it weren't for our commitment to our goals.

Surely in relation to our eternal values we are motivated to change because of our love of God. Love is the motive. We can change and accept new roles and challenges as we make the mental adjustments. We simply choose to change.

—Ed J. Pinegar

> . . . the type of changes that lead to growth are the result of far more than the capacity to change our minds in favor of something better. They also involve building up new mental and spiritual concepts; improving skills, such as speaking or writing; acquiring better attitudes or emotions—or suppressing undesirable ones.
> —**David S. King**[9]

CHALLENGE:
My bishop has called me to a leadership position, but I'm a bit embarrassed by my handicap.

OPPORTUNITY:

If what you refer to as a "handicap" involves lack of experience or skills, just identify the more critical ones and work hard to acquire them. With diligent practice, your confidence and competence will increase. If what you call your "handicap" is a physical situation, consider how the Lord's looks at it. Does he regard your "handicap" as a reason to forfeit a chance to serve? Does he regard your "handicap" as a reason not to share the gifts you have? Of course not. In the eyes of the Lord, physical "handicaps" are irrelevant.

Some people even regard age as a "handicap." My grandfather said dealing with age is simply mind over matter: "If you don't mind, it doesn't matter."

And consider the inspiration you can be to others. I recall an experience years ago in my home ward. A young man was just ordained a priest and it was his turn to administer the sacrament for the first time. He had a severe hearing disorder, and this affected his speech. When he tried to offer the sacrament prayer, he stumbled over the words. Because this is a priesthood ordinance that must be word-perfect, the young priest had to say the prayer five or six times before he got it right. I've heard the sacrament prayers thousands of times over the years, and they have never been more beautiful to me than when that faithful young man struggled past his "handicap" to request

> The gospel brings a spirit into people's lives which heals and also covers many of the so-called differences we have. I've also learned that before the Lord, all people are equal . . .
> —**Christoffell Golden**[10]

the blessings of heaven in behalf of our congregation.

All of us have "handicaps." Some of them are obvious, as when President Howard W. Hunter, paralyzed from an illness, stood braced at the podium to speak in the Tabernacle. Many "handicaps" are not so obvious. The question for us is do we trust the Lord to accept our offerings of faithful service. You can be sure that He does.

—Rodger Dean Duncan

CHALLENGE:

Some of the people I lead are not doing their duty. I've dealt with this in other settings, and have some good ideas on how to handle it. Is it necessary to ask the Lord for guidance if I already know what to do?

OPPORTUNITY:

Counsel with the Lord in all thy doings, and he will direct thee for good.

—**Alma 37:37**

The missionary was struggling. He had many concerns. He was frustrated and overwhelmed, he came to me wanting to go home. He was tired of the work and unable to perform. As I looked at him, my heart was saddened. And yet my empathy for him was deep and I wanted to help. As we began to visit, I realized he needed something more than just, "Come on, you can do it." Suddenly the Spirit spoke to me. Section 121 came into my heart and I said, "Elder, you're not keeping your commitments. Elder, you're not doing what the Lord asked you to do. You're not being the person you're supposed to be." This comment from his mission president caused him to be a bit downtrodden. Then the Spirit began to work with him and he said, "You're right, President. I've got to change and I can do it." Within a matter of seconds he realized who he was and what he needed to do and he made a commitment and everything was just wonderful. He said, "I'll stay. I'll work hard." And the elder did stay and he did work hard.

Well, following this event of success, through chastisement as inspired by the Spirit, I had occasion to visit another elder. Similar situation—didn't like to work, struggling a little bit, thought about maybe going home. I thought, "Oh, I know what to do." So, without taking the time to pray I just lit in and began to chastise the elder. "You aren't working hard. You know you should be doing better," and all those things without any direction of the Spirit, because I'd had success previously. Success was my worst enemy. Everyone is different and everyone needs special care. I failed to practice empathy, and so this elder said, "You're right. That's where I am and that's why I'm going home. I'm not going to work. I'm no good," and the interview was simply horrible. I suggested that he think about it and we would get together soon to make the plans.

He returned to his area and I was just sick. I thought, "What have I done?" The next day, not being able to sleep much

Wherefore, brethren, seek not to counsel the Lord, but to take counsel from his hand. For behold, ye yourselves know that he counseleth in wisdom, and in justice, and in great mercy, over all his works.

—Jacob 4:10

that night, I drove quickly down to the district meeting and met with the elder, begged his forgiveness and said, "Elder, we can work it out. We've just got to go a little slower. I understand, . . ." and lo and behold, the Spirit touched his heart, as the Spirit had touched my heart. Both elders were blessed and I learned an important lesson.

Success can be your worst enemy when you think the same treatment works for a different person. Each person is different, each person needs love, each person needs understanding. When you're counseling, counsel by the Spirit, for each individual has particular needs and concerns. Blanket solutions can be dangerous. I learned that when counseling someone we must always seek the direction of the Lord.

—Ed J. Pinegar

CHALLENGE:
My bishop gets involved in details of my calling that I feel I should handle. What should I do?

OPPORTUNITY:
First, pray for your bishop. He is a shepherd who is concerned about every member of his flock. His is an awesome responsibility, a very heavy load. By virtue of his calling, he has information and insights that no one else in the ward has. With this "big picture," he can see pieces of the ward mosaic not visible to others. Trust him. Love him. Sustain him.

If you feel you're being "micromanaged," revisit the ideas in chapter 12 on stewardship delegation. Consider, especially, the material on establishing clear, up-front, mutual understanding and commitment regarding expectations. Sometimes a lack of clarity on expectations causes a leader—unconsciously—to examine details of things he has delegated. It's sort of like pulling up the flowers to see if the roots are growing okay. A friendly discussion about what both you and the bishop hope for from your service will likely be helpful.

> Men must have trust in their leader in order cheerfully to follow him . . .
>
> —*Improvement Era*[11]

And whatever you do, beware the danger of trying to second-guess your leader. When I was stake president I went to a high priest who had been inactive for many years. He was a fine man with a wonderful wife and marvelous children. I asked him point blank why he chose not to be involved in the Church. He told me that many years earlier, in another part of the country, he was called as stake mission president. He had some ideas about how to do missionary work and took them to the stake president. The stake president listened, then asked that another approach be used. This man took offense and essentially dropped out of the Church.

"So," he said to me, "it all started with that stake president."

"I guess you showed *him* a thing or two," I replied.
"What do you mean?" he asked.

Let us support and
sustain our leaders ...
not only with our
hands but with our
actions . . .
—William T. Tew[12]

"Well, the stake president was doing his job, you didn't like it, and now you've made choices that have placed your temple blessings in jeopardy."

"How so?"

"The primary responsibility for missionary work—and everything else in your stake—resided with the stake president. He delegated some of that work to you, but he was still the presiding officer in the stake. You chose to resist his leadership. This was a violation of your temple covenants, and now your wife and children are sealed to a man who is out of harmony with the gospel."

It was very plain talk, offered in a spirit of love and caring. Fortunately the man's heart softened and for the first time he saw the implications of his actions. Because he allowed himself to be offended by a well-intentioned leader, he had wasted years that could and should have been devoted to faithful service.

—Rodger Dean Duncan

CHALLENGE:

My children seem to be frustrated and complain a lot. How can I better understand their problems so I can help?

OPPORTUNITY:

Jimmy came home from school and said,

"I hate school!"

As his father walked in and heard that, he said, "What do you mean you hate school? You should be grateful for school. You go upstairs and do your homework right now. We'll have no more of this talk." The boy sulked, and walked slowly upstairs.

His mother overheard this and went up to him and said, "Jimmy, you had a real bad day at school?"

"Yeah, Mom."

"Well, do you feel kind of upset and frustrated?"

"Feel upset? That's not the half of it! That mean Mr. Jones made me sit in the back of the classroom because I lost my paper. And that isn't all, Mom. He said if I don't get that done in two more days, I won't get credit for the class. That means I can't graduate."

"Do you feel overwhelmed?"

"That's not the half of it! There's no way I can finish that research paper. I can't even find my note cards."

"So you feel like you just can't make it?"

"I'm just tired. I'm sick. I hate everybody."
"Oh, I understand, Jimmy. I remember when we wrote those cards. I kept some pieces of paper that we wrote some of

> If you listen carefully to their feelings, you will find out something about the heart.
> —**Henry B. Eyring**[13]

that information on. How would it be if I took a little time to help you reconstruct that paper?"

"Oh, Mom, you mean you could . . . "

"Oh, sure, Jim, we can get that done. We'll just work together. I'll go get those papers right now and see what we can put together, because you already have some of the material written in rough draft."

"Right, I do, Mom! Oh, Mom, I love you."

"Oh, Jimmy, you're the best. We'll get it worked out."

In a matter of minutes this young man went from "I hate school" to "I love Mom." Why? Because his mother resisted the temptation to focus on her son's carelessness and blaming. She took the time to understand his needs and feelings before she made any judgment. Rather than stoke the flames of her son's anger, she simply listened, let him vent, and gently guided him in reaching a solution.

—Ed J. Pinegar

> As you listen, listen to the feelings being expressed more than to the descriptions of action . . .
> —**Martha Nibley Beck** and **John C. Beck**[14]

CHALLENGE:
I've held high profile leadership positions in the past, but now I'm only a teacher in my ward. Have I been retired from duty?

OPPORTUNITY:
Service in the kingdom of God is a sacred privilege, not a right. Throughout the

ages, prophets have told us that what really matters is *how* we serve, not *where*. Unlike work assignments in the secular world, there are no "promotions" or "demotions" in the Church. A man can be a stake president one day and an assistant scoutmaster the next.

I love the counsel from President Hinckley—whom we sustain as prophet, seer and revelator: "Your obligation is as serious in your sphere of responsibility as is my obligation in my sphere. No calling in this Church is small or of little consequence. All of us in the pursuit of our duty touch the lives of others. To each of us in our respective responsibilities the Lord has said: 'Wherefore, be faithful; stand in the office which I have appointed unto you; succor the weak, lift up the hands which hang down, and strengthen the feeble knees' (D&C 81:5)."[4]

No matter where we serve, we have the chance—the obligation, really—to be instruments for good in the lives of others.

Many years ago, I had a visit with Marion G. Romney, who at the time was a member of the Quorum of the Twelve. Elder Romney commented that he very much missed working with Church members on the "local" level. I particularly recall his saying, only half jokingly, that "everything above the office of bishop is mostly talk." He was underscoring the privilege that most Church members have

I sometimes wonder what would happen to this Church if we ran for office. We do not seek office, we do not resist calls to service, we accept releases willingly when they come, and we serve until we are honorably released. . . . In the Church and kingdom of God there is no unimportant office or calling or service. . . . It is essential to all we do in our ministry that it be done with "an eye single to the glory of God" (D&C 4:5). That should be our primary motive. We have not been called to build up ourselves, but to build the kingdom of God. We shall be instrumental in achieving this momentous goal as we magnify our callings and honor the Lord.
—**Ezra Taft Benson**[15]

to minister *closely* with the people they serve. Think about that. In reality, a Primary teacher can have a greater impact with a small child—"up close and personal"—than the prophet himself. Most Primary children will never meet the president of the Church. But every Primary child can be personally blessed by a faithful teacher who cares.

No matter *where* we serve, each of us can provide soul-building leadership. Sometimes the fruit of our labor is not evident until years after our release. It matters not. You can count the number of seeds in a single apple, but you can't count the number of apples in a single seed. The law of the harvest requires us to do our duty no matter where we're assigned in the orchard.

—Rodger Dean Duncan

The Church is the great reservoir of eternal truth from which we can constantly and freely drink. It is the preserver of standards, the teacher of values. Latch onto those values. Bind them to your hearts. Let them become the lodestar of your lives to guide you as you move forward in the world of which you will become an important part.

—**Gordon B. Hinckley**[16]

CHALLENGE:

My children don't feel the same way I do about the counsel from the prophet. How can I help them understand and appreciate the values and standards of the Church?

OPPORTUNITY:

Value collisions happen more at home than in regular Church settings. We must continually remember that our greatest leadership roles are in the home. Some of the values that we as parents and children have in the gospel not only must be understood, appreciated and shared, but above all they must be agreed upon. Agreed upon values bring unity to the home and family.

When our children were young we talked about dating. We discussed that sixteen years of age was the time they could begin dating—in groups. I thought we had covered the principle pretty well, but apparently it had not been internalized.

The time came. Our daughter was 15-and-a-half and a Christmas dance was coming up. She inadvertently let out that it wasn't a group going; the kids were kind of pairing off. When I heard that I said, "Well, Sweetheart, President Kimball counsels us not to date until we're 16. We need to sustain our Prophet and to be obedient." At first it was, "Why can't I go?". . . and pretty soon feelings were hurt, "You don't trust me!" . . . and then anger, "I'm mad at you!" . . . and then rebellion, "Don't talk to me." It seems to go that way. First we're hurt, then we're angered, and then we rebel.

As the week passed and our conversation was little or none, I became distraught and I went to my daughter and said, "Sweetheart, we've got to talk." So my lovely, gorgeous daughter sat down and I knelt down in front of her and said, "Sweetheart, Daddy's just trying to be a good daddy. He's just trying to help. You've got to help me so we can follow the prophet and be blessed. There are blessings associated with all of the things we're asked to do." I began to cry. As I began to cry, *she* began to cry. We stood up and hugged and expressed our love for

And all thy children shall be taught of the Lord; and great shall be the peace of thy children.

—Isaiah 54:13

Never forget that these little ones are the sons and daughters of God and that yours is a custodial relationship to them, that he was a parent before you were parents and he has not relinquished his parental rights or interest in these his little ones.

—Gordon B. Hinckley[17]

each other. To this day I don't know if it was the doctrine of obedience to the prophet or the doctrine of a pleading, caring parent. In any event, my daughter said, "I'm not going to that dance. I don't want to go to that dance anymore."

Of course parenting doesn't always work out that way. Sometimes our children reject good counsel and do things they shouldn't. But following the model of our Father in Heaven, we must love them unconditionally. When children feel the love and concern of their parents, the chance of their accepting counsel is improved. When they feel ordered around and "bossed," a natural inclination is to resist. Unity can prevail if we take the time to agree on values. And it's a good idea to "check up" on that agreement from time to time.

—Ed J. Pinegar

CHALLENGE:

There are things I'd like to do as a leader, but I honestly feel that I don't have the talents.

OPPORTUNITY:

There's a story that my father used to tell. It's become somewhat of a legend in the Duncan family, and it makes a good point about personal talents and gifts. Many years ago, Dad was driving on a highway out in the Oklahoma Panhandle and stopped in a little town called Slapout. Slapout apparently got its name back in the Indian Territory days when settlers drove their wagons to the general store there to shop for provisions. The proprietor invariably said "We're slap out of bacon" or "We're slap out of flour." The name stuck.

My Dad stopped in Slapout to gas up his car and have breakfast at a small diner. There was a waitress in the diner that the patrons good-naturedly called "Stingy Myrtle." It was unclear to Dad why the woman had that nickname, until she served him a bowl of oatmeal. Dad tore open the last small packet of sugar in front of him and sprinkled it on his oatmeal.

"May I please have some more sugar," he asked Myrtle.

"Nope. Ya ain't gettin' no more 'til you stir whacha got."

"Excuse me?"

"I said ya ain't gettin' no more 'til you stir whacha got."

Dad obediently stirred his oatmeal, he was served more sugar, then he enjoyed a good laugh with Myrtle and everyone else in the diner.

When Dad retold that story he always related it to personal gifts and talents. Few of us have all the gifts and talents we would like, but all of us *do* have gifts and talents. When we work hard, we can refine and improve the ones we already have. We can ask for additional gifts and talents, and they

Behold thou hast a gift, and blessed art thou because of thy gift. Remember it is sacred and cometh from above.
—D&C 6:10

You need never feel inferior. You need never feel that you were born without talents or without opportunities to give them expression. There is something of divinity in you. You have such tremendous potential because of your inherited nature. Every one of you was endowed by your Father in Heaven with a tremendous capacity to do good in the world. Cultivate the art of being kind, of being thoughtful, of being helpful. Refine within you the quality of mercy which comes as a part of the divine attributes you have inherited.
—**Gordon B, Hinckley**[18]

. . . and let virtue garnish thy thoughts unceasingly; then shall thy confidence wax strong in the presence of God.
—**D&C 121:45**

can be within our reach. But "we ain't gettin' no more 'til we stir what we got." I believe that is much more than pop psychology. It is pure doctrine (see D&C 46).

Sometimes we may lack certain gifts that we wish we had. In those cases, we often can make what's "lacking" less relevant by refining what we *do* have. For example, some people make their "lack" of speaking skill less relevant by loving and caring for others in ways that speak more eloquently than words ever could.

A key is to "stir" the gifts and talents we already have (see 2 Tim. 1:6). Of course another key is to trust in the Lord. Remember the words of Nephi. The Lord never asks us to do anything without also granting us the things (direction, resources, gift, talents, etc.) to accomplish what he asks (see 1 Nephi 3:7).

There's one more thing to bear in mind. When we "argue for our weaknesses" they are ours. When we invest energy in bemoaning our perceived shortcomings we rob ourselves of the strength to overcome them. On the other hand, when we focus on what we *can* do, and consistently do our best, our best gets better and better. There was once a young man who was shy and lacked confidence in his ability to express thoughts in a clear and compelling way. He worked for a university and deliberately placed himself in situations that *required* him to practice the very skills he felt he lacked. As he matured, he practiced more and more. He worked hard. He "stirred" what he had. He increased in capacity. That man is Neal A. Maxwell, today a member of the Quorum of the Twelve and known throughout the Church as a gifted thinker, teacher and speaker.

—Rodger Dean Duncan

CHALLENGE

When people have questions about their callings they sometimes want immediate answers . . . so they telephone the General Offices of the Church for information.

OPPORTUNITY:

I served for seven years on the General Board for the Young Men organization and when the calls came in we would suggest first that together we could review the manual and see if it could help us. Ninety percent of the time the answer was there. We would chat for a moment and then say how wonderful the manuals were in that they usually had an answer for our questions. The other ten percent of the questions were local Priesthood leader decisions that a Presidency or "Council" could decide. Sister Pinegar found the same thing to be true when she served for two and a half years in the General Presidency for the Young Women and then five years as General President of the Primary. The manuals and policy statements by the Brethren really do answer most all of our questions.

—Ed J. Pinegar

Early in my ministry as a member of the Council of the Twelve, I took to President Hugh B. Brown the experience of a fine person who could not serve in a ward position because he could not show mercy to himself. He could forgive others but not himself; mercy was seemingly beyond his grasp. President Brown suggested that I visit with that individual and counsel him along these lines: "I, the Lord, will forgive whom I will forgive, but of you it is required to forgive all men." (D&C 64:10) Then, from Isaiah and the Doctrine and Covenants: "Though your sins be as scarlet, they shall be as white as snow; though they be red like crimson, they shall be as wool." (Isaiah 1:18) "Behold, he who has repented of his sins, the same is forgiven, and I, the Lord, remember them no more." (D&C 58:42) With a pensive expression on his face, President Brown added: "Tell that man that he should not persist in remembering that

CHALLENGE:

Although I can satisfactorily answer all the questions in a temple recommend interview, and although I'm not guilty of any serious transgression, I wonder if I'm really worthy to serve.

OPPORTUNITY:

Let me share a story that may provide some perspective.

As stake president I worked closely with a woman who had lost her membership in the Church because of a serous transgression. Her bishop and I nursed her back to spiritual health, and she was rebaptized. But with Church members who have been excommunicated, priesthood and/or temple blessings are not automatically restored with rebaptism. That comes only after an additional time of careful rehabilitation, testing and healing.

A year or so after this sister's rebaptism, her bishop and I petitioned the First Presidency of the Church, asking that her temple blessings be restored. The brethren considered the matter, then sent to our stake a General Authority who was specifically authorized to perform the restoration of blessings ordinance. He met with the woman in a final interview. Finding everything in order, he invited her husband, her bishop and me into the room. And in a priesthood ordinance lasting only about three minutes, he restored to this sister the blessings of the temple that would tie her soul to God throughout the eternities.

It was a splendid day. We all wept with joy. The General Authority had another meeting, so he kindly bid us farewell. Then, just before he opened the door, he stopped. He returned to the sister, took her gently by the hand and said: "I know you have worked very hard for this day. It has been a long struggle. Now your spiritual healing is complete. But you do understand, don't you, that you did not *earn* this? It is a gift, a gift from the Savior who paid an unspeakable price for every one of us."

which the Lord has said He is willing to forget." Such counsel will help to cleanse the soul and renew the spirit of any who applies it.
                —**Thomas S. Monson**[19]

The principle taught that day applies to all of us in all things. What a tender moment that was. And what a tender moment it is when we come to the realization that we never fully *earn* the opportunities offered us by the Lord. That includes opportunities to serve. A call to serve is a precious gift. Our challenge, always, is to be as good as we can be. The Lord then makes up the difference.
                —Rodger Dean Duncan

QUESTIONS OF CONSCIENCE
1. Am I faithful in *studying* the scriptures?
2. Am I faithful in *studying* the counsel of the living prophets?
3. Do I carefully listen to the counsel and instruction of my local Church leaders?
4. Do I humbly obey the counsel and instruction I'm given?
5. Do I carefully follow correct principles in everything I do in my calling?
6. Am I prayerful in deciding how to solve problems?

7. Do I prayerfully consider the needs of individuals?
8. Do I "stick with the basics" of good leadership and avoid secular fads?
9. Do I affirm and encourage people more than I correct them?
10. As a leader, do I constantly remember that I am a servant?

APPLYING THE PRINCIPLES

1. Consider the various challenges you face in your leadership roles. Now carefully study Doctrine & Covenants sections 121 and 122. How do these revelations apply to your challenges? What principles can you apply to bless the people you're called to serve?
2. Consider any one of the challenges you face in your leadership roles. Which principles and practices discussed in this book can help you address that challenge in an effective, Christlike way?

YOU CAN DO IT!

Challenges and opportunities can come at any moment, especially when we are leaders. They've been part of human life from Adam to our very day. The prophets have endured and overcome just like the pioneers in our dispensation. In every ward and branch, and in every home and family, we are tested and tried. Remember that the Lord gives no commandment save he shall prepare the way to obey. Success and happiness come when we practice true principles. The Lord blesses us as we do our part with faith, diligence and patience. This is his work. We are instruments in his hands. When we are worthy, willing and available, and when we do our best, he does the rest.

You can do it!—in the strength of the Lord.

ENDNOTES FOR MAIN BODY TEXT

1. See Alma 57:21.

2. Neal A. Maxwell, *A More Excellent* Way (Salt Lake City: Bookcraft, 1967), 34.

3. Neal A. Maxwell, *For the Power Is in Them . . . Mormon Musings* (Salt Lake City: Deseret Book Co., 1970), 36.

4. Gordon B. Hinckley, "This is the Work of the Master," *Ensign*, May 1995, 71.

ENDNOTES FOR SIDEBARS

1. Lloyd D. Newell, *The Divine Connection: Understanding Your Inherent Worth* (Salt Lake City: Deseret Book Co., 1992), 174.

2. Marvin J. Ashton, *Be of Good Cheer* (Salt Lake City: Deseret Book Co., 1987), 48.

3. James E. Faust, "This Is Our Day," *Ensign*, May 1999, 17.

4. Ezra Taft Benson, *The Teachings of Ezra Taft Benson* (Salt Lake City: Bookcraft, 1988), 499.

5. Laura Gray, "Homing," *Improvement Era, 1942*, Vol. XIV, July, 1942. No. 7.

6. Elaine Cannon, *Adversity* (Salt Lake City: Bookcraft, 1987), 42.

7. Dean L. Larsen, "The Message: The Peaceable Things of the Kingdom," *New Era*, February 1986, 4.

8. David S. King, "Dealing Successfully with Change," *Ensign*, February 1981, 21.

9. Ibid., 21.

10. Christoffel Golden, as quoted by Chieko N. Okazaki, *Sanctuary* (Salt Lake City: Deseret Book Co., 1997), 105.

11. "Priesthood Quorums," *Improvement Era,* January 1929, vol. XXXII.

12. William T. Tew, *Conference Report,* April 1938, Afternoon Meeting, 109.

13. Henry B. Eyring, *To Draw Closer to God: A Collection of Discourses* (Salt Lake City: Deseret Book Co., 1997), 138.

14. Martha Nibley Beck and John C. Beck, *Breaking the Cycle of Compulsive Behavior* (Salt Lake City: Deseret Book Co., 1990) 231.

15. Ezra Taft Benson, *The Teachings of Ezra Taft Benson* (Salt Lake City: Bookcraft, 1988), 451, 453.

16. Gordon B. Hinckley, *Teachings of Gordon B. Hinckley* (Salt Lake City: Deseret Book Co., 1997), 117.

17. Gordon B. Hinckley, *Stand a Little Taller* (Salt Lake City: Eagle Gate, 2001), 344.

18. Ibid., 185.

19. Thomas S. Monson, "Mercy—The Divine Gift," *Ensign,* May 1995, 54.

INDEX